OFFICIAL
Netscape
Server-Side JavaScript
for Database Applications

WINDOWS NT & UNIX

OFFICIAL
Netscape
Server-Side JavaScript for Database Applications

WINDOWS NT & UNIX

NETSCAPE PRESS

An Imprint of Ventana
Communications Group

Design & Implement
Robust Internet/Intranet
Solutions

LUKE DUNCAN

VENTANA

Official Netscape Server-Side JavaScript for Database Applications
Copyright © 1997 by Luke Duncan

All rights reserved. This book may not be duplicated in any way without the expressed written consent of the publisher, except in the form of brief excerpts or quotations for the purposes of review. The information contained herein is for the personal use of the reader and may not be incorporated in any commercial programs, other books, databases, or any kind of software without written consent of the publisher or author. Making copies of this book or any portion for any purpose other than your own is a violation of United States copyright laws.

Library of Congress Cataloging-in-Publication Data
Duncan, Luke.
    Official Netscape Server-Side JavaScript for Database Applications/Luke Duncan.
        p. cm.
    Includes index.
    ISBN 1-56604-745-5
    JavaScript (Computer program language) 2. Netscape. 3. Web servers. I. Title.
QA76.73.J39D86 1997
005.7'13769—dc21

                                                                              97-34125
                                                                                 CIP

First Edition 9 8 7 6 5 4 3 2 1

Printed in the United States of America

Published and distributed to the trade by Ventana Communications Group
P.O. Box 13964, Research Triangle Park, NC 27709-3964
919.544.9404
FAX 919.544.9472
http://www.vmedia.com

Ventana Communications Group is a division of International Thomson Publishing.

Netscape Publishing Relations
Suzanne C. Anthony
Netscape Communications Corporation
501 E. Middlefield Rd.
Mountain View, CA 94043
http://home.netscape.com

Limits of Liability & Disclaimer of Warranty
The author and publisher of this book have used their best efforts in preparing the book and the programs contained in it. These efforts include the development, research, and testing of the theories and programs to determine their effectiveness. The author and publisher make no warranty of any kind, expressed or implied, with regard to these programs or the documentation contained in this book.
    The author and publisher shall not be liable in the event of incidental or consequential damages in connection with, or arising out of, the furnishing, performance or use of the programs, associated instructions and/or claims of productivity gains.

Trademarks
Trademarked names appear throughout this book and on the accompanying compact disk, if applicable. Rather than list the names and entities that own the trademarks or insert a trademark symbol with each mention of the trademarked name, the publisher states that it is using the names only for editorial purposes and to the benefit of the trademark owner with no intention of infringing upon that trademark.
    Netscape and Netscape Navigator are registered trademarks of Netscape Communications Corporation in the United States and other countries. Netscape's logos and Netscape product and service names are also trademarks of Netscape Communications Corporation, which may be registered in other countries.

President
Michael E. Moran

Associate Publisher
Robert Kern

Editorial Operations Manager
Kerry L. B. Foster

Production Manager
Jaimie Livingston

Brand Manager
Jamie Jaeger Fiocco

Art Director
Marcia Webb

Creative Services Manager
Diane Lennox

Project Editor
Rachel Pearce Anderson

Development Editor
Sarah O'Keefe, Scriptorium Publishing Services, Inc.

Copy Editor
Marion Laird

CD-ROM Specialist
Ginny Phelps

Technical Reviewer
Aaron Huslage

Desktop Publishers
Scott Hosa
Lance Kozlowski

Proofreader
Beth Snowberger

Indexer
Sherry Massey

Interior Designer
Patrick Berry

Cover Illustrator
Leigh-Erin M. Salmon

Outstanding Performance Employees of the Quarter
Arik Anderson, Mailroom Clerk
Chris Grams, Acquisitions Editor
Abiodun (Abbey) Oladosu, Jr., Accountant, Accounts Payable

About the Author

Luke Duncan is the Technology Director at catalogue.com in Chapel Hill, North Carolina. There he works on numerous enterprise applications using LiveWire with Enterprise Server 2.0 and Server-Side JavaScript with Enterprise Server 3.0. He is the author of the *Official Netscape Technologies Developer's Guide* and the *Official Netscape ONE Developer's Guide* with Sean Michaels.

Acknowledgments

I would like to thank the following Ventana employees and contractors who helped make this book possible: JJ Hohn, Rachel Anderson, Sarah O'Keefe, Aaron Huslage, Marion Laird, Scott Hosa, Lance Kozlowski, Beth Snowberger, Bob Kern, and Melanie Stepp.

I would also like to thank everyone else who had to put up with me while I did nothing but work all day long to get this book finished.

—L. D.

Dedication

This book is dedicated to Garland Greene.

Contents

Introduction i

SECTION 1
Developing Database Applications for Enterprise Server 3.0

Chapter 1 Understanding Web-Based Applications 1

    Using the Web as a Development Platform 2
        Advantages of the Web   3
        Disadvantages of the Web   4
        Working With Browsers   4
        N-Tier Web Applications   7
        Client-Server Applications   7

    Building a Dynamic Application Using a Database 9
        Designing Database Tables   9
        Designing Your Application Hierarchy   10
        Creating File Templates With Dynamic Content   11
        Intranets, Extranets & Security   12

Chapter 2 The Enterprise Server Application Framework 15
Writing Your Application Code 17
Compiling Your Application 18
    Using jsac   18
Using the JavaScript Application Manager 20
    Adding Applications   20
    What Defines a JavaScript Application   22
    Configuring the JavaScript Application Manager   25
    Starting Applications   26
    Stopping Applications   26
    Restarting Applications   26
Viewing Your Application 26
    Running Applications   26
    Debugging Applications   27

Chapter 3 Session Management Objects 31
The Lock Object 34
    Using the Lock Object   34
The Request Object 35
    Properties   36
The Client Object 38
    Properties   39
    Maintaining the Client Object   40
The Project Object 45
    Properties   45
    Locking   46
The Server Object 46
    Properties   46
    Locking   48

Chapter 4 Connecting to Your Database 49
Your Database Configuration 49
Database Connection Pools 51
    Creating a Database Connection Pool   51
    Using Database Connection Pools   52
    Sharing Pools   53
    Accessing Connections   54
    Using a Connection Across Multiple Requests   55

Contents

Running SQL Statements 56
    Displaying Database Queries   56
    Executing SQL   57
Cursors 58
    Using a Cursor   58
    Using Updatable Cursors   60
    Cursor Columns   62
Stored Procedures 62
    Using Stored Procedures   62
    Handling Data Returned From a Stored Procedure   65
Transactions 67
Database/JavaScript Data Types 68
    Using Binary Large Objects (BLObs)   70
Handling Errors 71

Chapter 5   Additional Server-Side JavaScript 73

Sending E-mail 74
    Using the SendMail Object   76
Working With Local Files 78
    Accessing a File   78
    File Position   79
    Reading From & Writing to a File   80
    File Information   81
    Using the File Object   82
Working With Response & Request Data 83
    Accessing the Request Header   83
    Accessing the Request Body   84
    Accessing the Response Header   84

Chapter 6   Using Java With LiveConnect 85

Working With Java in Your Application 85
    Built-In Java Classes   87
    Using Java Objects   88
    Sign-Out Board Example   89
Accessing JavaScript From Your Java Classes 97
    Using JavaScript Objects   97
    Writing to the Client   98
    Threading   98
    Expanding the Sign-Out Board   99
When to Use Java vs. JavaScript 107

SECTION II
Creating an Application

Chapter 7 Designing Your Web Application 111
   Creating Your Application Map 111
      The Pages   112
      The Map   113
   Designing Your Database Tables 115
      The Employee Table   115
      The Client Table   116
      The Hours Table   118
   Designing Your Application Objects 119
      The Employee Object   119
      The timeClient Object   120
      The Hours Object   120
      The Report Object   121
      The ReportHours Object   123
   Designing Your Interface 123
      The Menu Pages   124
      The General Access Forms   124
      The Administrative Access Forms   125

Chapter 8 Implementing Your Design 127
   The Preliminaries 127
      Creating Database Tables   127
      Setting Up the Application Directory   128
   Implementing Your Objects 129
      Creating Objects in JavaScript   130
      The Employee Object   130
      The timeClient Object   136
      The Hours Object   142
      The Report Object   145
      The ReportHours Object   150
   Writing Your HTML Pages 152
      Creating the Initial Page & the Home Page   153
      The Menus   156
      The Forms   161
   Writing Any Additional JavaScript Functions 180
   Server-Side vs. Client-Side JavaScript 184

Contents   xvii

Chapter 9 **Testing & Debugging** 185
 Adding Your Application 185
  Using the Application Manager   185
  Editing the jsa.conf File   187
  Running & Testing Your Application   188
 Debugging Your Application 189
  Using the Application Manager Debugger   189
  Adding Debug Messages   191
  Creating a Development Version   191
 Deciphering & Tracking Error Messages 191
  The Anatomy of an Error Message   192
  Database Errors   192
  Working Around Bugs   193
  Online Resources   195
 Other Test Options 196

SECTION III
References

Chapter 10 **Server-Side JavaScript Reference** 199

Chapter 11 **Server-Side JavaScript Object Reference** 263

SECTION IV
Appendices

Appendix A **About the Companion CD-ROM** 273

Appendix B **Viewing the Example Online** 275

 Index 277

Introduction

Server-side JavaScript was introduced into Netscape's Enterprise Server 2.0 as *LiveWire*. It allowed developers to write applications with Enterprise Server that could easily connect to a database. With the release of Enterprise Server 3.0, this technology was renamed *server-side JavaScript*.

Using server-side JavaScript, developers are able to create Web-based applications that are closely tied to the server. This allows faster access than using a CGI program, since the server doesn't have to do twice the work (by creating a second process or thread to handle the program as well as the request), as is the case with CGI.

Enterprise Server 3.0 introduced LiveConnect on the server. LiveConnect allows developers to add Java code to their applications and enables communication between Java and JavaScript. It also changed the way server-side JavaScript connects to your database. You can now use database pool objects to manage multiple connections to multiple databases instead of just a single database connection.

Who Can Use This Book?

This book is for Netscape developers who are using Enterprise Server 3.0 and want to create Internet, intranet, or extranet applications. Experience with client-side JavaScript will help in your understanding of the code examples. Only server-specific JavaScript is described in detail in this book. For more information about all aspects of JavaScript, please refer to the *Official Netscape JavaScript 1.2 Programmer's Reference,* also published by Ventana.

An Overview of This Book

This book is divided into three sections. Section I focuses on developing database applications for Enterprise Server 3.0. It covers everything you need to know about using the JavaScript Application Manager, compiling your applications, and using the server-specific features of server-side JavaScript.

Section II is about creating an application. It discusses everything from planning your application to testing and debugging it. Also included is a time-tracking example that illustrates how to create server-side JavaScript applications.

Section III is a reference section. It provides a comprehensive server-side JavaScript reference with an alphabetical listing of each object, method, property, and function, specific to server-side JavaScript. There is also a quick *object reference* that lists only the objects, with all the properties and methods of each.

SECTION 1

Developing Database Applications for Enterprise Server 3.0

Understanding Web-Based Applications

With the advent of the World Wide Web, the process of developing database applications has changed dramatically. You are no longer limited to creating an application for your users' computers. Your users can now come to your application over the Web. Because of Web-based communication, it is much easier to create applications that allow many users to access and share the same data sources, regardless of the users' geographical locations.

Using the Netscape Enterprise Server you can create database-driven applications that can be accessed by anyone in the world who has a connection to the Internet and a Web browser. This access can include gathering data as well as updating information for any other user to see. You can assign access to different classes of users based on an assigned user ID or based simply on the Internet location they're connecting from.

With growing Internet use, security has become a big concern. Your Web-based applications can have two levels of security. Your database server is protected by not allowing any outside connections to it. Only access by your Enterprise Server (or internal users) is needed to run your applications. You also have many options to protect your Enterprise Server. You can restrict access to your application through the *Secure Sockets Layer* (SSL) and *user authentication* or *client certificates*.

User authentication is a method by which the user's client displays a dialog box where the user can type in a username and password to access your site. Client certificates (signed by a designated third party) installed on the user's machine are a more secure way of verifying who a user is. Please see your Enterprise Server 3.0 documentation or *The Official Netscape Enterprise Server 3 Book* (published by Ventana) for more information on restricting access to your Web site and applications.

Using the Web as a Development Platform

Using the Web as your development platform gives you many advantages, but it also brings you a few unique problems to solve. Having the Enterprise Server and Netscape ONE as your platform of choice on the Web allows you to connect to Informix, Oracle, DB2, and Sybase database servers directly, as well as many other databases through ODBC. The applications you build on the Enterprise Server that connect to a database are called LiveWire applications.

Some of the following concepts may be familiar to you if you've already worked with Web-based applications. If so, you may want to skip to the next chapter, "The Enterprise Server Application Framework."

LiveWire: Enterprise Server 2.0 vs. 3.0

Between the releases of Enterprise Server 2.0 and 3.0 the definition of LiveWire has changed. In 2.0, LiveWire was a blanket term that referred to any application running on the server that used server-side JavaScript. In the administration server you would turn on LiveWire, which would enable you to access the Application Manager and create LiveWire applications.

In Enterprise Server 3.0, LiveWire only refers to those applications that connect to a database. You now enable the server-side JavaScript application environment. The applications you create are called server-side JavaScript applications unless they connect to a database. LiveWire can also be used to refer to a collection of JavaScript objects that are used when connecting to your database server. See Chapter 2, "The Enterprise Server Application Framework," for more information on setting up server-side JavaScript on your server and using the JavaScript Application Manager.

By standardizing on the Web, once you've created your application you can deploy it across your corporate intranet, your corporate extranet (which is similar to an intranet but with broader access among your business partners), or the whole Internet, without having to modify your application.

Advantages of the Web

Building on the Web offers three distinct advantages over more traditional application development environments: platform independence, ubiquitous client software, and stateless connections to your application server. The ability of users to access your application without having to download any special software makes the Web an obvious choice as your development platform.

Platform Independence

By creating your application using Netscape Enterprise Server 3.0 you allow any computer that's connected to the Internet with a Web browser to connect to your application. You don't have to worry about cross-platform development because most operating systems have a Web browser available to them.

Also, you don't necessarily have to worry about which Web browser people are using to connect to your application. There are some nice features that more advanced browsers include, but when using the Enterprise Server you can check out what type of browser is connecting and modify your display accordingly. Most users on the Internet have the most recent versions of browser software, so there will be only a few cases where users might see an application with a smaller feature set.

Ubiquitous Client Software

Since just about everyone connected to the Internet already has a Web browser, you don't need to worry about setting up a place to download software before users can access your application. You also don't need to worry about documenting how to use the Web browser because there are many sources on the Internet that explain the intimate details of each Web browser. (There are also many books available in the marketplace, such as *The Official Netscape Communicator 4 Book* published by Netscape Press, that describe how to use a Web browser.)

If you're deploying your application across your intranet, using the Web makes life easier for your computer support personnel because they don't need to maintain an additional piece of software on each employee's computer. It also makes it easier on the IS departments of your partner companies that may be accessing your application over your extranet.

Stateless Connections

Using HyperText Transfer Protocol (HTTP) allows many users to access your application at the same time without tying up your server. Since the browser sends a request to your application and then displays the response, there is no need for the user to stay connected while reading the response. In more traditional client-server models, you would have to limit the number of simultaneous users of your application based on how much you had invested in your server machines.

Using HTTP also makes it easier to balance the load across multiple servers without any extra development time. You can have multiple servers running the same application to increase performance without any noticeable difference to users.

Disadvantages of the Web

While the advantages of the Web can make our application development easier, there are a couple of disadvantages we have to contend with.

Since your application can possibly be open to the Internet, security is a bigger issue. You need to make sure that no one can access sensitive data they're not supposed to see. The Enterprise Server provides a few solutions for your security needs, including user authentication (by a username and password) and client certificates. (See your Enterprise Server documentation for more information.)

Because you may have requests from many users over a given time period, using a stateless protocol also causes some problems in trying to keep track of a user from one request to the next. The Enterprise Server Application environment has a client object that can keep track of users between connections. See the "Maintaining the Client Object" section in Chapter 3, "Session Management Objects," for more information on this topic.

Working With Browsers

One of the main problems with developing Web-based applications is that when you want to use advanced browser features, you can never be sure what browser will be connecting to your application. Hopefully, one day in the future all browsers will include a rich feature set so that everyone will be able to use all your application's capabilities. Until then you'll need to allow for certain rich features to be disabled for those clients that don't support them—otherwise you'll have to restrict access to your application.

Restricting access isn't necessarily a bad thing. Generally only a few percentage points of the Internet population will be blocked out by restricting access based on browser type. Depending on the application you're building, this might or might not be a problem.

Cookies

One of the nicest features of current browsers is *cookies*. Cookies allow you to save data, with the client browser, that will be sent back to the server on subsequent requests. This lets you maintain state without requiring a constant connection to your server. If you wish to use cookies, you can set up the JavaScript client object to handle them for you. See "Maintaining the Client Object" in Chapter 3, "Session Management Objects," for more information on using cookies in your application.

Advanced HTML Tags

As the Web has become more popular, browsers have added in new HTML tags. Sometimes these tags are part of the HTML 3.2 standard and sometimes they're custom tags. Some of these new tags have given developers the ability to display tables and frames in their HTML pages.

As new features are added, such as cascading style sheets and new client-side scripting abilities, there will still be browsers in use that don't support these features or don't support them well. If you wish to make your application accessible to users of browsers with fewer features, you'll need to include checks to make sure the appropriate HTML will be delivered to those browsers.

Usually the only time it may be necessary to include support for any and all browsers is when you're creating applications such as catalogs. In this case you'll want all users to be able to buy your products, regardless of the browser they're using—even if the catalog is not as nice-looking as it is to people using full-featured browsers.

Client-Side Scripting

You can use client-side scripting capabilities to handle some data processing before the data is sent to the Enterprise Server. This allows you to validate data so that there aren't extra requests to the server to validate the information.

You really need to check the browser type and version when using client-side scripting. Often, different browsers, such as Communicator and Internet Explorer, handle the same client-side code differently. You can modify the client-side code depending on the browser connecting to your application or simply allow only one type of browser to access your application.

Your current options for client-side scripting are JavaScript for Communicator, with partial support in Internet Explorer, and VBScript for Internet Explorer. Please refer to *The Official Netscape JavaScript 1.2 Book* or *The Comprehensive Guide to VBScript* (both published by Ventana) for more information on client-side scripting with these languages.

It is always a good idea to verify any data on your server before saving it to a database as a backup. Even if it's never needed, you'll feel safer having it there.

When "Outdated" Is an Understatement

Some people still use Web browsers purchased years ago, such as the .9 beta of Netscape Navigator, as well as early versions of Mosaic or obscure browsers that only five people even know about. For these users there may be nothing they can do except upgrade. They're missing out on a lot of what the Internet can offer them, so they should be happy to have the excuse to upgrade. You can avoid complaints from your site visitors by placing a message to let them know the minimum version of a browser they will need in order to get the most from your site.

N-Tier Web Applications vs. Client-Server

LiveWire applications have a three-tier framework, as seen in Figure 1-1. The three tiers are Web browser clients, the Enterprise Server (which is also a database client), and the database server. Other tiers can be added later without having to disrupt the end product of your application. For example, you might add another server between the Enterprise Server and your database server. This server would handle requests from the Enterprise Server and then gather data from multiple databases or other data sources.

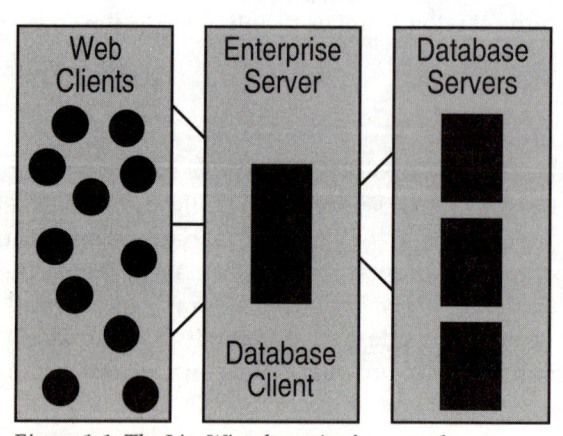

Figure 1-1: The LiveWire three-tier framework.

N-Tier Web Applications

The first tier, the Web clients, is the users' interface to your application. Some application data processing can be handled by the client, such as making sure form data is valid. This processing is done using client-side JavaScript. This type of processing requires a certain level of the browser feature set to support client-side JavaScript.

Using a feature such as client-side JavaScript means you have to be especially careful to anticipate potential problems with the browsers connecting to your application. Some client-side scripting that works perfectly in Communicator may not do anything in Internet Explorer. Be sure to test your applications in as many browsers as you can or in all the ones that will be accessing your application.

The second tier, the Enterprise Server, includes the capability to handle requests from the Web clients as well as to connect to the database server. Most of the logic and flow of the application are handled here. Your application security is also handled by this tier.

The third tier, the database server, contains all the data required by the application. Some of the application functionality may be implemented here through stored procedures. Extra security can be provided by securing this tier behind a corporate firewall.

Client-Server Applications

Client-server applications only have two tiers: the client and the server. Creating a client-server application generally requires you to create a client program for every platform you wish to be able to connect to your server. This can cause many headaches with porting issues.

Client-server applications are often run on closed networks because there are too many security issues when connecting over the Internet. Resolving these issues may add to development time as well as capital investments. Table 1-1 outlines the benefits of creating N-Tier applications over client-server applications.

Issue	N-Tier (With Enterprise 3.0)	Client-Server
Connection State	The Web browser doesn't keep a constant connection to the Enterprise Server. This helps to save network bandwidth. The Enterprise Server has built-in capabilities to manage state through multiple connections to the server.	The client remains connected to the server while it is running. It would require extra coding to drop this connection when unnecessary and maintain state across connections.
Platforms	Your application can be accessed from any platform that a Web browser will run on without any additional development time.	You must port your application to all platforms that you want to be able to access your server.
Processing	You can process data on any of the three tiers: Web client, Enterprise Server, or your database servers.	You can process data on your client or server.
Protocols	You use standard protocols for communication between each tier of your application: HTTP, TCP/IP, or ODBC.	You may have to create your own higher level protocol to communicate between your client and server that may run on top of any number of network protocols such as TCP/IP or IPX.
Security	You can use security features built into Enterprise Server 3.0, such as user authentication or client certificates, to make sure your users can have access to your application. You can also use Secure Sockets Layer to make sure no one can intercept any data traveling between the Web browser and the Enterprise Server. The connection between your Enterprise Server and your database server can be protected by being behind your corporate firewall.	You have to build in any additional security that your server doesn't provide. This may require additional man hours as well as additional software libraries to handle data encryption.
Usage	You may allow access from any user on the Internet without having to sacrifice security. You can also limit access to certain sites to build your extranet. This gives you great flexibility when building your application.	Any user who wants to connect to your server must download the client application for their platform. Users may also be restricted to only accessing the server from within your corporate LAN.

Table 1-1: This table describes the benefits of using Netscape's Enterprise Server for building N-Tier applications over creating traditional client-server applications.

Building a Dynamic Application Using a Database

Creating a database-driven Web application makes your applications more dynamic for your end users and makes the maintenance much easier on the content side. For example, on your Web site you may want to provide a way for an Internet user to search an employee database so that they know who to call when they need information or assistance. You could have an intranet application that allows employees to update their personnel information or find out how many vacation and sick days they have left and when their next evaluation is due. There could be another intranet application for use by management and human resources staff members to access and update salary and other sensitive information.

If the format of employee pages needed to change for Internet users, it would be easy to change the page or a function to print the new format. After making the change, the application would be rebuilt and restarted, and the whole world could see the new format.

You could store all your application content in your database, including the text, images, sounds, and/or video clips, by using Binary Large Objects (BLObs). Using the BLOb object methods you could then display your data in your application Web pages dynamically. See the section on BLObs in Chapter 4, "Connecting to Your Database," for more information on these methods.

Designing Database Tables

After deciding on the application you're going to build, you need to design your database tables. Designing your tables includes deciding on the tables you need to create, the field names you'll use, and which data type each field will be. You want to think ahead at this stage so that you don't need to go back and modify your tables at a later date—which could require you to modify some of your code.

Determining the Number of Tables

The number of tables you use is generally a matter of preference. In our employee example suggested above, you could include everything in one table. This would be the easiest approach but not necessarily the most secure.

If you created one table that included all the employee data to be displayed in the Internet application, you wouldn't include any sensitive data like salary or vacation days. This would ensure that confidential data could not slip out into the wrong hands.

A second table could include sensitive data that only the intranet application would see. If any employee was looking, they wouldn't be able to modify the data in the second table, but they could modify data from the first table if their ID matched the employee ID in the database.

Managers and HR personnel would have higher access that would allow them to browse and modify any of the information in either of the two tables. You could also include a third table, with data such as employee evaluations, for example, that the employee wouldn't be able to access within the database.

You could create informational tables as well that could map department IDs to full department names. Then you could store a numerical ID in the employee table that when displayed to anyone browsing would list the department name. This would make it easier to update if the department name ever changed due to a reorganization in the company.

Keeping Related Data Together

To reduce the number of queries you make to the database, you can keep all your related data in the same table. Using the tables described above, the Internet application would only need to send two queries when displaying an employee page: one to the employee table to display the information, and one to the department table to display the full department name.

You have various trade-offs in deciding whether to keep everything in the same table or possibly creating a maintenance nightmare by having the additional department table. If you included the department name in the employee table instead of an ID, you wouldn't need two queries for the Internet application, but you'd need to worry about making sure different intranet users used the exact same department name. The decision depends on the specifics of each particular company.

Designing Your Application Hierarchy

Once you've designed and created your database tables, you need to decide what pages you need for your application. For the Internet application we've been discussing, you might have a page to list departments, one to list employees (by department or a complete list), one to display the employee information, and possibly a search page as well. There might also be other pages you want to include, but this would be a bare minimum.

Application Levels

Our example application would then have three levels: department list, employee list, and employee page. Any other special pages would most likely fit into one of these levels—for example, the search page would be on the same level as the department list. The search page is a special case because it would have an extra level between clicking on Search and seeing a list of employees.

Using JavaScript Objects

JavaScript objects are a good way to make your application easy to understand and modify. In our example, the most logical objects to define would be an employee object and a department object. The employee object would have properties that would parallel the employee table and would also have methods to display the properties in HTML. The department object would include a list of the employees in that department and a method to display the list. These objects could be defined in JavaScript only as .js files.

With these objects, if you ever wanted to change the way either of these objects was displayed in the HTML pages, you would only need to change the HTML code in one place. You could also have multiple methods to display different types of information.

Creating File Templates With Dynamic Content

Once you have created the objects, you need to reference them from the HTML pages in your application. The first page would query the database to get a list of all the departments and list them with links to the employee list page. The employee list page would generate a department object based on the department ID passed to the page. The list of employees (viewed by calling the display method of the department object) would link each employee to the employee page. The employee page would generate an employee object based on the employee ID and then display the employee data.

You can now easily reuse code by calling to the objects already created. The search results page could list employees that matched the search and have links to the employee display page. You could make a new page that would display the employee of the month. This page would create an employee object from a statistically defined employee ID and display that employee. Any time you changed the display code, all these pages would be changed, making it much easier to modify your code.

Intranets, Extranets & Security

When building an application for your intranet or extranet, you are able to include much richer features. An extranet includes data and applications you want to share across multiple companies, using the Internet as a backbone but without allowing access to just any user on the Internet. This allows you to share data easily without a large investment, since most companies you deal with will already be connected to the Internet. Since you're creating an application for a limited set of users, you are better able to define what browser is being used. You may not be able to determine the exact browser in all cases, but you can expect a certain level of compliance with the latest features.

You also need to worry about keeping your data secure, since usually you want to make more sensitive data available to your employees and partners.

Restricting Client Browsers

By limiting the browsers that can view your application, you don't have to worry about whether or not to use frames. You also don't have to worry about how each page will look, because it will be easy to check each browser you're allowing. This would be an impossible task if you allowed just any browser.

By using the most recently available HTML tags as well as plug-ins and/or Java applets, you'll be able to create an application that is much friendlier to the user. Your application can be more dynamic and visually attractive.

Using Client-Side Processing

With browsers that support client-side JavaScript, you can include data processing on the client—to keep from having to do it on the server. Before a form is submitted, you can check to make sure the data is complete and in the correct form, and notify the user if it's not. If you were allowing access indiscriminately—that is, by any browser—you couldn't rely on this method to work and therefore you'd need to have backup data verification on the server.

You can also use the client to perform simple calculations before sending the data to the server. Using the intranet application as an example, you could show employees how putting more of their salary into their 401k plan would affect the amount of their take-home pay each pay period. Building these calculations into the client would save quite a few needless hits to your server.

Security Considerations With Extranets

When you're building for your intranet, the easiest way to keep security is to have the application only accessible from behind your firewall. This way, no outsiders can see your sensitive data. With extranets, you have to implement some other security scheme, since users will be accessing your application from the Internet.

You can also run your application on a secure server by activating SSL (Secure Sockets Layer) on your Enterprise Server. This way, any data and/or passwords sent to your server will be encrypted along the way so that no one on the Internet can intercept your data.

The best way to make your application secure is to restrict access. You have a few options when deciding how to do this. You could restrict access based on IP address or by requiring a user to log in. If you have multiple partner companies accessing your application, you could give them access based on their IP address. This would mean they could only connect from their company and not from an Internet Service Provider (ISP) account they might use at home. You could also allow different levels of access based on the company, but you couldn't assign different access rights within a partner company.

These are situations where restricting access by user ID is the best solution. You can assign IDs to various people in your partner companies, requiring them to log in with a password to see your data. You can restrict by IP and user ID if you want an added level of security. Of course, this type of security is only as reliable as the people who have access to it. If someone shares their password, you'll have to delete their account. You might lose some sensitive data, but you'll have legal recourse because you'll know where the leak in your security wall came from.

Moving On

In this chapter we've covered the underlying concepts of creating a Web-based application. We've seen the benefits of using the Web, such as platform independence, and what things we need to watch out for, such as security. We've also seen the benefits of creating N-Tier applications.

In the next chapter we'll focus on how the Enterprise Server can be used to create these applications and how to use the JavaScript Application Manager.

The Enterprise Server Application Framework

The Enterprise Server Application Framework consists of the JavaScript Application compiler, which you use to compile the JavaScript code, and the JavaScript Application Manager, which is your interface to working with the applications you've created and your server. There are also a lot of background pieces that the server does for you to handle reading your compiled application and serving it to your users.

The JavaScript Application Manager is actually a JavaScript application that comes with your server; you use it to manage the JavaScript applications. To access your Application Manager, you need to activate server-side JavaScript on your server. You can then access your Application Manager by going to http://www.yourdomain.com/appmgr/.

You activate server-side JavaScript by going to the administrative server for your Enterprise Server. The administrative server will be running on the port you selected when you installed your Enterprise Server. (Please see your Enterprise Server documentation for information on starting your administrative server if it isn't running.) Select the server to which you want to activate server-side JavaScript, then click the Programs button in the top frame and click Server Side Javascript in the left frame. Select Yes for both questions, then click OK. After following the instructions to apply your change, your browser should look like Figure 2-1.

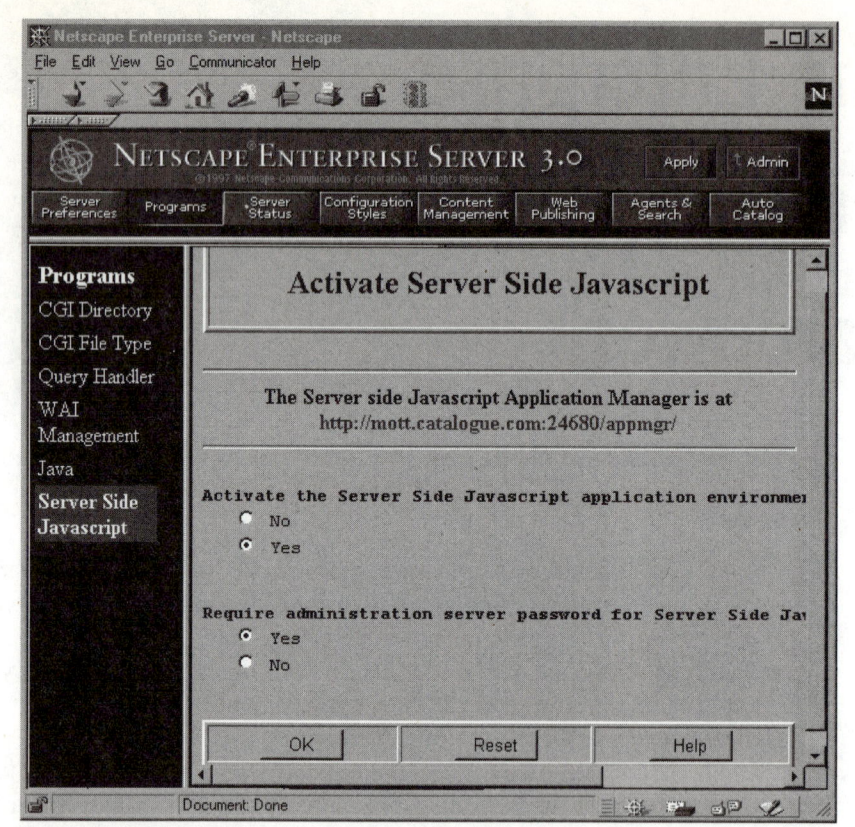

Figure 2-1: The Enterprise Server 3.0 administrative server: activating server-side JavaScript.

There should be a link to the JavaScript Application Manager on this page now. Click that link to access the JavaScript Application Manager. Your JavaScript application will consist of HTML (.html) and JavaScript (.js) files. After writing all the code for your application, you must compile it into a .web file that the Enterprise Server will use when serving your application.

Note: Netscape will soon be releasing a product called Visual JavaScript, which will help you create your applications in a visual development environment.

Writing Your Application Code

There are two types of files you can have in your application: HTML files and JavaScript files. HTML files have the extension .html or .htm, and JavaScript files have the extension .js. Whenever you want to run server-side JavaScript in your HTML files, you need to enclose the code within <SERVER> tags.

For example, to dynamically display the number of visitors you've had to your application's home page since it started, you could have the following code:

visits.html

```
<html>
<head>
<title>Application Visits</title>
</head>
<body>
<h1>Application Visits</h1>
<server>
write(There have been +project.visitors);
write( since this application started.<p>);
</server>
</body>
</html>
```

In your application's default page you would include the code to increment this variable each time it is loaded. Its code would look like the example below:

home.html

```
<html>
<head>
<title>Sample Application</title>
</head>
<server>
incrementVisitors();
</server>
<body>
<h1>Welcome</h1>
Welcome to the sample application.<p>
From here you can see how many <a href=visits.html>visitors</a> we've had to
this application.<p>
</body>
</html>
```

You'll notice that this page has a call to the function incrementVisitors( ). We also need to define this function, which we can do in a JavaScript source file such as the one shown below:

utils.js

```
function incrementVisitors() {
    project.lock();
    if ( !project.visitors )
        project.visitors = 1;
    else
        project.visitors++;
    project.unlock();
}
```

This function will lock the project object; it will also increment the project.visitors variable if it exists and initialize it if it doesn't. Chapter 3, "Session Management Objects," will cover the project object in more detail.

Compiling Your Application

You can compile your application files using the JavaScript Application Compiler. You must compile your application from a command prompt if you're using NT, or from a command shell if you're using UNIX. The compiler can be found in the bin/https/ subdirectory of the directory where you installed the Enterprise Server. The name of the program is *jsac*.

You must recompile your application any time you make any changes to the code. You must then restart the application from the JavaScript Application Manager before your application can be accessed again.

Using jsac

Now that we have a few files for this little application, we can compile it using the JavaScript Application Compiler, jsac. Many of the sample applications that come with the Enterprise server include a short shell script (or batch file) to build the application (aptly named "build"). The script for our example may look like the example that follows:

build

```
jsac -v -o sample.web utils.js home.html visits.html
```

Chapter 2: The Enterprise Server Application Framework

When we run this script or batch file, it will compile the application into the file sample.web. You should see the following output when running this script (the version number may be different):

```
JavaScript Application Compiler Version 21.9
Copyright (C) Netscape Communications Corporation 1996 1997
All rights reserved
Reading file utils.js
Compiling file utils.js
Reading file home.html
Compiling file home.html
Reading file visits.html
Compiling file visits.html
Writing .web file
```

See the sidebar titled "JavaScript Application Compiler Options" for more information on the options you can pass to jsac.

JavaScript Application Compiler Options

The following table shows the meanings for the jsac options. You must always include the -o option and you must have either a list of input files or use the -f option. Any arguments passed to jsac that aren't part of an option will be compiled into the .web file. These files must be html, .htm, or .js.

Option	Argument	Description
-c	none	It causes the compiler to only check the input files without building the .web file.
-d	none	It causes the compiler to display debugging output as it compiles.
-f	filename	This filename includes a list of files that will be compiled into the .web file. The filenames are separated by white space.
-h	none	It causes the compiler to display a help page explaining the options.
-i	filename	The filename will be compiled into the .web file. This option is optional and is only necessary if the filename starts with the switch character (-). These files can be .html, .htm, or .js files.
-l	character set name	It sets the character set to be used when compiling, such as: iso-8859-1.

Option	Argument	Description
-o	.web filename	This is the output file that will be generated after compiling.
-p	directory name	It sets the current directory to be used while compiling. If used, it should be used before the -f option.
-r	filename	Any error messages generated while compiling will be redirected to this file.
-v	none	It causes the compiler to display verbose output while compiling.

Table 2-1: The command line options for jsac.

Using the JavaScript Application Manager

Once you've written and compiled your application, you'll need to add it to the JavaScript Application Manager. Once it's been added, you'll be able to run and debug your application through its URL on your Enterprise Server.

Now you should go to the JavaScript Application Manager in a new browser window. You'll be asked to log in using the administrative server ID and password. The first time you see the Application Manager it should look like Figure 2-2.

Adding Applications

You can add an application by clicking the Add link in the left-side frame. This will display a form in the right-hand frame that allows you to type in the values for the fields to define your application. When you click OK, the Application Manager will check to make sure your .web file exists and will then add the application to the server. You will see your new application name appear in the selection box in the left frame.

Once you've added your application, your users can access it at http://www.yourdomain.com/*yourAppName*/.

Chapter 2: The Enterprise Server Application Framework

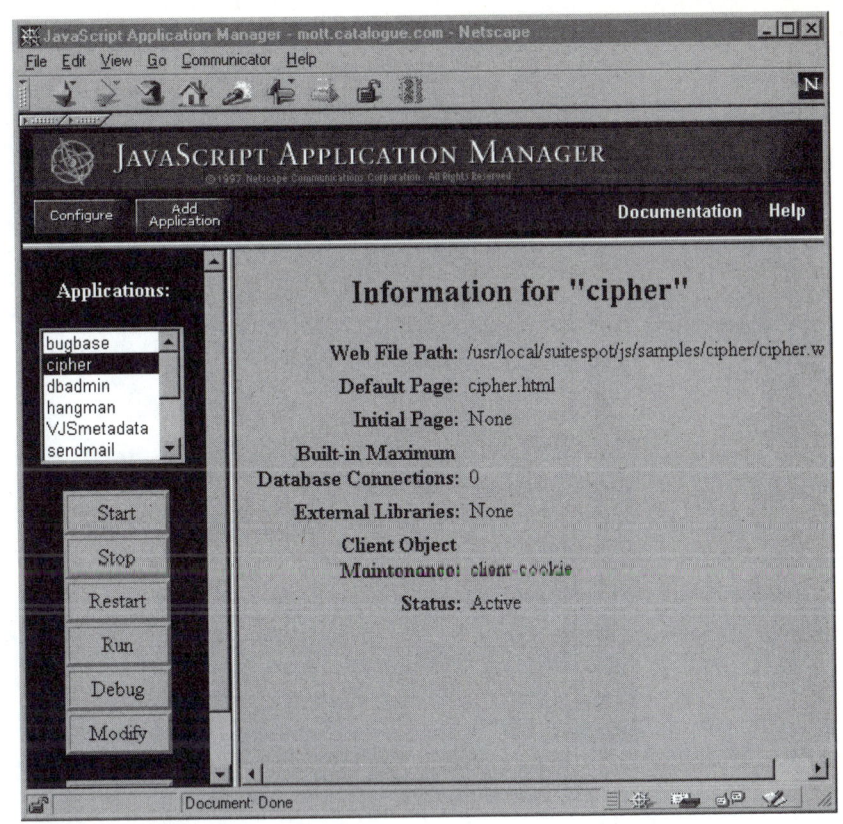

Figure 2-2: The JavaScript Application Manager.

Adding the Sample Application

Now that we understand how the JavaScript Application Manager works, let's add the sample application we built. Click the Add link and fill in the data as seen in Figure 2-3. Include the correct directory for your .web file.

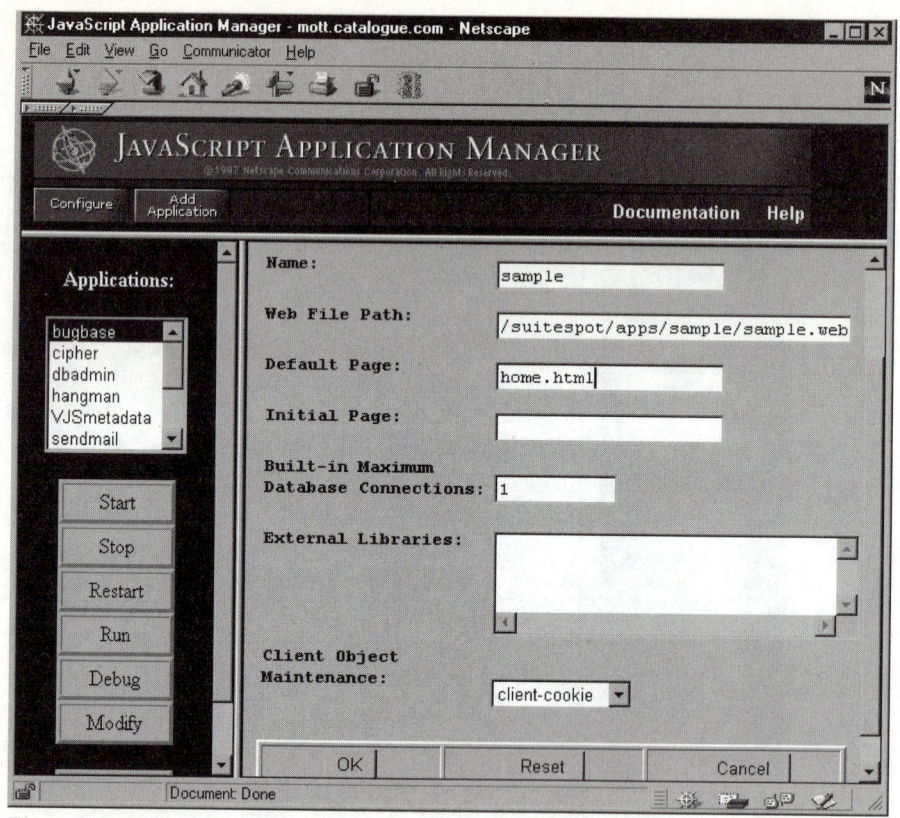

Figure 2-3: Adding the sample application.

Now click the OK button. You should now see sample selected in the list of applications in the left frame. Click the Run button to run the application in a new browser. Now if you type in the URL for the visits page (http://www.yourdomain.com/sample/visits.html) you will see how many visitors you've had to your application as shown in Figure 2-4.

What Defines a JavaScript Application

There are seven components involved in defining each JavaScript application you create. Required fields are marked by italics:

- **Name:** The name of the application is used to refer to the application from the Application Manager. It is also used as the URL of the application. You can access your application at http://www.yourdomain.com/*appname*/. This name must be unique among all the applications on the server.

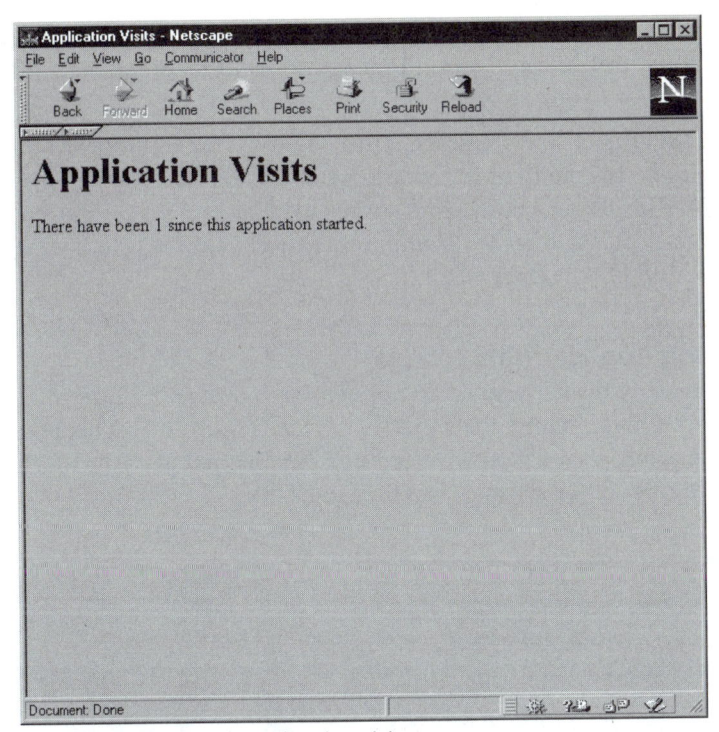

Chapter 2: The Enterprise Server Application Framework

Figure 2-4: The sample application visitors page.

- **Web File Path**: The .web file path tells the server where to find the compiled .web file for this application. The .web file (with the suffix .web) is created when you build your application.
- **Default Page**: The default page is the page that is displayed when a user doesn't request a specific page within your application (i.e., when they request http://www.yourdomain.com/*appname*/). It is generally the first page you want to be seen by someone accessing your application.
- **Initial Page**: The initial page is run the first time someone visits your application since it's been restarted. This page is only accessed once during the runtime of the application. You can use this page to initialize any application-wide variables.
- **Built-In Maximum Database Connections**: This setting is used to define the maximum number of database connections your application can have at one time. This setting only applies if you're using the built-in database object. This is mainly used for backward compatibility with 2.0 applications. With 3.0, you should use the DbPool object to maintain your connections instead of using the database object.

- **External Libraries**: Here you list any external libraries you wish to add to your application. These libraries can include C functions that you wish to call from your application.
- **Client Object Maintenance**: This is where you select how you want to maintain the client object. You have five choices: client-cookie, client-url, server-ip, server-cookie, and server-url. For more information on these choices, please refer to "Maintaining the Client Object" in Chapter 3, "Session Management Options."

Modifying Application Settings

You can modify the settings of an application by selecting it from the Applications list box and clicking the Modify link (see Figure 2-5). This page is similar to the Add page, except that you can't change the name of the application. You can change any other settings and then click OK.

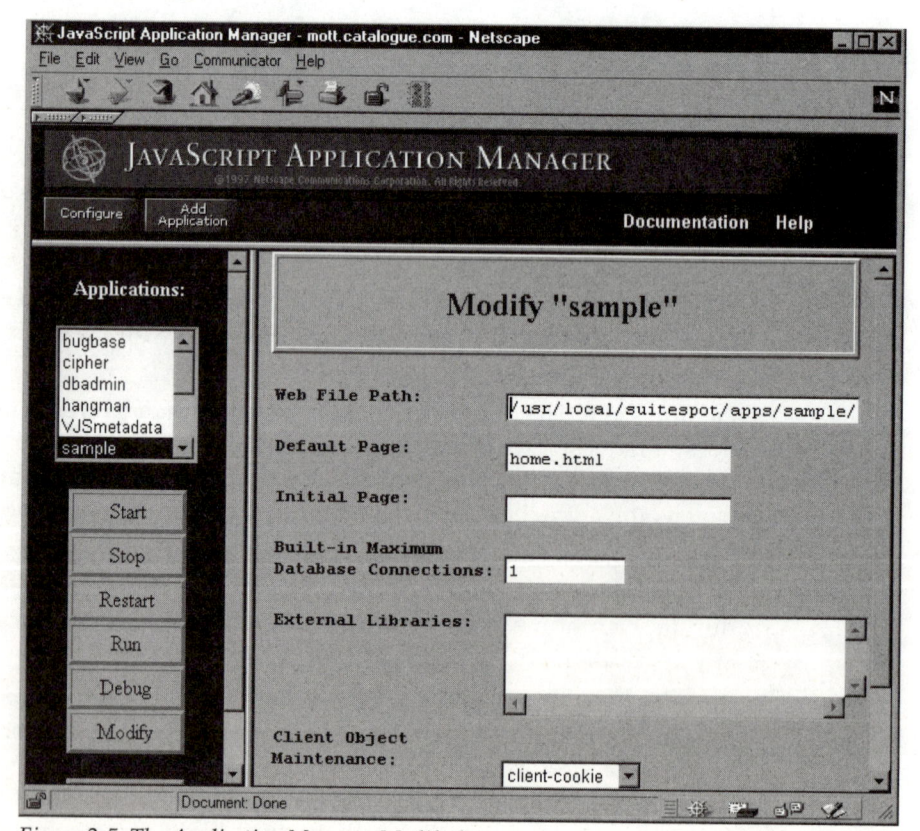

Figure 2-5: The Application Manager Modify frame.

Configuring the JavaScript Application Manager

If you're going to be adding a lot of applications, you may want to have an application template. You can set this up by clicking the Configure link. You can define default values for every setting except for application name (see Figure 2-6). Whatever you select here will be displayed in the Add form when adding any new applications.

You can also assign preferences when using the Application Manager. You can choose verification before removing, starting, stopping, or restarting an application. The default is to ask only before *removing* an application. You can also define where the debug information will be displayed when you debug an application. The default is to have the debug data shown in the same window as the running application, but you can choose to have it displayed in its own window.

These preferences will only apply to the current browser and machine you're using to access the Application Manager. If you change preferences and then access the Application Manager from a different machine you will again have the default preferences.

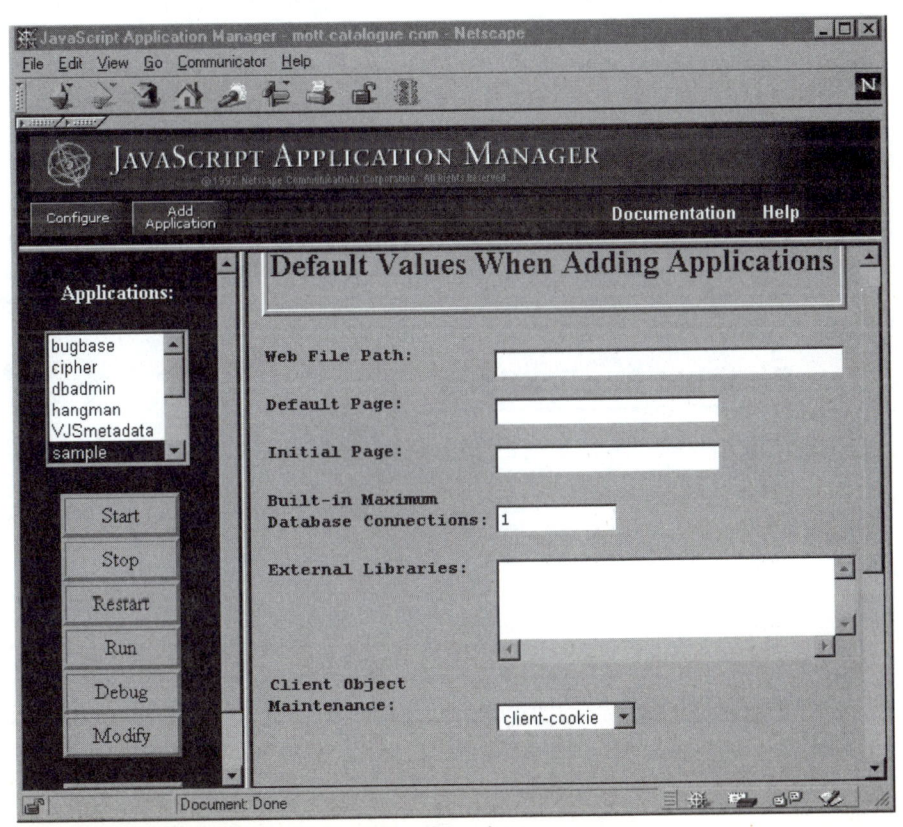

Figure 2-6: The Application Manager Configure frame.

Starting Applications

To start an application, select its name from the Applications list in the left-hand frame, then click the Start button. Users will now be able to access your application. Clicking Start on an application that is already running will have no effect.

Stopping Applications

To stop an application, select its name from the Applications list in the left-hand frame, then click the Stop button. Users will no longer be able to access your application. Clicking the Stop button while the application isn't running will have no effect. You need to stop the application before moving or replacing the .web file.

Restarting Applications

You can restart an application by selecting it from the Applications list and then clicking the Restart button. You need to restart an application any time you make any changes and rebuild the .web file. If you don't restart it, your changes won't take effect.

Viewing Your Application

You have two different ways of viewing your application. You can simply run it to make sure it's operating correctly. Or you can debug it, which will show you more specific information about what is going on as you use your application.

Running Applications

Simply click the Run button to access your application. A new window will appear with your application in it.

Debugging Applications

To debug, click the Debug button. A new window will appear with two frames (possibly more if your default page has more than one frame). The left-hand frame will include any debugging output. The right-hand side will display your default page. If you've changed your configuration to have the debug output appear in a window of its own, two windows will open when you click the Debug button.

Debugging the Sample Application

Even though the application worked as it should, we'll look at the debug output to see what it looks like. Figure 2-7 shows how the debug output will look. Table 2-2 gives a line-by-line description of the debug output. Please refer to Chapter 3, "Session Management Objects," for more information about the objects listed in this table.

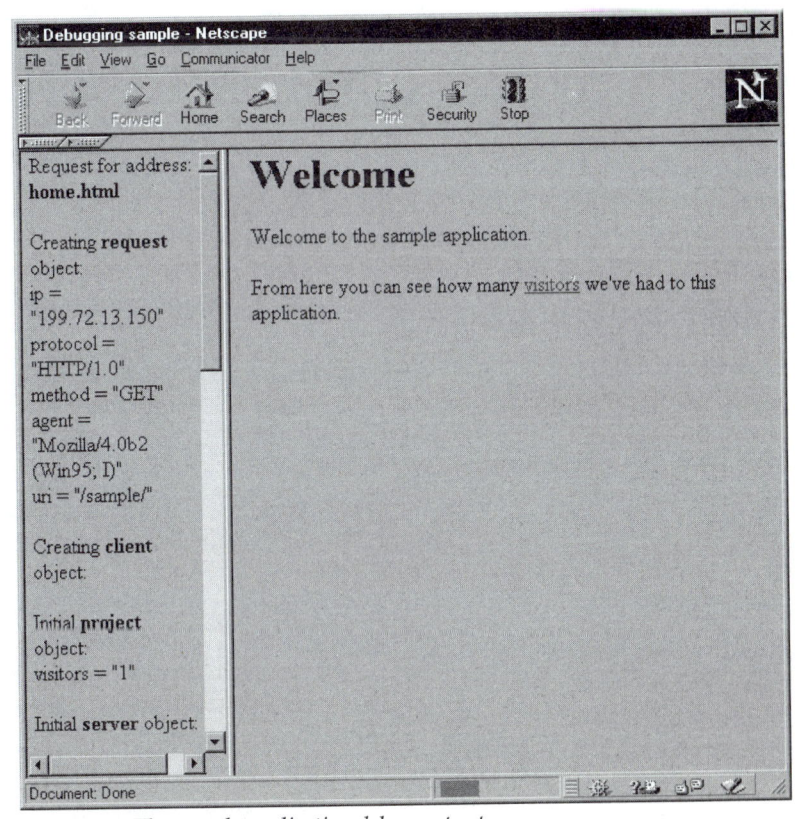

Figure 2-7: The sample application debug output.

Debug Output	Meaning
Request for address: **home.html**	This shows that the page home.html was requested from the application.
Creating **request** object:	This shows that the request object is being created. The request object contains information about the connection to the server.
ip = "199.72.13.150"	This shows there is a property named ip in the request object. It is set to the IP address of the machine requesting the page.
protocol = "HTTP/1.0"	This sets the value of the protocol property.
method = "GET"	This sets the value of the method property.
agent = "Mozilla/4.01 [en] (WinNT; U)"	This sets the agent property. It shows what browser is requesting the page.
uri = "/sample/"	This shows the URI that was requested. It is the part of the URL that comes after the machine name of the server.
Creating **client** object:	This shows that the client object is being created for this request. The client object is initialized with information sent from the client, which is *nothing* in this case.
Initial **project** object:	This shows the properties of the project object at the beginning of this request.
visitors = "1"	This shows that the visitors property has been set to 1. This was done the first time we accessed the home.html page.
Initial **server** object:	This shows the properties of the server object at the beginning of this request.
hostname = "edda.vmedia.com:18000"	This shows the value of the hostname property, which is the host and port of the machine where the server is running.
host = "edda.vmedia.com"	This shows only the hostname of the server.
protocol = "http:"	This shows the protocol of the connection to the server. It may be https: if you're running a secure server over SSL.
port = "18000"	This shows the port the server is running on. The default port is 80.
httpdlwVersion = "3.0 Solaris"	This shows the version of the LiveWire library for the server. In this case it is the 3.0 version of the Solaris server.

Debug Output	Meaning
jsVersion = "3.0 Solaris"	This shows the JavaScript version of the server, which is 3.0 running on Solaris.
Serving page...	This shows that the page is being sent to the client.
Final **request** object:	This shows the properties of the request object at the end of the request.
ip = "199.72.13.150"	See above.
protocol = "HTTP/1.0"	See above.
method = "GET"	See above.
agent = "Mozilla/4.01 [en] (WinNT; U)"	See above.
uri = "/sample/"	See above.
Final **client** object:	This shows the final properties of the client object.
Final **project** object:	This shows the final properties of the project object.
visitors = "2"	This shows that the visitors property has been set to 2 during this request.
Final **server** object:	This shows the final properties of the server object.
hostname = "edda.vmedia.com:18000"	See above.
host = "edda.vmedia.com"	See above.
protocol = "http:"	See above.
port = "18000"	See above.
httpdlwVersion = "3.0 Solaris"	See above.
jsVersion = "3.0 Solaris"	See above.

Table 2-2: The debug output of the sample application explained.

Moving On

In this chapter we've described how to use the JavaScript Application Manager to add applications to your server and how to use the JavaScript application compiler to compile applications.

In chapters that follow you'll learn about specific server-side JavaScript features that help you control user sessions. We'll also cover connecting to your database.

Session Management Objects

The JavaScript Application environment has a set of predefined objects to manage a user's session. This gives you a way to track users through multiple requests to your Enterprise Server. The creation and destruction of these objects are handled by session management services. These services are handled by the server-side JavaScript interpreter to create the session management objects as needed by user requests to your Enterprise Server.

By using these session management objects you can keep track of a user's progress through your application so that it becomes more coherent than just a bunch of hyperlinked Web pages. You can also share data among multiple users of your application—for example, by displaying the number of visitors daily or the hostname of the last visitor.

In the previous version of Enterprise Server, these objects were considered part of the LiveWire object framework. They are now referred to collectively as the object framework. Within the object framework, there are built-in capabilities to handle sharing data in the multithreaded Enterprise Server environment. Due to the threaded architecture, there may be more than one request to access a given object at the same time. Session management services provide capabilities such as object locking to protect your applications from data corruption in these cases.

The session management objects are: request, client, project, server, and lock:

- A **request** object is used to handle data specific to the current request. A request object is created each time a browser connects to the application and is initialized with data relevant to the request. This object is destroyed after the request has been served.
- A **client** object is used to hold data specific to the current client accessing the application. Client objects for one application on your server are separate from client objects for any other application on your server. The client object is destroyed when its expiration time is reached or if it's explicitly destroyed by your application.
- A **project** object holds data for the entire application. This object is created when the application starts; it is destroyed when the application ends. You use the project object to share application-specific data among all the clients connecting to the application.
- A **server** object holds data for the entire server. This object is created when the server starts; it is destroyed when the server is stopped. You can use the server object to share data across all the applications running on your server.
- A **lock** object is used to lock a critical section of code so that no other requests can access the lock until it has been unlocked. This protects against multiple requests to access the critical section at the same time, possibly corrupting the data.

Figure 3-1 shows how the session management objects are created through the duration of a server process on your machine.

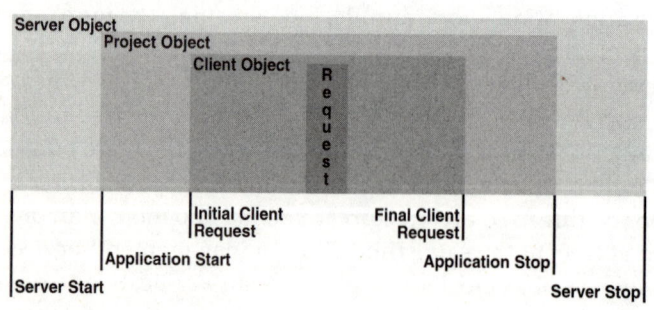

Figure 3-1: How session management objects are created and destroyed.

Except for the request and lock objects, these objects are used to maintain data across multiple requests to the application server. The lock object is used to provide protection for critical sections of code by restricting other requests from continuing while the lock is in effect. A *critical section* is a section of code in a multithreaded environment that can't be run by more than one thread at a time.

The following sections cover these objects in detail. We'll start with the lock object because it is something you may use at any time in your code to protect any critical sections. We'll follow with the rest of the session management objects in the order of length of lifetime: the request object for the life of a single HTTP request, the client object for the duration of a client's access to your application, the application object for the life of your application, and the server object that lives for the duration of your server process.

Table 3-1 outlines and compares various data about the session management objects.

Object	Scope	Lifetime	Use
Request	Can be accessed by one client connecting to a specific application.	Only exists as long as the request is being processed.	Can be used to store variables that are only needed for handling the current request.
Client	Can be accessed by one client connecting to a specific application.	The lifetime of this object depends on how the client object is maintained. See "Maintaining the Client Object" later in this chapter for more information.	Can be used to maintain state by storing information in the object. This information can be used on subsequent requests by the same client to customize the page displayed.
Project	Can be accessed by all clients connecting to a specific application.	Exists for the duration of the application on the server. It is destroyed when the application stops or restarts.	Can be used to store data that needs to be shared among all clients accessing a specific application.
Server	Can be accessed by all clients connecting to any application on the server.	Exists for the duration of the server. It is destroyed when the server stops or restarts.	Can be used to store data that needs to be shared among all clients accessing any application on the server.

Table 3-1: The scope, lifetime, and uses of the session management objects.

The Lock Object

Since the Enterprise Server is multithreaded, it is possible for more than one client to be requesting a page that will execute the same section of JavaScript code at the same time. This may cause problems if you're accessing a shared object, updating a database, or writing a file on the server.

The project and server objects already have a lock method to handle locking. If you've created your own shared object (or you're updating a database or writing a file), you'll want to create your own lock object to protect your changes. A lock object is generally stored as a property of the project or server object so that it can be accessed among all clients connecting to your application. You may also want to use a lock object if you're only accessing a few properties of a project or server object but don't want to lock access to the entire object.

Using the Lock Object

You can use as many locks as you want within an application. Once you've locked a lock object, any other requests that try to lock it will wait until it has been unlocked. Be sure to unlock the object once you've completed the critical section of code. As a safety measure, all locks will be unlocked at the end of a request so that your application doesn't hang during future requests.

You'll want to create any lock object you use as a property of a shared object, so that multiple requests can access it. To create a lock object, you simply make a new instance of the Lock class:

```
project.myLock = new Lock();
```

To lock the object, you call the lock method:

```
project.myLock.lock();
```

Once the object is locked, any other requests to access the lock will be blocked until the lock is available. When you're done with the critical code section, you unlock the lock like this:

```
project.myLock.unlock();
```

This will free the lock so that it's available for subsequent requests.

Let's say, for example, that you want to log a name that a user typed into an HTML form in your application along with a number you're incrementing to show how many people have accessed that page since your application started. You would use the following code:

```
project.myLock.lock();
var newVisitors = project.numVisitors +1;
logFile = new File("/path/name.log");
logFile.open(a);
logFile.write(request.name + "" + newVisitors + \n);
logFile.close();
project.numVisitors = newVisitors;
project.myLock.unlock();
```

You can see that there would be problems if one request set its copy of newVisitors and then a second request set its copy of newVisitors. Both requests would have the same number for newVisitors, which would make *project.numVisitors* incorrect; it would only have been incremented by one instead of two.

The section between the lock and unlock lines is considered a critical code section. This is because it is critical that only one thread should run this code at a time.

Refer to the information on lock object entry in Chapter 10, "Server-Side JavaScript Reference," for more details about the lock object.

The Request Object

The request object is created by session management services with each request to the application. It contains any data specific to that request. A request object is created for your application in the following circumstances:

- A user types in a URL within your application or selects a bookmark to your application.
- A user follows a hyperlink linked to your application or opens a page that references links to your application (such as within frames).
- Client-side JavaScript moves the current page to a page within your application.
- Server-side JavaScript redirects a user to a page within your application.

Once the server has responded to the request, the request object is destroyed. Generally the request object's lifetime is less than one second.

Properties

There are three different types of properties of the request object: *default*, *request specific*, and *assigned*. The default properties are created every time the request object is created and usually refer to information about the client or the request made to the server. The request-specific properties are created and set when a user submits a form, requests a URL with request properties encoded in the URL, or clicks on an image map. The assigned properties are defined by your application.

Default

The default request object properties are:

- **agent**—contains the name and version of the client software connecting to the application. You can use the agent property to determine what HTML features the browser supports. The agent information is in the format: browser/version (platform or other information). Netscape Communicator Preview Release 2 has the following agent value: Mozilla/4.0b2 (Win95; I). Mozilla means that it's a Netscape browser, 4.0b2 means that it's the second beta of Communicator (Navigator 4.0), Win95 means that it's running on Windows 95, and I means that it's running on an Intel-based processor.

- **ip**—contains the IP address of the client. You can use this property for logging purposes or to restrict access to certain operations of your applications. An example of an IP address is 199.72.13.1.

- **method**—contains the HTTP method associated with the request. The possible values for method in HTTP 1.0 are GET, POST, and HEAD. You will only see GET and POST as the request methods. GET is the method when a URL is requested. POST is the method when an HTML form is submitted to a page in your application with the METHOD attribute set to POST. The HEAD method is used by the browser to find only header information about your file. Since it doesn't actually request the whole file, the request object won't be created; therefore, you will never see it in your application.

- **protocol**—contains the HyperText Transfer Protocol (HTTP) level supported by the client, such as HTTP/1.0.

Assigned

You can assign any properties you want to the request object. These properties will only persist for the life of the request object. Assigning any new variable within one of your application pages will give it the same lifetime it would have if you assigned it within the request object.

```
var today = new Date();
```

has the same scope as:

```
request.today = new Date();
```

From Forms

Every element in a form submitted to a page in your application corresponds to a property of the request object. These properties are request-specific properties assigned by the session management services. The property name is defined by the NAME attribute of the element. The value typed or selected by the user is assigned to the property so that you can refer to the element's value, like this:

```
request.elementName
```

If you are using a SELECT form element that allows multiple OPTION selections, you'll need to use the getOptionValue function to retrieve the data. This is also true of any form elements that share the same name. For example, you may have a section of check boxes that share the same name, as in:

```
<INPUT TYPE=checkbox NAME=options value=verbose>Show extra output<br>
<INPUT TYPE=checkbox NAME=options value=links>Show link information<br>
```

Note: JavaScript applications do not support the ability to upload files to the application by using the file type of the <INPUT> tag. Any form input elements of this type will be ignored when session management services creates the request object.

URL Encoding

You can also encode request properties in a URL in the query string (a query string is any text in a URL that comes after a question mark):

```
URL?name1=value1&name2=value2
```

This will create the name1 and name2 properties in the request object. In the URL requested, you'll be able to access request.name1 and request.name2.

If you're using URL encoding for your client maintenance, you'll need to use the addClient function with any URLs you display in your page. See "Maintaining the Client Object" later in this chapter for more information on URL-encoding. If you have any special characters that aren't valid in a URL request (such as spaces, equal signs, or ampersands), you'll need to use the escape function to make sure the server can handle the URL. When session management services creates the request properties, it will unencode them appropriately.

You wouldn't want to store any sensitive data such as passwords through URL encoding because they will be displayed in the address area of the user's browser.

Image Maps

If you have an image map being sent to a page in your application, two new request object properties will be set: imageX and imageY. These properties will hold the integer values of the XY coordinates where the mouse clicked on the image. You can then use these values to determine where on the image the user clicked and display a new page accordingly.

The imageX and imageY properties will also be set when a form is submitted by clicking on an INPUT element that has the image TYPE, such as:

```
<INPUT TYPE=image SRC=mybutton.gif>
```

This button may have two sections: the left side to add new data, and the right side to update existing data. You can check the value of the imageX property to determine which side of the GIF the user clicked on.

The Client Object

The client object allows you to track a user through your application. This object allows you to maintain state through your application even though it's using HTTP, a stateless protocol. State is how you keep track of users across multiple requests to your application and distinguish one user from another, even if they're simultaneously accessing pages.

Every client that connects to your application has its own client object. If one user connects to two different applications on your server, it will have two client objects associated with it. There can be any number of client objects active at any given time.

Technically speaking, the client object only lives as long as the request object. Logically speaking, it lives for the duration of the session between the client and the application. At the end of each request, session management services saves the data in the client object and then destroys it. The next request that the user makes to your application will cause the client object to be created with the values from the saved data. How the data is saved depends on how you've decided to maintain the client object.

Properties

There are no default properties of the client object, only ones you assign to it. You can only store string data in client properties. This means that you can't assign objects to a client property, since objects can't be converted to a string.

If you need to store an object with each client, you can store an ID in the client object that refers to an object stored in the project or server objects. The following code fragment will refer an object, myObj, to an ID in the client object.

```
client.objID = getAvailableID();
project.savedObj[client.objID] = myObj;
```

Assume the getAvailableID function performs all necessary checks to make sure the ID returned is not being used by another client object.

Assignment Operator

You can assign values to the client object by selecting a property name and simply using the assignment operator:

```
client.name = "Joe Blow";
client.ID = 978;
```

The way the client object is saved depends on the method you chose when adding your application to the JavaScript Application Manager. If there are no properties assigned to the client object, session management services won't save the object, since it is unnecessary.

Some common uses for the client object are storing an ID associated with the user and storing a "shopping basket" of products that the user wishes to purchase.

Object Lifetime

The client object won't persist forever because there's no way to be sure that the client will ever connect to your application again. When the client object is created, its lifetime is set. The default expiration for a client object is 10 minutes of inactivity. What is defined as activity depends on the type of client maintenance you've selected. See the next section, "Maintaining the Client Object," for more information on how client maintenance affects the client object.

You can change the expiration time of a client object by using the expiration method:

```
client.expiration(3600);
```

This will set the expiration time to one hour. The expiration method takes its argument in seconds. You must declare the expiration on any page where you want the expiration to be different from the default. Setting it on one page in your application won't set it for every property you add to the client object from other pages.

For some types of client maintenance the expiration method doesn't apply—such as with client URL.

An explicit call to the destroy method of the client object will remove any properties that are set. Again, refer to "Maintaining the Client Object" below for information regarding varying behavior of the destroy method with different client maintenance methods.

Maintaining the Client Object

There are five different methods to maintain the client object in the Enterprise Server. They fall into two categories: client-side and server-side. If the client object is maintained on the server, there is usually some addressing scheme to associate data from the client software to data on the server.

Client-Side Methods

The two client-side methods are *client cookies* and *client URL encoding*.

When you're using any client-side method of client maintenance, you can't change any client properties after the requested page being served has been flushed. This is because the client object data is sent to the client software at the beginning of the output. Once the output has been flushed to the client software, the beginning of the output has been sent; therefore, any changes after that will be lost. Session management services automatically flushes the page after 64 kilobytes of output. To keep from losing any client data, you should assign all client properties before displaying 64K of content.

Client Cookies Method   When using the client cookies method, the browser stores all the client object information in a cookie file or in memory. This method is generally the best way to maintain the client object. It doesn't require any extra storing of data on the server, and it doesn't have any of the problems of client URL encoding. The only drawback it does have is that it requires browsers that support the cookie protocol, such as Netscape Navigator and Internet Explorer.

The client object properties are stored as cookies with the following name:

`NETSCAPE_LIVEWIRE.propertyName=propertyValue;`

Each of these cookies is limited to 4,096 characters. You are also limited to having only 20 client properties. If you try to use more than 20, the oldest property will be deleted.

If you use the destroy method when using the client cookies method, it won't affect any properties in the cookie file. If you want to delete the properties from the cookie file, you'll need to set the expiration of the client object to 0 seconds and then reset the property you want destroyed.

You can also never be sure how long the cookie will actually last. Any cookies in memory will be destroyed when the browser exits, and the user can remove the cookie file at any time.

Client URL Encoding Method   When using the client URL encoding method, the client object is stored as name/value pairs in the URL the client requests. This is done by using the query string of the URL. (The query string is any text in a URL after a question mark.) When using this method, all URLs in your application must be generated dynamically.

When using client URL encoding, you're limited to a maximum of 4K of name/value pairs with the URL. Any data past 4K is lost.

Any time you display a link on a page or use the redirect function, you need to use the addClient function. Without this, the client object will be lost. Due to the client being stored in the URL, the expiration method does nothing. The redirect function automatically stops the current request and causes the client to make a new request to the specified URL. The addClient function modifies the given URL argument to include the client object properties within the query string of the URL.

For example, the following code:

```
client.test1 = testing;
client.test2 = tested;
write(addClient("test.html"));
```

would produce this output:

```
test.html?test1=testing&test2=tested
```

If you want to destroy the client object, you should do so before any calls to addClient in the page. If you destroy the object after a call to addClient and the user clicks the link that the client was added to, the client object will remain (but not if any subsequent links are followed). Destroying the client at the end of the page has no effect either. You could also destroy the client by redirecting to a page without using the addClient function. Whenever a user submits a form using this method of client maintenance, all client properties are lost. A workaround is to include all the client properties in hidden form elements.

Server-Side Methods

There are three ways to store client data on the server: IP addresses, server cookies, and server URL encoding. Since all these methods store data on the server, all client objects are lost when the server stops or restarts. Restarting any particular application doesn't cause any problems. You should be careful when building your applications using one of these methods to allow for the server restarting in the middle of a user's session. Using one of the client-side methods resolves this problem.

Another disadvantage of the server-side methods is that each client object takes up disk space on the server. This could add up to quite a lot of space if you have many users connecting to your application.

When you're using any of the server-side methods, server management services checks out the client object from the server database when a request is made. If a second request is made for that client object before the first request is finished, that request won't get any data for the client object. This could cause problems for applications that use frames, since a client may be making multiple requests at one time. A workaround for this is to assign the client object variables in the document that contains the <FRAMESET> tags to client-side JavaScript variables, and then have the child frames refer to those variables instead of the client object.

IP Address Method   If you use the IP address method, the server stores the client object based on the client's IP address. This works fine as long as each client has a fixed IP address. You'll run into problems with dynamically assigned IP addresses or with users that have a proxy server. All users coming through a proxy server will share the same client object, which could cause problems.

Another problem with the IP address method is that if the user accesses two different applications on the server, the applications will share the client object. This could cause problems if the client property names overlap between the applications. If you use this method you should be careful to use unique property names between your applications.

Server Cookies Method   If you use server cookies, the server stores the client object data based on a generated ID. This ID is then assigned to the client as a cookie. On future requests, this ID is received, and session management services creates the client object based on that ID. This method requires the user's browser to support cookies. It keeps the client maintenance method transparent to the user (unless their browser notifies them every time a cookie is set).

Server URL Encoding Method   The server URL encoding method is similar to the server cookie method except that the ID is stored in the URL instead of in a cookie. When using this method you need to dynamically generate any URLs using the addClient function, as with the client URL encoding method.

Picking a Client Object Maintenance Method

The advantages and disadvantages of each client object maintenance method are outlined in Table 3-2.

Method	Advantages	Disadvantages
client cookies	Properties aren't lost by server restart.	Max. of 20 properties per application and only 4K per property.
		Increased network traffic since the cookies are transferred each time a request is made to the server.
		Requires a cookie-compliant browser.
client URL encoding	Works on all clients. Properties aren't lost by server restart.	Client properties are lost when submitting a form.
		Client expiration can't be controlled.
		You must use addClient for dynamic URLs or redirects.
		Large increase in network traffic due to the longer URLs that are being requested from the client.
		Properties lost when the user jumps to a bookmark or URL in the application.
		May lose some properties if the user uses the Back button.
IP address	Works with all clients. No increase in network traffic.	Doesn't support dynamic IP addresses or proxy servers (these users will share the same client object).
		Properties lost when server restarts.
		Takes up server disk space.
		All applications on the server accessed by a client share the same client object. This becomes an even larger problem when users from the same IP address access multiple applications on your server.
server cookies	Little increase in network traffic.	Properties lost when server restarts.
		Takes up server disk space.
		Requires a cookie-compliant browser.
server URL encoding	Works with all clients. Little increase in network traffic.	Properties lost when submitting a form.
		Properties lost when server restarts.
		Takes up server disk space.
		You must use addClient for dynamic URLs or redirects.

Table 3-2: The options for client object maintenance with their respective advantages and disadvantages.

The Project Object

The project object can be used to share data among all the clients accessing your application. A new project object is created by session management services when the application starts; it is destroyed when the application stops.

The project object is not created and destroyed at each request, as it was in previous versions of the Enterprise Server.

Properties

The only properties in the project object are ones that you assign. It is intended to keep data you want to share across your application.

> **TIP**
>
> *One excellent use of the project object is to store background image locations for all the pages in the application as well as server locations, so that you only need to update one variable if you need to change the background or any server names.*

You could also use the project object to track how many clients have connected to your application since it restarted and to assign client IDs based on this number. You may run into problems doing this if you restart your server often and you're using a client-side method to maintain the client object. If you do happen to restart your server often, you can store the ID number in a file on the server. This will be a little slower than using a project property. The following code fragments show the differences in these two methods:

```
project.IDlock.lock();
client.ID = project.currentID + 1;
project.currentID = client.ID
project.IDlock.unlock();
```

or

```
project.IDlock.lock();
IDFile = new File("IDFile.txt");
IDFile.open(r);
client.ID = eval(IDFile.readln()) + 1;
IDFile.close();
IDFile.open(w);
IDFile.writeln(client.ID);
IDFile.close();
project.IDlock.unlock();
```

You can see how the first method is much simpler and easier to read.

Locking

Any time you want to modify a property of the project object, you should lock it so that other requests don't try to modify it at the same time. In previous versions of the Enterprise Server, there was an implicit lock, but in this version you must explicitly lock it when you want to write data. You could also use a lock object if you don't want to use the project lock method.

While the project object is locked, no other clients can access its properties. Any requests that try to access the project object must wait until it's unlocked. If you have many pages that lock the project object, users may experience delays trying to use your application.

If you forget to unlock the project object, it will be unlocked at the end of the request.

The following code fragment shows how to use the project object's locking mechanism:

```
project.lock();
project.numVisitors = project.numVisitors + 1;
project.unlock();
```

The Server Object

The server object allows you to share data among all clients accessing any application on your server. The server object also contains some informational properties regarding your server.

A server object is created when the server starts and is destroyed when the server is stopped. If you have multiple servers running on one machine (either by using different ports or by using virtual servers), each of these servers has its own server object.

Properties

The main purpose of the server object is to share data among applications. Any property you assign to the server object will be accessible to any other application running on your server. There are a few default properties, however, giving information about the server.

Default

There are four default properties in the server object: *host, hostname, port,* and *protocol*:

- The **host** is the fully qualified name of the server machine (such as www.netscapepress.com).
- The **hostname** is the full hostname of the server, including a port number (such as www.netscapepress.com:80).
- The **port** is the port number of the machine that the server is using (such as 80).
- The **protocol** is the protocol that was used to access the server (such as http: or https:).

Assigned

Properties you assign to the server object can be of any valid JavaScript type. These properties are used in much the same way as the project object properties, except on a wider scale.

For example, you may have an application that anyone on the Internet can access to request more information about your company. You might have another application on the server that has restricted access, so that any users with access to that application can view how many people have asked for information since the server started.

The Internet application would include the following code when someone requested information:

```
server.lock();
server.numRequests = server.numRequests + 1;
server.unlock();
```

The intranet application would have a page to check the number with the following code:

```
write(server.numRequests + " people have requested information since the server started.<br>");
```

You could also store this information in a file on the server if you didn't want it to be lost when the server stops or restarts.

Locking

Since there is only one server object for all applications on the server, you need to lock that object before changing any of its properties. The server object is locked in the same way the project is locked. See the example above and "Locking" under the preceding "Project Object" section.

You must be even more careful about excessive locking of the server object because you may tie up many applications while it is locked.

Moving On

Now that you've learned all about the session management objects, you can create your own JavaScript applications using the Netscape Enterprise Server. You can process HTML form data using the request object. You can keep track of users with the client object and share data among users and applications using the project and server objects.

The next chapter focuses on how to connect your application to a database server. This will give you the ability to add dynamic content to your application through your database.

Connecting to Your Database

LiveWire is a collection of server-side JavaScript objects that allow you to connect your application to one or more database servers. Once connected, you can run queries and arbitrary SQL statements on the database server.

The supported database servers are DB2, Informix, Oracle, Sybase, and any database you can access through ODBC. In the previous version of the Enterprise Server, you were limited to only one database connection per request. With Enterprise Server Version 3.0, you can connect to multiple databases as well as connect multiple times to the same database, possibly with different users. All this functionality is handled through database connection pools.

This chapter will cover how you connect to your database and run SQL statements and queries. We'll see how to use transactions to make sure your data is consistent. Enterprise Server 3.0 has also added the capability to run stored procedures on your database server.

Your Database Configuration

No database client libraries ship with the 3.0 version of the Enterprise Server. This means that, unlike the previous versions of the Enterprise Server, you need to install the appropriate libraries on your server machine. Your database vendor can supply the appropriate libraries.

The supported databases with the required libraries for each platform are outlined in Table 4-1. The supported ODBC drivers are listed in Table 4-2.

Database	Solaris 2.5	NT 3.51/4.0	IRIX 6.2
DB2	CAE 2.1.2 with APAR #JR10150	CAE 2.1.2	CAE 2.1.2
Informix	Ifx Client 7.22	Ifx Client 7.22	Ifx Client 7.22
Oracle	Oracle Client 7.3.x	Oracle Client 7.3.x	Oracle Client 7.3.x
Sybase	OpenClient/C 10.0.3	OpenClient/C 10.0.3	OpenClient/C 10.0.3
ODBC Manager	Visigenic 2.0	MS ODBC Manager 2.5	Visigenic 2.0

Table 4-1: The client libraries required for each database and platform.

Database	Solaris 2.5	NT 3.51/4.0	IRIX 6.2
MS Access 7.0	N/A	MS Access Driver 3.5 (odbcjt32.dll)	N/A
MS Excel 7.0	N/A	MS Excel Driver 3.5 (odbcjt32.dll)	N/A
MS FoxPro x.0	N/A	MS FoxPro Driver 3.5 (odbcjt32.dll)	N/A
MS SQL Server 6.5	Visigenic MS SQL Server Driver version 2.00.0600 (vsmsssql.so.1)	MS SQL Server Driver 2.65 (sqlsrv32.dll)	Visigenic MS SQL Server Driver version 2.00.0200 (vsmsssql.so.1)
MS SQL Server 6.0	Visigenic MS SQL Server Driver version 2.00.0600 (vsmsssql.so.1)	2.50.0121 (sqlsrv32.dll)	Visigenic MS SQL Server Driver version 2.00.0200 (vsmsssql.so.1)
Sybase SQL Anywhere 5.0	N/A	Sybase SQL Anywhere Driver 05.05.0001 (wod50t.dll)	N/A

Table 4-2: The ODBC drivers required for each supported database and platform.

For more information on configuring your database with Enterprise Server 3.0, please refer to the documentation for Enterprise Server and your database server.

Some ODBC drivers and databases don't support all the features, as when directly connecting to your database. Table 4-3 outlines what features are supported when using ODBC to access your database server.

Database (Platform)	Connect	Read-only Cursor	SQL Passthrough	Stored Procedures	Updatable Cursor
Access (NT)	X	X	X	N/A	
Excel (NT)	X	X	X	N/A	
FoxPro (NT)	X	X	X	N/A	
MS SQL Server 6.0/6.5 (NT)	X	X	X	X	X
MS SQL Server (Solaris)	X	X	X	X	X
MS SQL Server (IRIX)	X	X	X	X	
Sybase SQL Anywhere (NT)	X	X	X		X

Table 4-3: *The capabilities of the supported ODBC drivers.*

Database Connection Pools

To connect to a database, you must first create a pool of connections to the database. When you need to access the database, you can pull a connection from the pool and call the connection object methods to run your queries.

Creating a Database Connection Pool

When you create a database connection pool, you have the option of connecting to the database at that time, or you can create a generic pool and connect to it later. You create the pool by creating a new DbPool object. If you've created a generic DbPool object, it won't have any connections available. To make sure you always have available connections, it's generally better to connect to the database when you create the pool.

When you create a pool and connect it, you must specify the connection configuration. This configuration consists of the following parameters of the DbPool object:

- The type of database you're connecting to: INFORMIX, ORACLE, SYBASE, or ODBC.
- The name of the database server. The name of the server is defined when the database is installed. Consult your database administrator if you're not sure what to use here. If you're using ODBC, you should put the name of the ODBC service here.
- The username to connect to the database.
- The password for that user.
- The name of the database on the server to connect to. (Some database servers allow multiple databases per server.)
- The number of available connections to create in the database connection pool.
- A Boolean flag to denote whether to commit open transactions at the end of the request.

The last two parameters are optional and they default to 1 and false, respectively. The following code will create a new DbPool object:

```
myPool = new DbPool("ORACLE", "db", "www", "password", "", 5, true);
```

If you do wish to create a generic DbPool object, you simply create a new object without passing any parameters. You need to be sure to call the connect method on this object before you can access any database connections from your pool.

```
myPool = new DbPool();
myPool.connect("ORACLE", "db", "www", "password", "", 5, true);
```

Using Database Connection Pools

When you have a connected DbPool object, all the connections within it are associated with a particular connection configuration to a database. In other words, all connections allocated from your pool will be connected to the same database using the same user ID and password, as long as you don't disconnect and reconnect the pool.

There are two main ways to connect to multiple database servers or to the same server as a different user with possibly different access:

- The *standard method* is to create a pool for each configuration you want and store the DbPool object in a project property. This is the most efficient and safest way of using multiple connections configurations.
- The second method is called the *serial approach*. Using this method, you connect and disconnect the same pool each time you need to change the configuration of the connection pool. You should only use this method if there is a large number of database configurations that you will be connecting to through the life of your application.

Before you can disconnect a database connection pool, all the connections in the pool must be released. If there are connections still in use, the Enterprise Server will wait until the connections have been released before disconnecting the pool.

Sharing Pools

Sometimes you may find that all the users of your application need to share a set of connection pools. If you only have a few possible configurations, you can create a pool for each configuration and store them all in the project object. This allows you to quickly access the database connection you need without having to create a new pool with each client request.

In the employee database applications we've discussed in previous chapters, you may want to have multiple database configurations in the intranet application. Depending on the user's access rights, a different connection can be used:

```
project.normal = new DbPool("INFORMIX", "db", "employees", "password",
"employee", 5, true);
project.restricted = new DbPool("ORACLE", "otherdb", "hr", "password", , 2);
```

This would create two pools that your application can access at any time. You should include this code in the Initial Page of your application that so it will be run the first time the application is accessed after it has been started.

When users are accessing your application you don't need to worry about connecting to the database; you just need to decide which pool to use and then allocate a connection from it.

If your connection configuration changes often and you're using the serial approach, you shouldn't store your connection pool in the project object. Doing so may adversely affect other users accessing your application. In this case you should create the DbPool as part of the request. If the connection needs to be available across multiple requests, then you will need to use the project object. The next section talks about how to do this. You could also store an associative array of connection pool objects in the project object and store the key in the client object. Then the next time that client connects, it can access its configured pool.

Accessing Connections

Now that you have a pool of connections, you need a way to access a connection from that pool. You can do this by calling the connection method of the DbPool object. It will return a connection object based on the connection configuration of the pool.

To get a connection from our normal connection pool, as defined in the previous section, we would use:

```
myConnection = project.normal.connection('employee connection', 30);
```

The parameters to the connection method are both optional. The first sets a name to the connection (which may be useful when debugging), and the second sets a timeout (in seconds).

If the pool has an available connection, it will assign it to the myConnection variable. If not, the Enterprise Server will wait 30 seconds (as specified by the timeout) for a connection to become available. If no connection becomes available, the connection method will return without a connection. If you don't specify a timeout period, the server will wait until a connection is released and then return that connection.

Once a connection has been allocated from the pool, it can be released by one of two methods: by calling the connection's release method or by having the variable that refers to the connection go out of scope.

Before you call the release method, you should close any open cursors. If you don't close open cursors, the system will wait until all cursors have been closed before releasing the connection back to the pool. When all cursors have been closed, the connection becomes available for the next connection request to the pool.

Depending on how you've stored the connection object, it may go out of scope at different times. If the connection is a property of the project object, it will remain until the application stops. If the connection is a property of the server object, it will remain until the server stops. It would be very rare to have a connection you wanted to last for the life of the server. In any other case, the connection will be part of the client request. It will go out of scope when the server completes the request.

Note: If you create a cursor from your connection object and then pass that cursor to a function, you must also pass the connection object, or the cursor will fail because it can't find its connection.

See the connection object entry in Chapter 10, "Server Side JavaScript Reference," for more information on the connection object methods.

Using a Connection Across Multiple Requests

In some cases you may want to have a connection object live across multiple requests. You'll need to have your pool of connections in the project object, but you'll need a different way to manage it than the method described above.

> **TIP**
>
> *You should be very careful when your connections span multiple requests. There's no way to guarantee that a client will complete the next request, and thus a connection may be left unreleased. If this happens enough times, your connection pool may be used up, and any subsequent connection requests will hang until a connection is released.*

One reason you might want to have a connection span multiple requests is if you want a transaction to span the requests as well. That way, if an error occurs two requests into the transaction, you can still roll back all of your changes.

Using our employee database from earlier sections, let's say we have two pages that need to be filled out when an employee gets promoted. The first page assigns a new title; the second page assigns a new salary. We don't want to commit the transaction until both changes have been successfully made. We use a client ID to keep track of the connection across requests.

The first page that sets the title would include this code:

```
client.id = request.id;
project.sharedPool = new DbPool("ORACLE", "db", "hr", "password", "", 5);
var myConnection = project.sharedPool.connection();
project.connections[client.id] = myConnection;
myConnection.beginTransaction();
addTitle = myConnection.cursor("select title,id from employees where id ="
    +request.employee);
addTitle.next();
addTitle.title = "VP";
addTitle.updateRow("employees");
addTitle.close();
```

The second page that sets the new salary would include this code:

```
var myConnection = project.connections[client.id];
addSalary = myConnection.cursor("select id,salary from salaries where id ="
+request.employee);
addSalary.next();
addSalary.salary = 120000;
addSalary.updateRow(salaries);
addSalary.close();
myConnection.commitTransaction();
myConnection.release;
delete project.connections[client.id];
```

After updating the salary and committing the open transaction, this page releases the connection back to the connection pool and then deletes the connection from the project associative array.

Running SQL Statements

Once you've made a connection to your database, you have two ways to run SQL statements. You can run a query and have it displayed to the user in an HTML table, or you can run an arbitrary SQL statement that doesn't return any data to the user. These two functions don't allow you to manipulate the data returned (if there is any data). See the "Cursors" section that follows to learn about manipulating the data returned from your SQL queries.

Displaying Database Queries

If you want to view the results of a query without having to write a lot of code, you can use the SQLTable method of your connection object. This method will create an HTML table with the names of the columns as headers in the first row of the table, with each of the following rows representing a record from the database.

If you use the SQLTable method, you don't have any control over how the data is displayed. If you want to customize the data display, see the "Displaying Query Results Using a Cursor" section that follows.

Let's say for example you want to display a table of all employees' salaries in your company (assuming you're allowed to see such data). You could use the following code (assume you've already created a connection object named myConnection):

```
myConnection.SQLTable("select employee_name, salary from employees order by salary desc");
```

That's it. The output from this command would be:

```
<TABLE BORDER>
<TR>
<TH>employee_name</TH>
<TH>salary</TH>
</TR>
<TR>
<TD>Joe Blow</TD>
<TD>30000</TD>
</TR>
<TR>
<TD>Bill Gates</TD>
</TD>data out of range</TD>
</TR>
...
```

Executing SQL

If you want to run a SQL statement that doesn't return a cursor, you can use the execute method of the connection object. A few of the most common statements you might run are data definition language statements, such as ALTER, CREATE, or DROP, or you might use control statements like DELETE, INSERT, or UPDATE.

Unless you're updating or deleting a large number of rows, you should use cursors instead of using DELETE, INSERT, or UPDATE in the execute method. This keeps your application more independent from the SQL server you're using. Cursors also provide support for Binary Large Objects (BLObs). See the "Using BLObs" section below for more information.

To execute the statement, pass it to the execute method:

```
myConnection.execute("update employees set salary = salary + 1000");
```

TIP

When executing SQL statements, the statement must conform to the syntax required by your database server. Some servers require all statements to end in a semicolon (;), for example. Your database server documentation should explain the syntax required.

If you haven't explicitly begun a transaction, any SQL statement that you run using the execute method will automatically be committed. See the "Transactions" section that follows for more information on managing database transactions.

Cursors

When you want to do more with your database queries than just display them in a table, or if you want to customize the display, you need to use cursors. When you make a query to the database through a SQL SELECT statement, the matching data is returned in a table to the cursor. You can then access the rows of the table by working your way through the cursor.

When using server-side JavaScript, database cursors are represented by a cursor object. The columns requested by the query are made into properties of the cursor object. You can find out information about the cursor columns as well as move through the cursor by using the cursor object methods.

You can only move one way with a cursor object: to the next row. Anything you do to the cursor will affect the current row of the cursor.

Server-side JavaScript also has the concept of updatable cursors. When using updatable cursors, you can modify information and delete or add rows to the database table. Once you've finished all your operations on a cursor, you should close it. All cursor objects are automatically closed at the end of the request.

Using a Cursor

You can create a cursor object by calling the cursor method of a connection object. The cursor method takes two arguments: the SQL query to run, and a Boolean flag to indicate whether the cursor is updatable or not. The second argument is optional and defaults to false.

If you want your application to be easily portable, allowing it to be used with other or multiple database servers, you should be careful to include only SQL standard syntax when creating a cursor object. If you don't, you will run into problems and delays when moving your code.

The following JavaScript statement will create a cursor object that holds the data requested from the employees table in the database. The cursor will have a property set for each column in the table that is requested (ID, name, title, department), ordered alphabetically by the name of the employee.

```
employees = myConnection.cursor("select ID,name,title,department from
employees order by name");
```

You can now manipulate the data returned by the cursor by calling methods of the cursor object or by accessing the ID, name, title, and department properties.

> **TIP**
>
> *Because most database column names aren't case-sensitive, the cursor property names aren't case-sensitive. All other JavaScript properties are.*

The SQL statement can be any valid string object, so you can access other objects, such as the request object, when writing your query. You may want to have a statement similar to the one below if you have a search page in your application.

```
found = myConnection.cursor("select * from employees where name like' %" +
request.searchTerm + "%'");
```

This will return a cursor with all the records that include the search term selected by the user. This search will be case-sensitive. Some database servers have custom SQL features that allow you to do more complex searches.

Displaying Query Results Using a Cursor

You can iterate through the rows of a cursor by using the *next* method. When a cursor is created, its current position is before the first row; so you must call the *next* method before being able to access any of the property data.

Using the first cursor created in the previous section, you could display the data of the current row by using the following code:

```
write("<table border=0>");
write("<tr><th align=right>Name:</th>");
write("<td>"+employees.name+"</td></tr>");
write("<tr><th align=right>Title:</th>");
write("<td>"+employees.title+"</td></tr>");
write("<tr><th align=right>Department:</th>");
write("<td>"+employees.department+"</td></tr>");
write("<tr><th align=right>ID:</th>");
write("<td>"+employees.ID+"</td></tr>");
write("</table>");
```

You can also access the properties of the cursor by treating the cursor object as an array. The first column of the query can be accessed by this:

```
employees[0]
```

You can iterate through all the properties of the current row of the cursor using a *for* loop and accessing the cursor as an array, like this:

```
for ( i = 0; i < employees.columns(); i++ ) {
    write(employees[i] + "<br>");
}
```

For a larger example of using a cursor, see the cursor object entry in Chapter 9, "Testing & Debugging."

Using Aggregate Functions in SQL

Sometimes when you make complex queries to the database, there isn't a column name associated with the data returned to the cursor. In these cases you have to use the array index to access the values of the data.

If you wanted to find out your total salary cost for all your employees, as well as the average salary, you could do this:

```
salaryInfo = myConnection.cursor("select SUM(salary), AVG(salary) from employees");
salaryInfo.next();
write("Total Salary:" + salaryInfo[0] + "<br>");
write("Average Salary:" + salaryInfo[1] + "<br>");
```

Cursor Navigation

Whenever you call the *next* method to iterate through the rows in your cursor, you can tell when you've reached the last row because the *next* method will return false. The most common way to iterate through all the rows in a cursor is by using a *while* loop:

```
while ( employees.next() ) {...}
```

Using Updatable Cursors

When you create an updatable cursor, you are able to modify the contents of your database tables. Remember to set the second argument of the cursor method to true when you want to have an updatable cursor, as in:

```
newEmployee = myConnection.cursor( "select * from employees, true" );
```

To be able to create an updatable cursor, the SQL statement you pass to the database must have the ability to be updated. Cursors that request data from more than one table or have a GROUP BY clause cannot be updated. If you're inserting new data, you must also be sure that you've retrieved all the columns from the table that can't be assigned null values.

Inserting a New Row

To insert a new row into the table, follow these steps:

1. Assign the new values to the cursor properties:
   ```
   newEmployee.name = "Joe Blow";
   newEmployee.salary = 20000;
   newEmployee.title = "Peon";
   ...
   ```

2. Call the insertRow method:
   ```
   newEmployee.insertRow("employees");
   ```

If you've already called the *next* method of the cursor, any properties you don't explicitly assign will be assigned the values from the current row of the cursor. If you haven't called the *next* method, any unassigned columns will contain the null value. The same is true for any columns that didn't exist in the cursor but are in the database table.

Updating Information in an Existing Row

To update the information in an existing row, follow these steps:

1. Call the *next* method until you've reached the row you wish to update. If you used a WHERE clause in your database query to find the record you wish to update, you'll only need to call *next* once, assuming there aren't multiple rows matching your conditions.
   ```
   newEmployee.next();
   ```

2. Assign the new values:
   ```
   newEmployee.salary = 22000;
   ```

3. Call the updateRow method:
   ```
   newEmployee.updateRow("employees");
   ```

Removing a Row From the Table

To remove a row from the table, follow these steps:

1. Call the *next* method until you've reached the row you wish to delete. If you've used the WHERE clause to find the data you want removed, you'll only need to call the *next* method once, assuming there aren't multiple rows matching your conditions.

2. Call the deleteRow method:
   ```
   newEmployee.deleteRow("employees");
   ```

Cursor Columns

You can use the columns method of the cursor object to find out the number of columns in the cursor. You can use this method to iterate across all the columns in the cursor. An example of this that mimics the SQLTable method can be found near the cursor object entry in Chapter 9, "Testing & Debugging."

You can use the columnName method to determine the name of a column in the table based on the zero-based index of the column. See the sidebar titled "Using a Cursor Object to Mimic & Customize the SQLTable Method" in Chapter 9, "Testing & Debugging," for an example of using the columnName method.

Stored Procedures

Stored procedures are a part of your database server. They are used to automate tasks you need to perform often for convenience. Other benefits of stored procedures are:

- **Data management**. You don't have to worry about user error when performing complex transactions because the user can simply call the stored procedure. This also guarantees that your data is stored consistently, so you always know what to expect in future queries.
- **Efficiency**. When a stored procedure is called, it remains in memory. This makes future calls to the stored procedure much faster. This results in less traffic and a smaller work load on the database server. Stored procedures also help in managing your modular programming.
- **Security**. A stored procedure can have more access rights than the user calling the procedure. This can allow limited access to sensitive data without having to worry about giving too much access.

The two JavaScript objects you will use to handle stored procedures are StoredProc and ResultSet. By using the methods of these objects, you can call stored procedures and work with their results.

Using Stored Procedures

Stored procedures work differently depending on the database server you are using. Be careful to note what database server is being discussed, to make sure the content is appropriate for your application. In the current version (3.0) of the Enterprise Server, there is no support for stored procedures when using ODBC to connect to your database.

Stored Procedures in Sybase & Oracle Databases

Sybase and Oracle databases have three methods of passing data between your application and the stored procedure:

- **Input & Output Arguments**. The arguments to a Sybase or Oracle stored procedure can be one of three types: input (to pass arguments to the procedure), output (to store output from the procedure), and input/output (to pass arguments to the procedure and then store the output). You use the outParamCount and outParameters methods to access output parameters.

- **Return Value**. Sybase and Oracle stored procedures can have a single return value that can be accessed via the returnValue method of the StoredProc object.

- **Result Sets**. A Sybase stored procedure may generate result sets depending on whether any SELECT statements were executed during the stored procedure. There is a result set for each such SQL query. These result sets are very similar to a cursor (except they can't be updated). You use the resultSet method to access a stored procedure's result sets.

> **TIP**
>
> *The current release of the Enterprise Server doesn't support result sets for Oracle stored procedures. Future releases should support this functionality.*

Stored Procedures in Informix Databases

Informix databases handle information differently between the application and the stored procedure:

- Informix stored procedures can only accept input arguments to pass data to the procedure. The outParamCount and outParameters always return 0 for Informix databases.

- Informix databases can have multiple return values, but they have no result sets. Since there are multiple return values, they are accessed through the resultSet method as a ResultSet object. The returnValue method returns 0 for Informix databases.

Registering a Stored Procedure for DB2 Databases

DB2 includes system tables where stored procedures can be recorded. It is generally optional to register your stored procedures in these tables, but for LiveWire it is required.

If you're using the DB2 common server, you must create a DB2CLI.PROCEDURES system table where all the stored procedures must be entered. If you're using DB2 for MVS/EA V4.1 or later, you must enter your stored procedures in the SYSIBM.SYSPROCEDURES catalog table.

Since DB2 stored procedures are written in an external language like C or C++, you need to be sure to enter the DB2 data type in the stored procedure parameters instead of the C/C++ data types. Please refer to your DB2 documentation for more information on stored procedures.

Defining a Prototype for DB2, Sybase & ODBC Databases

Stored procedure prototypes are only necessary for calling DB2, Sybase, or ODBC stored procedures. For these databases your application can't determine the argument types for the stored procedures at run time. For this reason, you must create a prototype for each stored procedure your application will be calling after you connect to the database.

You use the storedProcArgs method of the DbPool object to define the prototypes. You only need to define one prototype per stored procedure; any additional prototypes will be ignored.

The arguments to storedProcArgs are the name of the stored procedure followed by the argument types for each argument: input (IN), output (OUT), or input/output (INOUT). The following prototype declaration defines a prototype for a procedure called "fire" with one input argument:

```
myPool.storedProcArgs("fire", IN);
```

Running Stored Procedures

All database servers call stored procedures in the same way. You create a StoredProc object via a call to the storedProc method of the Connection object. The arguments to storedProc are the name of the procedure and any arguments the procedure may take.

The "fire" stored procedure takes one argument, the ID of the employee that was fired. This stored procedure can be called by:

```
myProc = myConnection.storedProc ("fire", 12457);
```

The steps to run your stored procedure are different for each database. The following table briefly outlines which steps are necessary for each database. If the step is required for your database, it will have an 'X' beside that step.

Step	DB2	Informix	Oracle	Sybase	ODBC
Register the stored procedures in the necessary system tables. (This must be done outside of the JavaScript Application Environment.)	X				
Define a prototype.	X			X	X
Run the stored procedure.	X	X	X	X	X
Access the ResultSet object to handle the return data.	X	X	X	X	X
Access the output parameters to handle the return data.	X		X	X	X
Access the return value to handle the return data.			X	X	

Table 4-4: The steps for using stored procedures for each database.

Handling Data Returned From a Stored Procedure

There are three ways to handle data returned from a stored procedure: result sets, return values, and output parameters.

The following table shows how you can retrieve data from a stored procedure object. See the following sections for more information on each type.

Database	Result Sets	Return Values	Output Parameters
DB2	X		X
Informix	X		
Oracle	X	X	X
Sybase	X	X	X
ODBC	X		X

Table 4-5: The possible ways data is returned from a stored procedure for each database.

Informix databases don't actually have a result set; however, Informix databases return their return values through a ResultSet object. Since Informix sends the return values through a result set, only Oracle and Sybase use return values.

Result Sets

Calling the resultSet method of the StoredProc object returns the first result set from the stored procedure. If you're using Informix, there will only be one result set, but all other databases may have multiple result sets.

These result sets act exactly like cursors that can't be updated. You can access the columns of the result set as a property of the result set object. Any unnamed columns can be accessed as an array index. Result sets also have the notion of a current row, therefore you can use the *next* method of the ResultSet object to iterate through the result set values, as in:

```
myResult = myProc.resultSet();
while (myResult.next()) { ... }
```

Informix result sets never have named columns, so you must always access the returned data through the array indices:

```
while ( myResult.next() ) {
    write(myResult[0] + "<br>");
    write(myResult[1] + "<br>");
}
```

Since a stored procedure may call multiple SELECT statements, it may have multiple result sets. You can access subsequent result sets by multiple calls to the resultSet method:

```
myResult1 = myProc.resultSet();
while ( myResult1.next() ) { ... }
myResult2 = myProc.resultSet();
while ( myResult2.next() ) { ... }
```

> **TIP**
>
> *Be sure to access all the result sets created by your stored procedure before accessing the return value or output parameters. If you don't, the unclaimed result sets will be lost.*

Return Values

You can use the stored procedure's return value to pass any data back to the application from the stored procedure. DB2, Informix, and ODBC stored procedures always have a return value of 0.

You might use the return value to determine if the stored procedure executed correctly to know whether or not to access any result sets or output parameters.

Output Parameters

Output parameters aren't relevant to Informix-stored procedures. If you're using an Informix database, the output parameter methods will always return 0.

You can determine how many output parameters there are by the outParamCount method of the StoredProc object. You can then view the output parameters by passing a zero-based index to the outParameters method.

You could use the following code to display all the output parameters returned from the procedure:

```
for ( i = 0; i < myProc.outParamCount; i++ ) {
    write("output parameter" + i + ":" + myProc.outParameters(i) + "<br>");
}
```

Transactions

A database transaction is a collection of actions that are grouped together. Either all the actions succeed, or they all fail. When you attempt to execute all the actions, you are committing the transaction. If you decide to cancel the actions, you can roll back the transaction.

Transactions are useful for making sure your data remains consistent. If you modify one table to debit an account, you want to make sure that another account is credited by the same amount. If one of the actions fails and you didn't have transaction control, you'd be rich (and probably thrown in jail).

You can use transactions for any set of SQL statements that you want to execute, but they are most useful when you're modifying the database. These modifications may be made either through cursors or the SQL DELETE, INSERT, or UPDATE statements.

If you are using cursors in your transaction, any open transactions will be committed or rolled back when the cursor closes. This depends on whether the *commitFlag* was set to true or false when the connection configuration was defined in the DbPool object. If you're using multiple cursors within a transaction, you should be sure to commit or roll back the transaction before closing any of the cursors—otherwise you may get unexpected behavior.

If you don't want to deal with managing transactions, each statement you send to the database will be part of an implicit transaction. This transaction will begin before the statement and will attempt to be committed after the statement.

You can explicitly manage a transaction using the beginTransaction, commitTransaction, and rollbackTransaction methods of the connection object:

- **beginTransaction** starts a new transaction.
- **commitTransaction** attempts to commit all statements since a call to beginTransaction.
- **rollbackTransaction** cancels any statements since a call to beginTransaction.

The scope of a transaction is limited to the life of the connection object that began the transaction. This is usually for one request but may be different if you're using connections across multiple requests. See the section "Using a Connection Across Multiple Requests" earlier in this chapter for more information on this topic. If the connection object goes out of scope before being committed or rolled back, the default behavior will be determined by the *commitFlag* set when the DbPool object was configured.

The LiveWire database connectivity libraries don't support nested transactions. Nested transactions are multiple calls to beginTransaction without a call to commitTransaction or rollbackTransaction. If you do make multiple calls to beginTransaction, the next call to commit or roll back the transaction will refer to the first beginTransaction statement.

Database/JavaScript Data Types

Different databases have various data types. When you access these data types in LiveWire, they will be converted to JavaScript data types. JavaScript numbers are stored with a double-precision floating-point value. LiveWire generally converts database character types to strings, numeric types to numbers, and dates to a date object. Nulls remain as a JavaScript null.

When assigning JavaScript data types to an updatable cursor, make sure the JavaScript type can be converted to the database type; otherwise you may get an error or corrupt data. See the following tables that map the database data types to JavaScript data types.

Table 4-6 shows a comparison of the JavaScript data types to the corresponding database types.

Chapter 4: Connecting to Your Database

JavaScript	DB2	Informix	Oracle	Sybase	ODBC
BLOb	blob	byte	raw(255), long raw	binary(b), image, varbinary(n)	SQL_BINARY, SQL_LONGBINARY, SQL_VARBINARY
date	date, time, timestamp	date, datetime	date	datetime, smalldatetime	SQL_DATE, SQL_TIME, SQL_TIMESTAMP
number	decimal, double, integer, smallint	decimal(p,s), double precision, float, integer, money(p,s), serial, smallfloat, smallint	number(p,s), number(p,0), float(p)	bit, decimal(p,s), double precision, float(p), int, money, numeric(p,s), real, smallint, smallmoney, tinyint	SQL_BIGINT, SQL_DECIMAL, SQL_DOUBLE, SQL_FLOAT, SQL_INTEGER, SQL_NUMERIC, SQL_REAL, SQL_SMALLINT
string	char(n), varchar(n), long varchar	char, nchar, nvarchar, text, varchar	char, long, mislabel, rowid, varchar2(n)	char(n), nchar(n), nvarchar(n), text, varchar(n)	SQL_CHAR, SQL_LONGVARCHAR, SQL_VARCHAR
Not supported		interval			

Table 4-6: JavaScript to database data type conversions.

Going back to the employee database example, let's assume that we're using an Oracle database. We've created a date type birthdate field in the employee table. When accessing this column as a property of a cursor, it will be a JavaScript date type, so you can use any method associated with the JavaScript date object:

```
employee = database.cursor("select name,birthdate from employees");
employee.next();
write(employee.name +  "was born on" );
write(parseInt(employee.birthdate.getMonth()+1) + "/");
write(employee.birthdate.getDate() + "/");
write(employee.birthdate.getYear() + ".<br>");
employee.close();
```

This may display the following output:

```
Joe Blow was born on 5/19/63.<br>
```

Please refer to your JavaScript documentation or the Official Netscape JavaScript Programmer's Reference for more information on the date object and its methods.

Using Binary Large Objects (BLObs)

Since we're creating dynamic Web pages, you might want to store large binary files such as images, sounds, or video clips within your database. The data type you use for this data will depend on your database, but in JavaScript they will be BLObs. In some cases, you may just have a character field that refers to a path on the server where the binary data can be found, but you can also store the binary data directly in the database and use the BLOb object methods to access the data through LiveWire.

Continuing with our employee database example, let's say you have an image field in the employees table that is a BLOb. When you access this column in a cursor, it is converted to the JavaScript BLOb data type.

There are two useful methods for dealing with BLOb images in LiveWire: blobImage and blobLink. blobImage will create an HTML <IMG> tag with a link to the BLOb data that will be held in memory until it is served to the user. blobLink will create an HTML anchor tag to the BLOb data in a temporary file.

When you call blobImage, the server pulls out the BLOb data and stores it in memory. It then creates the appropriate HTML code to display the image inline. The memory will be reclaimed after the user requests the image. The blobImage requires one argument to specify the type of image that is stored in the BLOb (such as gif or jpeg). There are optional arguments to blobImage to define optional attributes to the IMG tag. Please refer to the blobImage entry in Chapter 9, "Testing & Debugging," for more information.

When you call blobLink, the server stores the BLOb data in a temporary file. It then creates the appropriate HTML to display a link to the data. If the link hasn't been accessed within 60 seconds, the temporary file will be removed. The blobLink method has two required arguments: the MIME type of the BLOb data and the text to be hyperlinked.

We would create a linked image of the employee by using the following code:

```
write(employee.image.blobLink("image/gif", employee.image.blobImage(gif)));
```

If you wish to update BLOb data into your database, you can use the BLOb function to read in a file off your server and convert it to a BLOb data type. You can then assign this BLOb to an updatable cursor:

```
addImage = myConnection.cursor("select ID,image from employees where ID = 23443");
addImage.next();
addImage.image = blob("/pics/bob.gif");
addImage.updateRow("employees");
```

Handling Errors

If any of your SQL statements fail for any reason, the database server will return an error message stating the reason for the failure. There are two ways you can check for an error: you can check the status code returned by the method you're calling, or you can use one of the four error methods of the connection object.

The following methods of the connection and cursor objects return status codes based on the database server: beginTransaction, commitTransaction, deleteRow, execute, insertRow, rollbackTransaction, and updateRow. These methods will return a status code of 0 if the method was completed successfully. See the majorErrorCode entry in Chapter 9 for a complete list of status codes and their meanings.

The four error methods are: majorErrorMessage, majorErrorCode, minorErrorMessage, and minorErrorCode:

- The *majorErrorMessage* method returns the major error message that was returned by the database server or from ODBC.
- The *majorErrorCode* method returns the major error code returned from the database server or from ODBC.
- The *minorErrorMessage* method returns the secondary error message returned from the database vendor library.
- The *minorErrorCode* returns the secondary error code returned from the database vendor library.

For more information on the error methods, please refer to their entries in Chapter 9.

Moving On

In this chapter, we have learned about all the LiveWire database connectivity objects built into server-side JavaScript. With this knowledge, you should be able to build a dynamic database-driven application using your Enterprise Server.

The next chapter will cover how to tie in Java with your application using LiveConnect.

Additional Server-Side JavaScript

This chapter will introduce the additional server-side specific JavaScript objects and functions you may find useful in your applications. These objects and functions will allow you to send Internet e-mail, access files on your server, and give you the ability to access and modify client requests and server responses.

JavaScript Object Properties

There are two different ways to access properties on a JavaScript object: *object.property* and *object* ["*property*"]. The general practice is to always use the '.' method for assigning and retrieving property values. The second (*array*) method is useful when the property name isn't valid in the normal context of a variable name—for example, using a "-" in the name.

The *array* method is also handy when you've assigned property names that include a number as part of the property. You can then cycle through all the values without having to use the *eval* function. The following example shows how you could do this. Assume you had a set of messages in the application object named msg1 through msg10. You could use the following code to randomly display one of the messages:

```
var msgNum = Math.round(Math.random()*9+1);
write("<i>" + application["msg"+msgNum] + "</i><p>");
```

Sending E-mail

To send e-mail from your application, you need to create an instance of a *SendMail* object using the new function. Then you set the necessary properties for your e-mail and call the *send* method. The send method returns true if the message was sent, and false if an error occurred. If it returns false, you can check the *errorCode* and *errorMessage* methods for more details.

The properties of the SendMail object correspond to the header of an e-mail message with the addition of the Body property and the Smtpserver property. The most important properties are listed in Table 5-1 below.

Object	Property
To	This is the recipient of the e-mail message. You can have multiple addressees separated by commas. You must have this property set to send the message.
From	The e-mail address of the person sending the message. You must have this property set to send the message.
Cc	(Carbon copy) A comma-delimited list of e-mail addressees who will be copied on the message.
Bcc	(Blind carbon copy) A comma-delimited list of e-mail addressees who will be copied on the message, which won't be seen by the others receiving the message.
Subject	The subject of the e-mail message you're sending.
Body	The main portion of the message you're sending.
Smtpserver	This is the location of the SMTP server to use for transmitting the message. If you don't set this property, it will use the value of the MTA Host setting in your Enterprise Server. This property is under Server Preferences|Network Settings. See Figure 5-1.

Table 5-1: SendMail object properties.

Once you set all the necessary properties, you can send the e-mail by calling the send method on the SendMail object. This method will return false if any errors occurred in sending the message. You can then use the errorCode and errorMessage methods to determine what the error was. Table 5-2 explains what the possible error codes may be.

Chapter 5: Additional Server-Side JavaScript

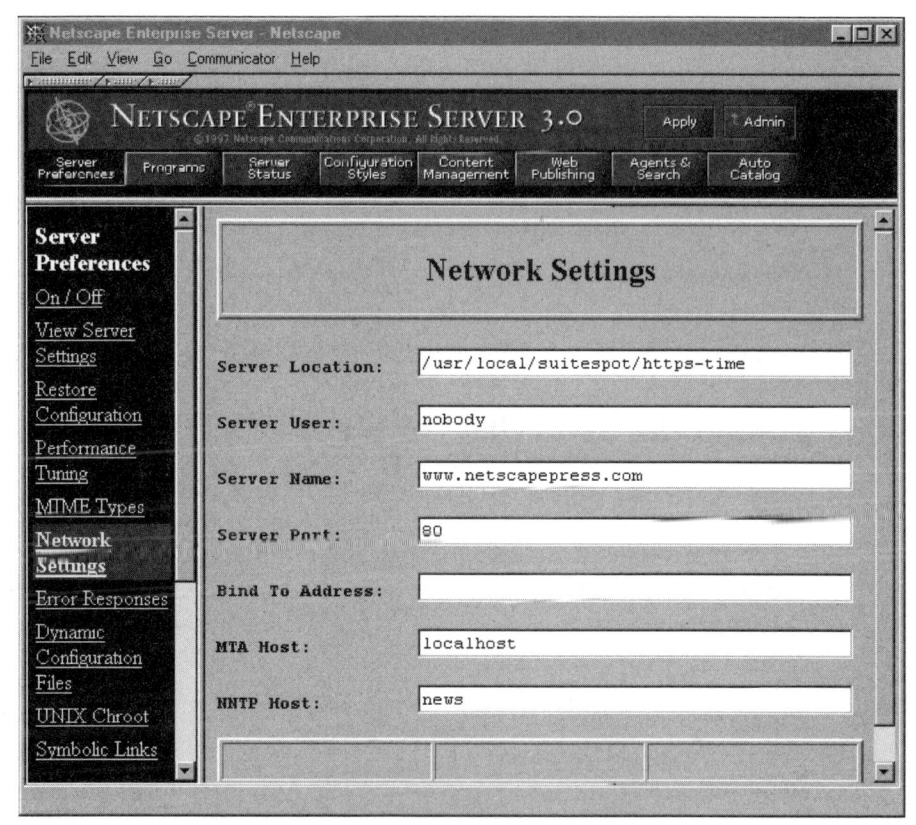

Figure 5-1: The Network Settings form on the Enterprise Administration Server.

Error code	Deciption
0	The message was sent (no error occurred).
1	The SMTP server wasn't specified.
2	The mail server (either through the Smtpserver property or the MTA Host setting) wasn't responding or doesn't exist.
3	The To property wasn't set.
4	The From property wasn't set.
5	There was an unspecified error connecting to the SMTP server. The message wasn't sent.

Table 5-2: SendMail error codes.

These error checks can only determine if the message was accepted by the SMTP server or if the required properties were set. They won't detect if an invalid e-mail address was used. The message will bounce to the From property if the To address is invalid (or can't be sent to for some reason). You could also set the Errors-to property of the SendMail object so that any bounces would be sent to that e-mail address instead of the From address. The following code is the best way to set the Errors-to property:

```
mail["Errors-to"] = "postmaster@netscapepress.com";
```

Another property you might find useful to use is Organization. This will simply set the organization in the header of the message being sent.

Using the SendMail Object

The following example is a page you can include in your JavaScript application that will display a form to allow someone to send e-mail. In the interest of space, this example doesn't check to make sure the form was filled out correctly. Figure 5-2 shows this form in action.

email.html
```
<html>
<head>
<title>Send Email</title>
</head>
<body>
<server>
// Check to make sure that a form is being
// submitted.  If so then send the mail.
if ( request.method == "POST" ) {
    var mail = new SendMail();
    mail.To = request.To;
    mail.From = request.From;
    mail.Subject = request.Subject;
    mail.Body = request.Body;
    mail.Smtpserver = "localhost";
    if ( !mail.send() ) {
        write("Mail not sent: "+mail.errorMessage() + "<p>");
    } else {
        write("Your message was sent.<p>");
    }
}
```

```
</server>
This form allows you to send an email.<p>
<form method=POST>
<table border=0>
<tr>
    <th align=right>To</th>
    <td><input size=40 name="To"></td>
</tr><tr>
    <th align=right>From</th>
    <td><input size=40 name="From"></td>
</tr><tr>
    <th align=right>Subject</th>
    <td><input size=40 name="Subject"></td>
</tr><tr>
    <th align=right>Body</th>
    <td><textarea name="Body" cols=50 rows=5
        wrap=soft></textarea></td>
</tr><tr>
    <th colspan=2><input type=submit
        value="Send Email"></th>
</tr>
</table>
</form>
</body>
</html>
```

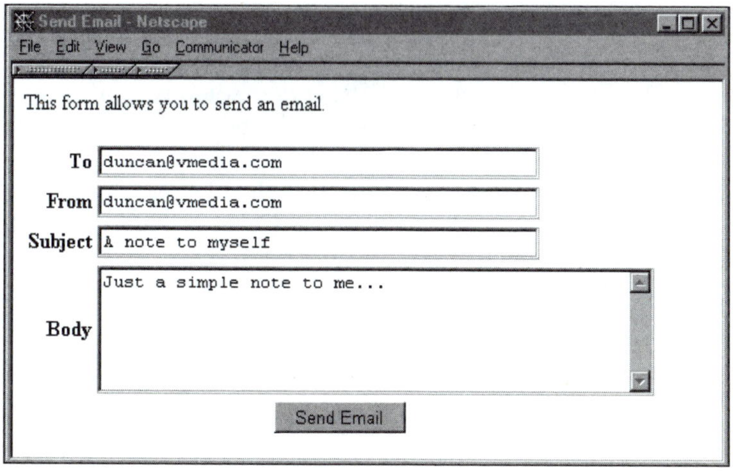

Figure 5-2: The SendMail object example.

Working With Local Files

You can access local files on the machine running your Enterprise Server by using the File object. You can only access files that the running Web server has permission to access. See your documentation on the Enterprise Server to determine what access your Web server has.

Accessing local files on your server allows you to log data or write files with information you may want later, such as number of visitors. (Remember, if you keep this in the server or application object, it will be reset when the server or application restarts.) You can also use file access to write an order invoice that can be sent to other departments of your organization when a user completes an order using your application.

Accessing a File

The first thing you need to do to access a file is to create a file object using the new function. You pass the path to the file when you do this:

```
myFile = new File("/path/to/file");
```

The format of the path is dependent on the operating system that your server is running on. After creating the object, you use the object variable to access the file. You can display the name of the file by passing the file object to the *write* function:

```
write("Filename is: "+myFile);
```

Once you've created the file object, you use the *open* method so that you can read from or write to the file. The *open* method takes an argument that is the mode the file should be opened in. The *open* method returns true if the file was opened successfully, and false otherwise. The possible modes are listed in Table 5-3.

When you're finished reading or writing the file, you can close it by using the *close* method. If you don't explicitly close it, it will automatically be closed when the current page finishes loading.

```
myFile.close();
```

Mode	Result
r	The file is opened for reading. If the file doesn't exist, the *open* method returns false.
w	The file is opened for writing. If the file exists, it will be overwritten; if it doesn't exist, it will be created.
a	The file is opened for appending. If the file exists, any new data will be added to the end of the file; if it doesn't exist, it will be created.
r+	The file is opened for reading and writing at the beginning of the file. If the file doesn't exist, the method will return false.
w+	The file is opened for reading and writing. If the file exists, it will be overwritten; if it doesn't exist, it will be created.
a+	The file is opened for reading and writing at the end of the file. If the file doesn't exist, it will be created.
b	This mode can be added to any of the above modes. If present, the file will be opened in binary mode. This mode is only relevant on a Windows operating system.

Table 5-3: The file modes for the open method.

File Position

The file position is used to determine where the next *read* or *write* method will occur in the file. When a file is opened, the current position will be either the beginning or the end of the file, depending on the mode you chose when you opened the file.

You can find out what the current position is by using the *getPosition* method. This method will return –1 if an error occurs. The beginning of the file will return 0.

You can change the position of the file explicitly by using the *setPosition* method. The first argument to setPosition determines how much to change the position; it can be a positive or negative integer. The second argument is optional and determines where to start from when moving the position. Table 5-4 shows what the possible values for the second argument can be.

Argument	Result
0	The position is moved relative to the beginning of the file.
1	The position is moved relative to the current position.
2	The position is moved relative to the end of the file.
Anything else	The position is moved relative to the beginning of the file.

Table 5-4: Acceptable values for the setPosition method.

To jump back in the file you're reading by 10 bytes, you would use the following command:

`myFile.setPosition(-10, 1);`

You can use the *eof* method to determine if you've reached the end of the file. This method will return true only after you try to read past the end of the file.

Reading From & Writing to a File

There are three methods used for reading from a file and four methods for writing to a file.

The *read* method takes an argument that is an integer representing how many bytes to read from the file. It will return a string of the bytes read. The *readln* method will return the next line from the file. It will read from the current position up to a linefeed. If there is a carriage return as well (on Windows), it will be ignored. The string won't include the carriage return or linefeed characters. The *readByte* method reads the next byte from the file and returns its numeric value.

The *write* method writes the string passed to it to the file at the current position. It will return true if it succeeded, and false otherwise. The *writeln* method writes the string followed by a linefeed (or carriage return and linefeed on Windows if the file isn't in binary mode). Like write, it returns true if it succeeded, and false otherwise. The *writeByte* writes a character to the file based on the number passed to it. Any time you use one of the write methods, it isn't necessarily written to the file. The server keeps the data in a buffer. You can force the data to be written to the file by using the *Flush* method.

Converting Bytes

There are two methods to convert between binary and text data. Binary data is what you read and write using the *readByte* and *writeByte* methods. You can use the *byteToString* and *stringToByte* methods to convert between the two. The byteToString method will return a one-character string corresponding to the number passed to it. The stringToByte method will return a number corresponding to the first character in the string passed to it or 0 if there was no string.

These methods are called using the File object itself and not an instance of the object; for example:

```
myByte = File.stringToByte("a");
myChar = File.byteToString(56);
```

File Locking

Since there may be many people accessing your application at the same time, you'll need to use the project or server lock methods or use a lock object before you do any reading or writing from a file. If you don't, users may see incorrect or corrupted data.

The following example uses the project object to lock access before writing to a file. Assume that myFile is an instance of a File object and newData is an initialized variable.

```
project.lock();
myFile.open("a");
myFile.writeln(newData);
myFile.close();
project.unlock();
```

File Information

There are two methods for retrieving information about the file and two for dealing with errors.

The *getLength* method returns the number of bytes in the file. It will return –1 if an error occurred. The *exists* method returns true if the file exists, and false if it doesn't.

The *error* method returns the current error status of the file or –1 if the file isn't open or can't be opened. If there is no error, it will return 0. The status codes that may be returned are platform-specific. The *clearError* method clears the error status and the value of *eof*.

Using the File Object

The following example will append what a user submits to the bottom of the page, as in a running "comments" page. Figure 5-3 shows this page in action.

comments.html
```
<html>
<head>
<title>Comments</title>
</head>
<server>
if ( request.method == "POST" ) {
    project.lock();
    comments = new File("/tmp/comments.txt");
    comments.open("a");
    comments.writeln(request.comment);
    comments.writeln("<hr>");
    comments.close();
    project.unlock();
}
</server>
<body>
<form method=POST>
<textarea name=comment rows=5 cols=50 wrap=soft></textarea><p>
<input type=submit value="Add Comment">
</form>
<hr>
<server>
project.lock();
comments = new File("/tmp/comments.txt");
comments.open("r");
write(comments.read(comments.getLength()));
comments.close();
project.unlock();
</server>
</body>
</html>
```

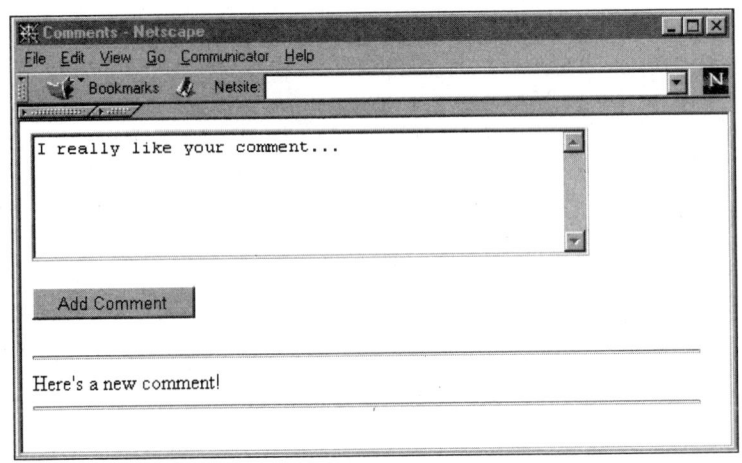

Figure 5-3: The file object example page.

Working With Response & Request Data

Normally you'll never need to deal with the response and request data directly. You can usually access the information you need from the request object. The JavaScript engine parses the request data if it's of the standard MIME type (application/x-www-form-urlencoded). You may have a different content type in your application if you so desire. You can change the content type of data that is posted to you by changing the ENCTYPE attribute of the FORM HTML tag. You can then access the request body to parse and handle your content type.

This section discusses how you can use JavaScript functions to work with the request header and body and the response header on data you send back to the client.

Accessing the Request Header

You can retrieve the request header by calling the *httpdHeader* method of the request object. This will return an object with the name/value pairs set as the properties of the object.

The following code will display all the header properties of the current request:

```
var headerInfo = request.httpdHeader();
for ( name in headerInfo ) {
    write(name + " = " + headerInfo[name] +
        "<br>\n");
}
```

Accessing the Request Body

If the request is of a type different than the standard, you can access the body of the request by using the *getPostData* method of the request object. You must pass the number of characters you want to get to this method. If you pass 0, it will return the entire request body.

If you want to know the length of the entire body without pulling it all into a variable, you can access the *content-length* property of the header object:

```
PostLength = parseInt(headerInfo["content-length"]);
```

Accessing the Response Header

You can change any of the response header name/value pairs by using the *deleteResponseHeader* and *addResponseHeader* functions. The deleteResponseHeader function takes one argument: the name to be removed. The addResponseHeader takes two arguments: the name of the field to be added and the value to set it to.

You can use these methods to change the header before it's sent to the client. Before you can set a header field, you must first delete it. You must also be sure to call these functions before the data is flushed to the client. The server buffers up to 64K of data before flushing it.

One case where you might need this is if you wanted to change the content type being displayed to something like "text/plain."

```
deleteResponseHeader("Content-type");
addResponseHeader("Content-type", "text/plain");
```

Moving On

In this chapter, we explored some other features of JavaScript specific to the server-side environment. These features help add the functionality you expect when programming on a Web server.

The next chapter will covers how to tie in Java with your application using LiveConnect.

Using Java With Live Connect

LiveConnect allows your JavaScript application to access built-in Java objects, as well as objects you create. LiveConnect is a technology that was originally developed by Netscape on the client side in Navigator 3.0. It allowed JavaScript to communicate with Java applets and Java applets to communicate with plug-ins. With Enterprise Server 3.0, Netscape has added LiveConnect functionality on the server side. Any Java objects you create can access JavaScript objects that are passed to them.

To benefit from the information in this chapter, you need to have a basic understanding of Java programming, but in-depth knowledge and experience are not required.

For more about LiveConnect, please visit the DevEdge Web site at http://developer.netscape.com/.

Working With Java in Your Application

Server-side LiveConnect allows your JavaScript application to create instances of Java classes. Once an instance is created, you can access any of the public methods and properties of that object, enabling you to add functionality to your application that wouldn't be possible without LiveConnect. You can have Java objects that connect to custom data sources or allow you to do anything Java can do within your JavaScript application.

You can only access objects that your application has created or that have been created by other applications on your server and stored in the server object. You can't access any built-in Java objects on the server, such as WAI or NSAPI extensions, or any applets embedded in your application pages. Applets wouldn't be part of your server-side JavaScript application code. This is different from client-side JavaScript, where you can access any of the objects embedded in the Web page.

When invoking Java methods on an object, you can pass JavaScript objects as arguments. This allows the Java code to manipulate JavaScript objects. This is the only way you can access a JavaScript application from Java. Java code can't access the application unless JavaScript code created an instance of a Java class and called a method.

Any Java classes you wish to access must be in the CLASSPATH of your Enterprise Server. There are two ways to do this: you can add the directory to your CLASSPATH environment variable before starting up your Enterprise Server, or you can add the directory in which you're storing your classes to the classpath directive in the obj.conf configuration file. This file can be found in the config subdirectory of your Web server's directory. Refer to your Enterprise Server documentation if you're unsure where this directory is.

Modifying Your CLASSPATH Environment Variable

UNIX—You simply need to set your CLASSPATH before starting the server. You'll need to start the server from the command line instead of from the Administration server, however. You can also modify the start script to set the CLASSPATH before the server starts, so that you can start it from the Administration server.

NT—You can use the System control panel to set the CLASSPATH environment variable. You may need to restart your system in order for the change to take effect.

The code should look like the example below. Simply add a colon and then the path to your class directory, or store your Java classes in one of the listed directories.

```
Init classpath=
"/usr/local/suitespot/wai/java/nisb.zip:
/usr/local/suitespot/js/samples:
/usr/local/suitespot/plugins/java/classes/serv3_0.zip:
/usr/local/suitespot/plugins/java/local-classes" ldpath=
"/usr/local/suitespot/plugins/java/bin" fn="SJavaBootInit"
```

One good way to keep all your JavaScript and Java code in one place is to have one directory for all your JavaScript applications. Let's assume this directory is /usr/local/suitespot/apps. In this directory you'll create subdirectories for each of your applications. Let's say we're creating a database-driven periodic table of the elements, so we'll call our subdirectory "elements." Since we're going to use Java in this application, we can create all our classes in a package named "elements" as well. Now all you need to do is add "/usr/local/suitespot/apps" to the CLASSPATH (either in the environment variables or in the obj.conf file); since all the classes are in the elements package, they'll be found by the server when it runs your application. This is because when the server is trying to load the class, it looks for the file *packageName/className*.class within one of its CLASSPATH directories.

See the "Calling Java From Your JavaScript Application" subsection later in this chapter for more information on creating and invoking your Java classes.

Built-In Java Classes

Your Enterprise Server has a set of Java packages built into a file named *server3_0.zip*. You can access any of these packages from your application without having to write any Java code or modify any environment variables or server configurations. A few of these packages are listed in Chapter 10, "Server-Side JavaScript Reference."

All the java and sun packages are included in this file, so there's no need to include the classes.zip file from the JDK in the server's CLASSPATH. There is also a *netscape.net* package that replaces *sun.net*.

Two packages that may come in handy while creating your own Java classes for use in your JavaScript applications are *netscape.javascript* and *netscape.server*. The netscape.javascript package allows your Java code to access and manipulate JavaScript objects. The netscape.server package allows you to send output to the server, similar to the JavaScript *write* function. The classes in these packages are discussed in Chapter 10 and will be used in the "Accessing JavaScript From Your Java Classes" section later in this chapter.

Calling Java From Your JavaScript Application

You can access Java from your application by creating an instance of the Java class and then calling its methods or accessing its properties. If you need to pass another Java object as a parameter for creating one, you'll need to create an instance of that class first.

Using Java Objects

There are two ways to access Java objects: you can create a new instance of a Java class or you can access static methods and/or properties from a Java class.

Creating an Instance of a Java Object

You create an instance of a Java class by using the JavaScript *new* function followed by the name of the class you wish to create. You can refer to the class by using the JavaScript Packages object and the name of the package the class is in:

```
javaObj = new Packages.packageName.className();
```

You don't need to use the Packages object if you're creating an instance of a class within the netscape, java, or sun package (e.g., Packages.java.lang.String is the same as java.lang.String).

Once you've created an instance of the object, you can access its methods and properties the same way you do for JavaScript objects:

```
javaObj.methodName
javaObj.propertyName
```

Using Static Methods & Properties

You can access static methods and properties simply by accessing them through the Java class:

```
var pi = Packages.java.lang.Math.PI;
var maxNum = Packages.java.lang.Math.max(1,2);
```

If you were trying to access only the Java Math object, you could simply use the JavaScript Math object; these examples are just to show the syntax. Using the Packages object is also optional—the following code would work equally well:

```
var pi = java.lang.Math.PI;
```

JavaScript to Java Data Types

When you access Java code through LiveConnect, your JavaScript data values are converted to Java values. These conversions are the same using client-side LiveConnect as they are with server-side LiveConnect.

JavaScript strings, numerics, and Boolean values are converted to Java String, Float, and Boolean objects. Java objects with JavaScript wrappers are unwrapped, and JavaScript objects are wrapped within an instance of JSObject.

Sign-Out Board Example

Now we'll create a simple JavaScript application that uses LiveConnect to access Java objects. For this example we'll create a Web application to keep track of employees on a sign-out board. Normally, we'd want to store this data in a database, but for this example, to save space, we'll maintain the board in the JavaScript project object.

We'll begin by creating the Java objects we'll need and then tie them into Web pages in a JavaScript application. We'll create an *inout* directory in our application directory (/usr/local/suitespot/apps) to hold all our source code and the .web file of the application.

Writing Java Code

For this example, we'll create two Java classes within a package named "inout." The classes will be Employee and InOut. The Employee class will keep data about the employee, and it will include methods to return the name of the employee and to return an HTML table with all the employee data. The InOut class will include properties that hold the list of employees that are checked in and checked out, as well as the time they checked in or out. This class will have methods to return the in and out lists in an HTML table.

These classes were written using the JDK 1.1 API and compiled with the JDK 1.1.2 Java compiler. You can download the latest version of the JDK from http://www.javasoft.com/.

Employee.java
```
package inout;

public class Employee {
    private String        FirstName;
    private String        LastName;
    private String        Department;

    // This is the constructor for the employee
    // class
    public Employee(String first, String last,
        String dept) {
        this.FirstName = first;
        this.LastName = last;
        this.Department = dept;
    }
```

```java
// This method will return the full name
// of the employee
public String getFullName() {
    return new String(this.LastName + ", " +
        this.FirstName);
}

// This method will return an HTML table
// of the employee data
public String toHTML() {
    StringBuffer EmpData = new
        StringBuffer("<table border=2>\n");
    EmpData.append("<tr><th ➔
        align=right>Employee</th><td>" +
        this.getFullName() + "</td></tr>\n");
    EmpData.append("<tr><th ➔
        align=right>Dept.</th><td>" +
        this.Department + "</td></tr>\n");
    EmpData.append("</table>");
    return EmpData.toString();
}
}
```

InOut.java

```java
package inout;
import java.util.*;
import java.text.*;

public class InOut {
    private Hashtable    In;
    private Hashtable    Out;

    public InOut( int initialSize ) {
        this.In = new Hashtable(initialSize);
        this.Out = new Hashtable(initialSize);
    }
    public InOut() {
        this.In = new Hashtable(10);
        this.Out = new Hashtable(10);
    }

    public void checkIn( Employee who ) {
        this.In.put( who, new Date() );
        this.Out.remove( who );
    }
```

```java
public void checkOut( Employee who ) {
    this.Out.put( who, new Date() );
    this.In.remove( who );
}

public String toHTML() {
    StringBuffer inOutTable = new
        StringBuffer("<table border=2>\n");
    Boolean seenIn = Boolean.FALSE;
    Boolean seenOut = Boolean.FALSE;
    DateFormat df = DateFormat.getInstance();
    TimeZone tz = TimeZone.getTimeZone("EST");
    df.setTimeZone(tz);

    for ( Enumeration whoIn = this.In.keys();
        whoIn.hasMoreElements(); ) {
        if ( !seenIn.booleanValue() ) {
            inOutTable.append(
                "<tr><th>Employee</th>" +
                "<th>In Since</th>" +
                "</tr>\n");
            seenIn = Boolean.TRUE;
        }
        Employee curEmployee =
            (Employee)whoIn.nextElement();
        Date inDate =
            (Date)this.In.get(curEmployee);
        inOutTable.append("<tr><td>" +
            curEmployee.getFullName() +
            "</td><td>" +
            df.format(inDate) +
            "</td></tr>");
    }
    for ( Enumeration whoOut = this.Out.keys();
        whoOut.hasMoreElements(); ) {
        if ( !seenOut.booleanValue() ) {
            inOutTable.append(
                "<tr><th>Employee</th>" +
                "<th>Out Since</th>" +
                "</tr>\n");
            seenOut = Boolean.TRUE;
        }
        Employee curEmployee =
            (Employee)whoOut.nextElement();
```

```
            Date outDate =
                (Date)this.Out.get(curEmployee);
            inOutTable.append("<tr><td>" +
                curEmployee.getFullName() +
                "</td><td>" +
            df.format(outDate) + "</td></tr>");
        }
        inOutTable.append("</table>");
        return inOutTable.toString();
    }

}
```

Compiling Your Java Code

When you're compiling your Java code, be sure to have the JavaScript application directory in your CLASSPATH (/usr/local/suitespot/apps) so that it will find the necessary classes when compiling. You should also compile the Employee class first so that your compiler can find it when it compiles the InOut class. You could also use the *–depend* option if you're using javac from the JDK. This will tell the compiler to compile any classes this class "depends" on that it can't find (the Employee.java class in this case).

```
javac -depend InOut.java
```

Writing the HTML Pages

Now we need to build the application pages to tie everything together. We'll need four main pages for the application: the sign-in page, the sign-out page, the view board page, and the home page, which has links to the other three. We'll also create a start page with some JavaScript code that will be executed the first time the application is accessed.

Create these pages in the inout subdirectory of your applications directory with the Java code. The start.html page simply creates a new instance of the InOut class and stores it in the JavaScript project object. The signin.html page creates a new instance of an employee object and checks the employee in with the InOut object. The signout.html page is the same as the sign-in page, except that it checks the person out with the InOut object. The view.html page displays all the employees, whether they checked in or out, and what time they checked in or out.

start.html

```
<server>
project.board = new Packages.inout.InOut();
redirect("home.html");
</server>
```

home.html

```
<html>
<head>
<title>Sign Out Board</title>
</head>
<body>
<font size=+1>
<a href="signin.html">Sign-In</a><br>
<a href="signout.html">Sign-Out</a><br>
<a href="view.html">View Board</a>
</body>
</html>
```

signin.html

```
<html>
<head>
<title>Sign-In</title>
</head>
<body>
<h2>Sign-In</h2>

<server>
if (request.method == "POST") {
    var employee = new
        Packages.inout.Employee(request.first,
        request.last, request.dept);
    project.board.checkIn(employee);
    write("You are now signed in.<br>");
    write("<a href=home.html>");
    write("Back to the Main Page</a>");
} else {
</server>
<form method=POST>
<table border=0>
```

```
<tr>
    <th align=right>First Name</th>
    <td><input name=first></td>
</tr><tr>
    <th align=right>Last Name</th>
    <td><input name=last></td>
</tr><tr>
    <th align=right>Department</th>
    <td><input name=dept></td>
</tr><tr>
    <th colspan=2>
    <input type=submit
    value=" Sign In! "></th>
</tr>
</table>
<server>
}
</server>
</body>
</html>
```

signout.html
```
<html>
<head>
<title>Sign-Out</title>
</head>
<body>
<h2>Sign-Out</h2>

<server>
if (request.method == "POST") {
    var employee = new
        Packages.inout.Employee(request.first,
        request.last, request.dept);
    project.board.checkOut(employee);
    write("You are now signed out.<br>");
    write("<a href=home.html>");
    write("Back to the Main Page</a>");
} else {
</server>
<form method=POST>
<table border=0>
```

```
<tr>
    <th align=right>First Name</th>
    <td><input name=first></td>
</tr><tr>
    <th align=right>Last Name</th>
    <td><input name=last></td>
</tr><tr>
    <th align=right>Department</th>
    <td><input name=dept></td>
</tr><tr>
    <th colspan=2><input type=submit
    value=" Sign Out! "></th>
</tr>
</table>
<server>
}
</server>
</body>
</html>
```

view.html
```
<html>
<head>
<title>View Sign-Out Board</title>
</head>
<body>
<h2>The Board</h2>
<server>
write(project.board.toHTML());
</server>
<br>
<a href="home.html">Back to the Main Page</a>
</body>
</html>
```

Compiling Your Application

Now we can compile the application using the JavaScript Application Compiler (jsac), which can be found in the bin/https directory of your Enterprise Server installation. See Chapter 2, "The Enterprise Server Application Framework," for more information on compiling your applications with jsac.

```
jsac -o inout.web *.html
```

Adding the Application to the Server

Now go to your server's Application Manager to add our new application. Fill out the form as shown in Figure 6-1, replacing the path to the .web file with the one you used.

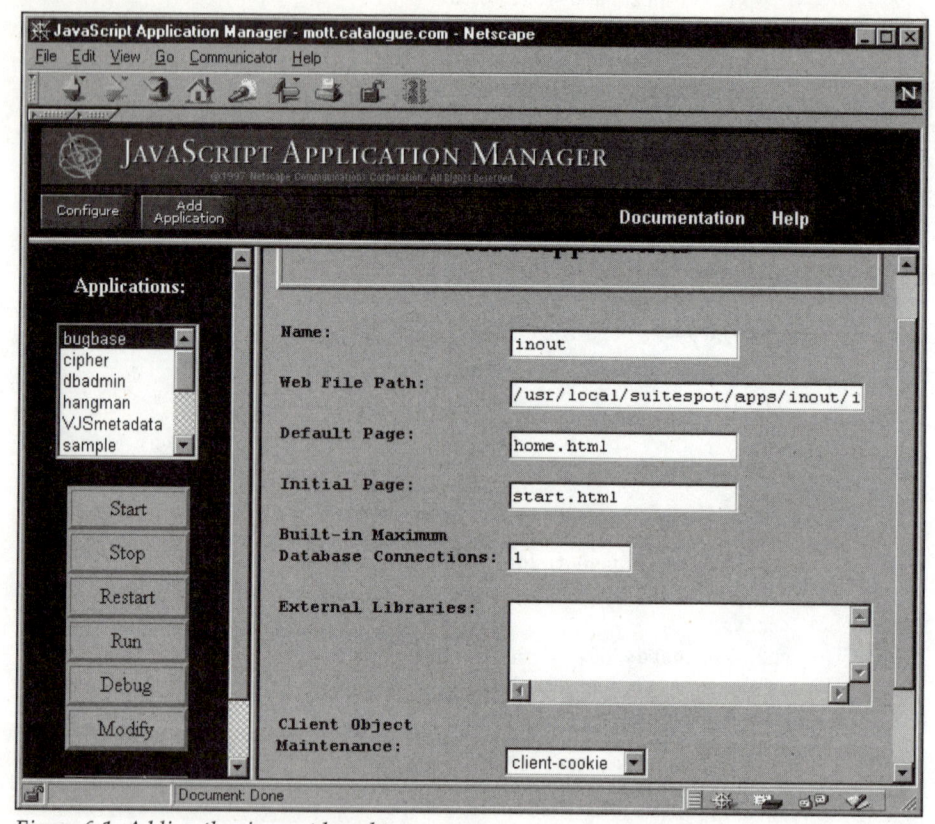

Figure 6-1: Adding the sign-out board to your server.

Running the Application

Now click the Run button in the left frame of the Application Manager to run the new application. You can sign in and out a few employees and then view the table of who's in and who's out.

Accessing JavaScript From Your Java Classes

Netscape has provided three classes to enable you to access JavaScript from your Java classes: JSObject, JSException, and NetscapeServerEnv. The first two provide capabilities to interact with JavaScript objects and handle errors from JavaScript code. The third class doesn't technically give you access to JavaScript, but it allows you to access the outgoing connection buffer with a method like the JavaScript *write* function.

Using JavaScript Objects

When you want to use JavaScript objects from your Java code, you need to import the netscape.javascript package. This is where the JSObject and JSException classes are. You can find detailed information about these classes in Chapter 10, "Server-Side JavaScript Reference."

Any time you pass a JavaScript object from your application to a Java object, it is wrapped by an instance of JSObject. Any methods you create in your class that take a JavaScript object should accept the type JSObject:

```
public String getIt(JSObject reqObj) { ... }
```

You can use the getMember method of JSObject to retrieve properties of your JavaScript object. It takes one argument: the name of the property to retrieve. Be sure to cast the return of this method to the type of object you're expecting. There is also a getSlot method, which takes an indexed number that refers to a property of the object.

You can assign values to properties of your JavaScript object using the setMember and setSlot methods.

You can use the *call* method to invoke a method on your object. The eval method will simply evaluate arbitrary JavaScript code. Table 6-1 lists some JavaScript code with the equivalent code in Java.

JavaScript	Java
var temp = this.prop1	String temp = (String)this.getMember("prop1")
var temp = this[1]	String temp = (String)this.getSlot(1)
this.prop1 = temp	this.setMember("prop1", temp)
this[1] = temp	this.setSlot(1, temp)
this.runIt(temp)	this.call("runIt", temp)

Table 6-1: Calling JavaScript from Java.

Data Types

When you pass Java data types to JavaScript, the following conversions are made by LiveConnect:

- The Java types byte, char, short, int, long, float, and double are converted to a JavaScript number.
- The Java Boolean type is converted to a JavaScript Boolean.
- A JSObject is converted to the equivalent JavaScript object.
- JavaScript wraps any other Java objects. The methods and properties on these objects can be accessed like any other JavaScript objects.
- Java arrays are converted to an object similar to the JavaScript Array object, giving you the ability to access it via indices using [ ]. You can determine the size of the array using the *length* property.

Writing to the Client

If you want to write output to the client accessing your application from your Java code, you can do so by importing the netscape.server.serverenv package and calling the static writeHttpOutput method of the NetscapeServerEnv class.

The following Java class has a method that will write to the client when it is created:

```
import netscape.server.serverenv.*;
public class Boo {
    public Boo() {
        NetscapeServerEnv.writeHttpOutput("Boo!");
    }
}
```

> **TIP**
>
> *Don't forget to have the Enterprise Server Java classes in your CLASSPATH when compiling any Java classes using JavaScript or the Netscape server environment.*

Threading

If it is necessary for your Java code to create new threads, you must be careful when you use them. Any threads you create can't interact with your JavaScript application or write data to the client. This is because the server handles the request to your application in a thread. When you access Java from that thread, it can interact with the state of that thread, but any subsequent threads that are created aren't within that state framework.

Expanding the Sign-Out Board

Now we're going to expand the sign-out board we created in the previous section to make it easier to track and identify the employees based on the JavaScript client object. This application will also pass JavaScript objects to Java methods.

We'll place this application in the *board* directory of our application directory.

Writing the Java Code

First, we create a new package called "board," to go with the application. This package will include classes similar in design to the ones we used before, but it will use Java/JavaScript communication more effectively.

We'll start with the Employee class again, which has been modified to include a constructor that takes the JavaScript request and client objects as arguments and then uses the getMember method to initialize the properties of the Employee object. The constructor then sets a property in the client object so that we can recognize the employee when he or she accesses the application later.

The Board class will include a new hash table that will keep track of all the employees based on an employee code. This will make signing in and out easier so that employees won't have to retype all their personal information each time.

employee.java
```
package board;
import netscape.javascript.*;
import netscape.server.serverenv.*;

public class Employee {
    public String      Code;
    private String     FirstName;
    private String     LastName;
    private String     Department;

    public Employee(String code, String first,
        String last, String dept) {
        this.Code = code;
        this.FirstName = first;
        this.LastName = last;
        this.Department = dept;
    }
    // create an instance of an Employee object
    // from a JavaScript request object
    public Employee( JSObject JSRequest, JSObject
        JSClient ) {
```

```java
            this.Code =
                (String)JSRequest.getMember("code");
            this.FirstName =
                (String)JSRequest.getMember("first");
            this.LastName =
                (String)JSRequest.getMember("last");
            this.Department =
                (String)JSRequest.getMember("dept");
            JSClient.setMember("code", this.Code);
    }

    public String getFullName() {
        return new String(this.LastName + ", " +
            this.FirstName);
    }

    public String getFirstName() {
        return this.FirstName;
    }

    // display the Employee object
    // to the client.
    public void writeHTML()
    throws java.io.IOException {
        NetscapeServerEnv.writeHttpOutput(
            "<table border=2>\n");
            NetscapeServerEnv.writeHttpOutput(
            "<tr><th align=right>Code</th><td>" +
            this.Code + "</td></tr>\n");
        NetscapeServerEnv.writeHttpOutput(
            "<tr><th align=right>Employee</th>"+
            "<td>" +
            this.getFullName() + "</td></tr>\n");
        NetscapeServerEnv.writeHttpOutput(
            "<tr><th align=right>Dept.</th><td>" +
            this.Department + "</td></tr>\n");
        NetscapeServerEnv.writeHttpOutput("</table>");
    }

}
```

Board.java

```java
package board;
import java.util.*;
```

```
import java.text.*;
import netscape.javascript.*;
import netscape.server.serverenv.*;

public class Board {
    private Hashtable    In;
    private Hashtable    Out;
    private Hashtable    EmployeeList;

    public Board( int initialSize ) {
        this.In = new Hashtable(initialSize);
        this.Out = new Hashtable(initialSize);
        this.EmployeeList = new Hashtable(initialSize);
    }
    public Board() {
        this.In = new Hashtable(10);
        this.Out = new Hashtable(10);
        this.EmployeeList = new Hashtable(10);
    }

    public void newEmployee( Employee who ) {
        this.EmployeeList.put( who.Code, who );
    }

    public Employee getEmployee ( String code ) {
        return (Employee)this.EmployeeList.get(code);
    }

    public Employee checkIn( String code ) {
        Employee who = (Employee)this.EmployeeList.get(code);
        if ( who != null ) {
            this.In.put( who, new Date() );
            this.Out.remove( who );
        }
        return who;
    }
    public Employee checkIn( JSObject JSClient ) {
        String code = (String)JSClient.getMember("code");
        return this.checkIn(code);
    }
    public void checkIn( Employee who ) {
        this.In.put( who, new Date() );
        this.Out.remove( who );
    }
```

```java
public Employee checkOut( String code ) {
    Employee who = (Employee)EmployeeList.get(code);
    if ( who != null ) {
        this.Out.put( who, new Date() );
        this.In.remove( who );
    }
    return who;
}
public Employee checkOut( JSObject JSClient ) {
    String code = (String)JSClient.getMember("code");
    return this.checkOut(code);
}
public void checkOut( Employee who ) {
    this.Out.put( who, new Date() );
    this.In.remove( who );
}

public void writeHTML()
throws java.io.IOException {
    NetscapeServerEnv.writeHttpOutput("<table border=2>\n");
    Boolean seenIn = Boolean.FALSE;
    Boolean seenOut = Boolean.FALSE;
    DateFormat df = DateFormat.getInstance();
    TimeZone tz = TimeZone.getTimeZone("EST");
    df.setTimeZone(tz);

    for ( Enumeration whoIn = this.In.keys(); whoIn.hasMoreElements(); )
    {
        if ( !seenIn.booleanValue() ) {
            NetscapeServerEnv.writeHttpOutput(
                "<tr><th>Employee</th>" +
                "<th>In Since</th></tr>");
            seenIn = Boolean.TRUE;
        }
        Employee curEmployee = (Employee)whoIn.nextElement();
        Date inDate = (Date)this.In.get(curEmployee);
        NetscapeServerEnv.writeHttpOutput(
            "<tr><td>" +
            curEmployee.getFullName() +
            "</td><td>" +
            df.format(inDate) +
            "</td></tr>");
    }
    for ( Enumeration whoOut = this.Out.keys();
        whoOut.hasMoreElements(); ) {
```

```
            if ( !seenOut.booleanValue() ) {
                NetscapeServerEnv.writeHttpOutput(
                    "<tr><th>Employee</th><th>" +
                    "Out Since</th></tr>\n" );
                seenOut = Boolean.TRUE;
            }
            Employee curEmployee = (Employee)whoOut.nextElement();
            Date outDate = (Date)this.Out.get(curEmployee);
            NetscapeServerEnv.writeHttpOutput(
                "<tr><td>" +
                curEmployee.getFullName() +
                "</td><td>" +
                df.format(outDate) +
                "</td></tr>");
        }
        NetscapeServerEnv.writeHttpOutput(
            "</table>");
    }
}
```

Compiling Your Java Code

When you're compiling your Java code, be sure to have the JavaScript application directory in your CLASSPATH (/usr/local/suitespot/apps) so that it will find the necessary classes when compiling. You should also compile the Employee class first so that your compiler can find it when it compiles the Board class. You could also use the *–depend* option if you're using javac from the JDK.

```
javac -depend Board.java
```

Writing Your HTML pages

The HTML pages in this application perform the same function as in the inout application, except that the pages are modified for the new Java package classes and methods, and they make use of the client object.

start.html

```
<server>
project.board = new Packages.board.Board();
redirect("home.html");
</server>
```

home.html

```
<html>
<head>
<title>Sign Out Board</title>
</head>
<body>
<font size=+1>
<a href="signin.html">Sign-In</a><br>
<a href="signout.html">Sign-Out</a><br>
<a href="view.html">View Board</a>
</body>
</html>
```

signin.html

```
<html>
<head>
<title>Sign-In</title>
</head>
<body>
<h2>Sign-In</h2>

<server>
if ( client.code != "" && project.board.getEmployee(client.code) != null ) {
    employee = project.board.checkIn(client.code);
    write("You are now signed in, "+employee.getFirstName()+"<br>");
    write("<a href=home.html>Back to the Main Page</a>");
} else if (request.method == "POST") {
    var employee = new Packages.board.Employee(request, client);
    project.board.newEmployee(employee);
    project.board.checkIn(employee);
    write("You are now signed in, "+employee.getFirstName()+"<br>");
    write("<a href=home.html>Back to the Main Page</a>");
} else {
</server>
<form method=POST>
<table border=0>
<tr><th align=right>Code</th><td><input name=code></td></tr>
<tr><th align=right>First Name</th><td><input name=first></td></tr>
<tr><th align=right>Last Name</th><td><input name=last></td></tr>
<tr><th align=right>Department</th><td><input name=dept></td></tr>
<tr><th colspan=2><input type=submit value=" Sign In! "></th></tr>
</table>
```

```
<server>
}
</server>
</body>
</html>
```

signout.html

```
<html>
<head>
<title>Sign-Out</title>
</head>
<body>
<h2>Sign-Out</h2>

<server>
if ( client.code != "" && project.board.getEmployee(client.code) != null ) {
    employee = project.board.checkOut(client.code);
    write("You are now signed out, "+employee.getFirstName()+"<br>");
    write("<a href=home.html>Back to the Main Page</a>");
} else if (request.method == "POST") {
    var employee = new Packages.board.Employee(request, client);
    project.board.newEmployee(employee);
  project.board.checkOut(employee);
    write("You are now signed out, "+employee.getFirstName()+"<br>");
    write("<a href=home.html>Back to the Main Page</a>");
} else {
</server>
<form method=POST>
<table border=0>
<tr><th align=right>Code</th><td><input name=code></td></tr>
<tr><th align=right>First Name</th><td><input name=first></td></tr>
<tr><th align=right>Last Name</th><td><input name=last></td></tr>
<tr><th align=right>Department</th><td><input name=dept></td></tr>
<tr><th colspan=2><input type=submit value=" Sign Out! "></th></tr>
</table>
<server>
}
</server>
</body>
</html>
```

view.html

```
<html>
<head>
<title>View Sign-Out Board</title>
</head>
<body>
<h2>The Board</h2>
<server>
project.board.writeHTML();
</server>
<br>
<a href="home.html">Back to the Main Page</a>
</body>
</html>
```

Compiling Your Application

Now we can compile the application using the JavaScript Application Compiler (jsac) just as we did with the inout application. This application can be found in the bin/https directory of your Enterprise Server installation. See Chapter 2, "The Enterprise Server Application Framework," for more information on compiling your applications with jsac.

```
jsac -o board.web *.html
```

Adding the Application to the Server

Now go to your server's Application Manager (http://www.domain.com/appmgr/) to add our new application. Fill out the form as shown in Figure 6-2, replacing the path to the .web file with the one you used. Note that this application uses the client-cookie method of client object maintenance.

Running the Application

Now click the Run button in the left frame of the Application Manager to run the new application. You can sign in, and when you go to the sign-out page it will remember who you are. To sign in as another employee you'll need to close and reopen your browser so that your cookie will be cleared.

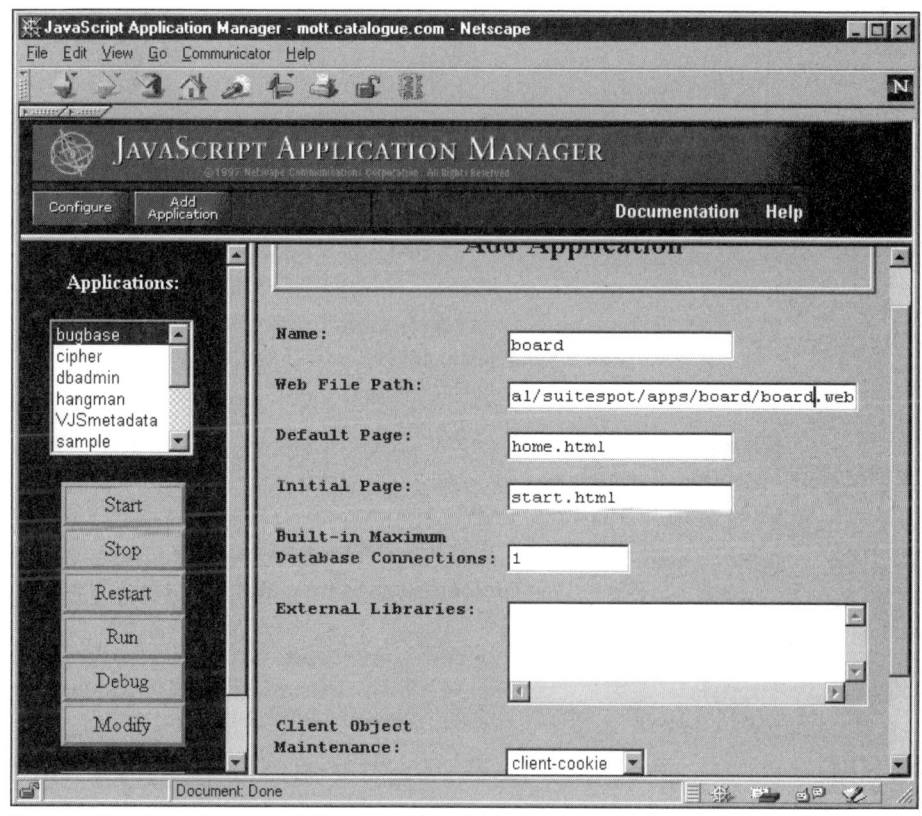

Figure 6-2: Adding the expanded sign-out board to your server.

When to Use Java vs. JavaScript

Now that you've seen how to use Java objects in your application and have these objects access JavaScript, you might be wondering when you should use Java instead of JavaScript.

The most obvious choice for adding Java to your application is when you want to do something that JavaScript can't do, such as connecting to an unsupported external data source. You also may want to use a Java vector object instead of JavaScript's built-in array object for the added functionality. You can do this without writing any Java code at all:

```
myVector = new java.util.Vector(10);
myVector.addElement(newData);
write(myVector.firstElement()+"\n");
```

There may be other instances where you prefer to use a Java object for the extra features. Some Java objects you may find useful are java.util.Calendar, java.util.Dictionary, java.util.Hashtable, java.util, java.util.Stack or java.util.StringTokenizer. For most of these objects, you could write JavaScript code to mimic their behavior, but the Java objects may produce more elegant code. Elegant code generally leads to fewer bugs.

If you're more familiar with Java, you may find it easier to create Java classes to do most of the work of your application, and then create the HTML pages to tie it all together with a minimum of JavaScript code. This way you're also able to distribute your application to others without their seeing the meat of your code, since your Java classes are compiled.

Moving On

In this chapter you learned how to add Java to your server-side JavaScript applications, adding functionality that you wouldn't otherwise have. You also learned how to access JavaScript from Java and Java from JavaScript—through LiveConnect.

In the next chapter, we begin the second part of this book, which explores a large database example using all the features of server-side JavaScript that you learned about in the first part of the book.

SECTION 2
Creating an Application

Designing Your Web Application

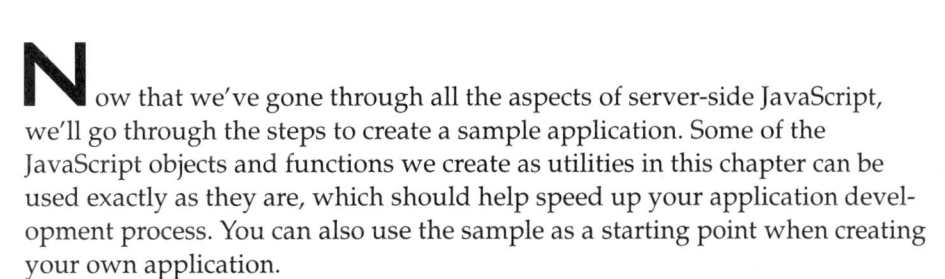

Now that we've gone through all the aspects of server-side JavaScript, we'll go through the steps to create a sample application. Some of the JavaScript objects and functions we create as utilities in this chapter can be used exactly as they are, which should help speed up your application development process. You can also use the sample as a starting point when creating your own application.

The sample application is a time-tracking system for your intranet. It can easily be modified to create an extranet application so that your customers can log trouble tickets and job requests easily.

There are two main parts to the application. The first part provides a way for employees to log their hours, describe the client or project, and see where they've been spending their hours. The second part allows managers to evaluate the projects employees have been working on, view reports to see how much time was spent on a specific client or project, and determine how much a client should be billed (if the time was billable). This section also includes an area to add employee logins and new client or project information.

Creating Your Application Map

Generally at this point in the development process you'd create a flow chart to map out how your application will work. Actually, you'd probably first write up a more detailed specification than what was covered at the beginning of this chapter. The following section, "The Pages," goes into more detail about the pieces of this application.

Since this is a Web-based application, we're going to create an application map instead of a flow chart; this will be similar to a Web site map. We'll start with the home page of the application and show the links to the subsequent pages.

The Pages

The nine pages described below are all we need to create our time-tracking application; they cover all the necessary tasks. The next section, "The Map," describes how these pages link together in the application map.

- **Home Page**. The home page will be a form where an employee can type his or her login name and password to access the application. This login serves two purposes: restricting access to your application and tracking the number of hours an employee spends using the application. You can also add a level of security to your application by using the restricted access portions of the Enterprise server. We'll see how to do this in Chapter 8, "Implementing Your Design." Once an employee logs in, we'll use the client object to identify that employee.

- **Main Menu**. The main menu will consist of two links: the general access menu page and the admin access menu page. Only employees with administrative access will see the admin access menu page; employees without admin access will see only the general access menu page.

- **General Access Menu**. The general access menu page will consist of two links: the "log hours" page and the "view hours" page. These are the most common tasks that employees will be using in this application.

- **Admin Access Menu**. The admin access menu page will consist of three links: view reports, administer employees, and administer clients. These cover any administrative tasks needed to manage the application. This page will most likely use frames to make application management easier. It isn't necessary to decide whether or not to use frames at this point—we'll be covering that in the "Designing Your Interface" section later on.

Chapter 7: Designing Your Web Application

- **Log Hours**. The log hours page is a form that will allow an employee to select from a list of clients and log the number of hours spent and the work done during those hours. There will be check boxes to determine whether the time is billable or part of a project, and if it was a rush job that would cost more than a normal job.

- **View Hours**. The view hours page will allow employees to select a specific date range and then see what clients or projects they were working for and how much revenue they generated within that time period. Of course, you may choose not to display the revenue, or your application may be project-based instead of client-based.

- **View Reports**. The view reports page will consist of a form on which the administrator can choose a date range and either a client (or project) or an employee. The administrator can then generate a report to see how much time was spent on the client (and how much money the client owes) or where the employee was spending his or her time.

- **Administer Employees**. The administer employees page will allow the administrator to add and remove employees from the employee log in the database. The administrator can also set a flag to determine whether the employee has administrative access or not.

- **Administer Clients**. The administer clients page will allow the administrator to add clients to the client database. The client list will be displayed on the "log hours" page so employees can log hours to that client. This database can also consist of internal projects to simply track time instead of time and money.

The Map

When employees come to this application, the home page is displayed, which lets them log in and make choices from a menu. If an employee has administrative access capabilities, he or she can choose between doing general access tasks and doing administrative access tasks. If an employee doesn't have administrative access, only the general access menu will be displayed. This will consist of two options: logging hours and viewing hours. The administrative menu will give the employee the ability to either view a report based on an employee or client and a date range, or administer employee accounts and clients in the database.

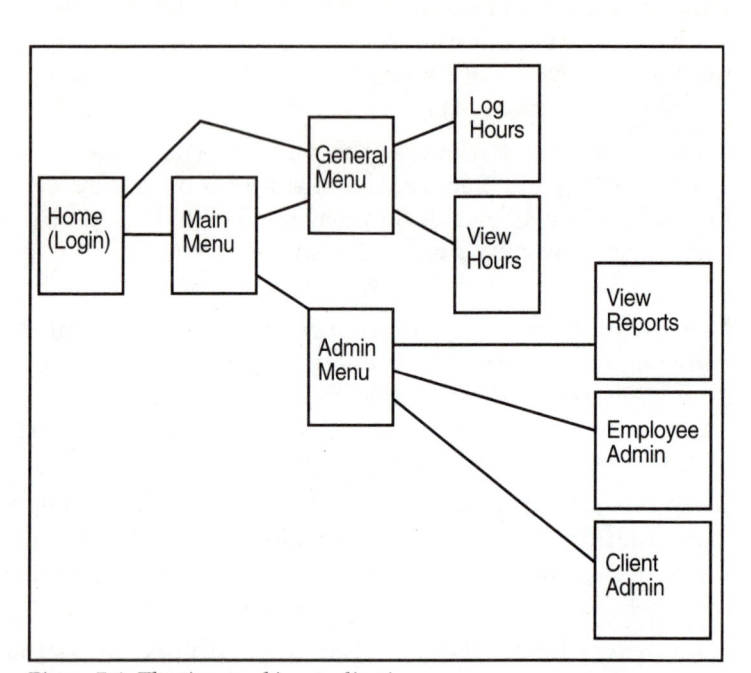

Figure 7-1 shows the pages users will see in this application.

Figure 7-1: The time tracking application map.

We will come back to these pages in more depth later in this chapter in the "Designing Your Interface" section. At that point we'll decide how the pages will look and when and where to use frames or other client-specific features.

> **TIP**
>
> *Remember that using more advanced features in your application may limit the browsers that can view it. This is generally not a problem for intranet and extranet applications.*

Designing Your Database Tables

Now that we know basically what the application will do and how users will access it, we need to begin designing the database tables. This example was created using an Informix database on Solaris 2.5, but it will work with any database supported by Enterprise Server 3.0.

For the time-tracking application, we'll create three tables: an employee table, a client table, and an hours table. The following sections discuss each of these tables, their fields, and how they'll be used in this application.

> **Creating Database Tables**
>
> How you create database tables will differ depending on your database server. You may have a nice GUI or program to create tables, or you may have to simply execute a SQL statement. Refer to your specific database server documentation for more information. For nearly all SQL database servers, you should be able to execute the following command to create a new table:
>
>   create table tableName (field1 datatype1, field2 datatype2);
>
> You can also give more information about each field such, as "unique" or "not null," after the data type to limit what data must be entered or whether or not there can be duplicate data.

The Employee Table

The employee table's main purpose is to hold the login names and passwords for all employees who will be accessing your application. It will also contain a flag to determine whether the employee has administrative access or not. Any other fields will be purely informational and can be added as you see fit. You could also later add in levels of access if it makes sense for your application.

The following table lists the fields we'll be creating for this database table with the appropriate data type and a description. The data type you use may differ depending on your database.

field name	data type	description
login	variable character length (maximum 16)	The login field will be what employees use to identify themselves to the application. It will correlate to a field in the hours table so that employees can be mapped to the hours they spend. This field must be unique and not allow any null values. Once an employee logs in to the application, this value will be stored in the client object so that in subsequent requests the employee will be recognized.
password	variable character length (maximum of 8)	The password field is used to verify the employee's identity. In this example it won't be encrypted when it is stored, but you may wish to add in a step to encrypt and decrypt when dealing with the passwords. This field must not allow any null values.
admin	integer	This field will be set to 0 if the employee doesn't have administrative access. If the employee does, the value will be 1. You may later expand this to have numerical levels of access to the application.
firstname	variable character length (maximum of 12)	This field will hold the first name of the employee. It is only used when displaying reports regarding this employee.
lastname	variable character length (maximum of 24)	This field will hold the first name of the employee. It is only used when displaying reports regarding this employee.

Table 7-1: The employee table.

You may wish to add a position or title field; if you're in a large organization, you may also want to add a phone or extension number or e-mail address for contacting the employee.

The Client Table

The client table's main purpose is to hold information on all the clients and/or projects your employees will be working with. The most important fields are the id, name, and rate, used to identify the client and the standard hourly rate for that client. The rest of the fields are purely for informational purposes.

The following table lists the fields we'll be creating for this database table with the appropriate data type and a description. The data type you use may differ depending on your database.

field name	data type	description
id	integer	An identifier for the client. This will be used to correlate entries in the hours table to the client (or project) the time was spent on. It must be unique and not null.
name	variable character length (maximum of 64)	This field will be used when generating reports to show the name of the client and on the "log hours" page in the list of clients for the employee to choose from. It must be unique and not null.
rate	float	This field determines how much the client must pay per hour. It may be overridden depending on the circumstances but is most often used as a default. If you're using this table for internal projects as well as clients, you will probably put 0 in this field. This field must not be null.
desc	a text blob	This field will contain a brief description of the client.
contact	variable character length (max: 64)	This is the name of the person at the client company who should be contacted for any inquiries.
address	variable character length (max: 64)	This is the address of the client where any bills should be sent.
city	variable character length (max: 24)	The client's city.
state	variable character length (max: 16)	The client's state
zip	variable character length (max: 16)	The client's zip code.

Table 7-2: The client table.

You may wish to include more informational fields in this table such as a phone number or e-mail address—or even a Web site address—for the client.

The Hours Table

The hours table's main purpose is to log the hours spent by each employee. Each entry in this table will represent a block of time spent by an employee on a specific client or project.

The following table lists the fields we'll be creating for this database table with the appropriate data type and a description. The data type you use may differ depending on your database.

field name	data type	description
day	date	This field is the date on which the employee spent time working on the client or project. It must not be null.
hours	float	This field is the number of hours spent working for the client or project. It must not be null.
desc	text blob	This field is a description of what the employee did during the time worked.
employee	variable character length (max: 16)	This field correlates with the login field in the employee table. It identifies the employee who spent the time on the client or project. It must not be null.
client	integer	This field correlates with the id field of the client table. It determines which client the time was spent on. It must not be null.
rate	float	This field determines how much the client should be charged per hour for this time. If this field is null or 0, then the default rate for the client will be used instead.
billable	integer	This field determines whether the time is billable or not. If the value is 0, then the time won't be charged to the client; if it's 1, it will be charged. This is because some time may be spent fixing problems that are not the client's fault; these time periods cannot be billed to the client.
rush	float	If this flag is anything other than 0 or 1, then it will be a multiplier for the cost of the time. This is generally used for a rush job that has to be done immediately and thus costs more. It could also be used as a discount field if the value is between 0 and 1.

Table 7-3: The hours table.

Designing Your Application Objects

Now we'll determine where we can create objects in our application. You can create these objects in either Java or JavaScript, depending on the capabilities you require. We'll be using JavaScript for most of them and Java for one as an exercise in using LiveConnect on the server.

We'll create five objects for this application: three that correspond to the three database tables and two for handling running reports on the data.

The Employee Object

This object will be implemented in JavaScript. The employee object will include properties for each of the fields in the employee table. We will also need to create methods to handle the data.

There will be three possible constructors for the employee object. One will be passed a login name to be used to query the database for the employee information. The object properties will then be seeded with this information. A second constructor will be passed the request object from an HTML form. This will then create the object from the request properties. The third constructor will create a blank employee object.

The following table lists the methods we'll be creating for the employee object.

method	description
check	Checks the validity of the object to make sure all the properties contain valid values so that the object can be saved to the database.
checkPassword	Compares the password passed to this method with the password property of the object. If they match, it returns true; otherwise it returns false.
displayForm	This method will create an HTML form with all the properties of the object. If the properties are blank then the form will be blank, and if the properties exist they will be used as the default values of the form.
getName	Returns the full name of the employee from the firstname and lastname properties. If these properties don't exist or are null, then it returns the login name of the employee.
save	Saves the properties of the object to the database. It will be passed a flag to determine whether it should update information if the employee already exists in the database or only create a new employee entry.

Table 7-4: The employee object methods.

The timeClient Object

This object will be implemented in JavaScript. The timeClient object corresponds to the client database table. We won't use the name "client," to avoid confusion with the JavaScript client object.

There will be three possible constructors for the timeClient object. One will be passed a client id that will query the database to seed the object properties from the database. The second will be passed a request object to create the object from an HTML form submission. The third constructor will create a blank timeClient object.

The following table lists the methods we'll be creating for the timeClient object.

method	description
check	Checks the validity of the object to make sure all the properties contain valid values so that it can be saved to the database.
DisplayAddress	Displays the name and address of the client to the Web browser.
DisplayForm	This method will create an HTML form with all the properties of the object. If the properties are blank, then the form will be blank; if the properties exist, they will be used as the default values of the form.
DisplayFull	Displays the name, contact, address, and description of the client to the Web browser.
getDesc	Returns the description of the client.
getName	Returns the name of the client.
getRate	Returns the hourly rate the client usually gets.
save	Saves the properties of the object to the database. It will be passed a flag to determine whether it should update information if the client already exists in the database or if it should only create a new client entry.

Table 7-5: The timeClient object methods.

The Hours Object

This object will be implemented in JavaScript. The hours object will be similar to the timeClient and employee objects by having properties to correspond with the fields in the hours table. The only difference will be that the employee property will be an employee object, as opposed to simply the login, and the client property will be a timeClient object instead of the client ID.

Chapter 7: Designing Your Web Application

There will only be two constructors for the hours object. The first will take a request object and create an hours object with the properties set based on the value of the properties in the request object. The second will create a blank hours object.

The following table lists the methods for the hours object.

method	description
check	Checks the validity of the object to make sure all the properties contain valid values so that the object can be saved to the database.
display	Displays a formatted view of the time spent and the client to the browser.
displayForm	This method will create an HTML form with all the properties of the object. If the properties are blank, then the form will be blank; if the properties exist, they will be used as the default values of the form.
save	Saves the properties of the hours object to the hours table.

Table 7-6: The hours object methods.

The Report Object

This object will be implemented in JavaScript. The report object will be used to generate and display reports from the data stored in the hours table. When a user or administrator runs a report, a report object will be created with the parameters of the report. Table 7-7 lists the properties of the report object.

property	description
employee	This property will contain a single employee login or a list of logins, or will be blank to indicate all employees. It will be used to determine which employees the report will display information about.
client	This property will contain a client id or a list of id's, or will be blank to indicate all clients. It will be used to determine which clients the report will display information about.
start	This property will be a JavaScript date object which determines the starting date to run the report for.
end	This property will be a JavaScript date object which determines the ending date to run the report for.

property	description
clientTotals	This property will be a hash table that will associate a client id with a ReportHours object that contains the total hours for each client. Using LiveConnect, this property will be an instance of a Java Object.
employeeTotals	This property will be a hash table, which will associate an employee login with a ReportHours object that contains the total hours for each employee. Using LiveConnect, this property will be an instance of a Java Object.
dateTotals	This property will be a hash table, which will associate each date showed by the report with a ReportHours object that contains the total hours for each date. Using LiveConnect, this property will be an instance of a Java Object.
total	This will be a ReportHours object with the total hours for the entire report. Using LiveConnect, this property will be an instance of a Java Object.

Table 7-7: The report object properties.

There will be only one constructor for the report object. It will take four parameters: a list of employees, a list of clients, a start date, and an end date. If either the employee list or the client list is empty, then the report will display data for all employees or clients respectively.

The following table lists the methods for the report object.

method	description
query	This is an internal method used to determine the database query that will pull the necessary data out of the database to create the report.
display	The display method will call all the appropriate display methods from the hash tables stored in this object, as well as the total numbers for the report.
displayClient	This method will display a table of the total hours and amounts of money owed for each client of the report. If the report is only showing data for one client, then this will not display anything, as the total numbers will be the same.
displayEmployee	This method will display a table of the total hours and amounts of money owed for each employee of the report. If the report is only showing data for one employee, then this will not display anything, as the total numbers will be the same.
displayDate	This method will display a table of the total hours and amounts of money owed for each date of the report.

Table 7-8: The report object methods.

The ReportHours Object

This object will be implemented in Java. The ReportHours object is used by the report object to store totals for each piece of the report. Table 7-9 lists all the properties for this object.

property	description
name	An identifier for the data being totaled.
hours	The total hours for this specific set of data.
amount	The total amount of revenue generated for this set of data.
start	The starting date for this set of data.
end	The ending date for this set of data.

Table 7-9: The ReportHours object properties.

There will only be one constructor for this object that will be passed the name to be associated with the set of data.

The following table lists the methods for the ReportHours object.

method	description
add	Adds the hours and amounts of revenue to the current totals for this object. If the starting date hasn't been set, it will be, and the ending date will then be set. This assumes that once the object is initialized, each subsequent call to add will be a later date than the previous one.
display	Displays a row in a table with the data stored in this object.
displayHead	This is a static method; it will display an HTML table with headers for the row that will be returned by the display method.

Table 7-10: The ReportHours object methods.

Designing Your Interface

Now we're getting close to being able to implement our application. We just need to decide what each page will look like. This can be broken down into three main sections: the menu pages (including the login page), the general access forms, and the administrative access forms. We'll also decide in pseudocode what the code will be doing when forms are submitted.

Of course, this is just a basic overview of the pages. When we begin implementing, we can make minor changes if necessary.

The Menu Pages

The menu pages are the first few pages of the application. They include the home page, the main menu, the general access menu, and the administrative access menu.

- **Home Page**. The home page will be a frameset page with two frames: a thin one at the top and a larger main page at the bottom. When it first loads, the top frame will be a form with a place for a login name and password and a submission button. This frame will have a simple black background, and the form will be formatted in a table with white text. The bottom frame will be a blank white page. When the employee submits the login page, an employee object will be created from the login name. If the passwords match, then the employee will be given a menu page in the top frame (the main menu if there's administrative access and the general menu if not).

- **Main Menu**. The main menu page will consist of two text links. These links will be in a one-row table, each in its own column. These two links will simply lead to the general access menu or the administrative access menu, which will both load in the top frame.

- **General Access Menu**. The general access menu page will be very similar to the main menu page. There will be two links in a single row of a table. These links will load in the lower frame and will link to the "log hours" and the "view hours" pages. If the user has administrative access, there will also be a left-justified second row with a link to the administrative access menu page, which will load in the top frame.

- **Administrative Access Menu**. The administrative access menu will be similar to the previous two windows except that the first row will consist of three columns with links to the "view reports," "administer employees," and "administer clients" pages; these pages will all load in the lower frame if selected. The second row will have a link to the general access menu page, which will load in the top frame.

The General Access Forms

The general access forms consist of two forms: one that employees will use to log hours and one that shows the hours they've spent over a specified time range. Both of these forms will load in the lower frame.

- **Log Hours**. When the log hours page is loaded, a blank hours object will be created. The displayForm method will be called on this object. This form will consist of an HTML form with a field for each property of the hours object. When the employee fills out and submits this form, an hours object will be created from the request object. If the check method returns that the data is acceptable, then the save method will be called to log the hours to the database. If the check method fails, then an error message will be displayed and the form redisplayed.
- **View Hours**. The view hours page will simply consist of two sets of drop-down boxes to select the beginning date and the ending date for the range. Each date will be in a row of a table. When the form is submitted, the date form will be redisplayed with the selected dates as the default values, and below the table the report will be seen. The report will consist of the total number of hours spent per client for the date range as well as a daily breakdown of the hours spent. This page will only display the time spent by the employee who is viewing the page.

The Administrative Access Forms

The administrative access forms consist of three forms, which administrators will use to view time-tracking reports, administer employees, and administer clients. All these forms will load in the lower frame.

- **View Reports**. The view reports form will be a table similar to the one used with the view hours page. It will have two rows each with a set of drop-down boxes to select a beginning and ending date for the report. There will also be a two-column third row where the administrator can select from a list of employees or clients (or any combination of the two) to view the reports on them. When the form is submitted, the total hours spent on and total amount owed from each client for the date range will be displayed on the page. If only a single client is selected, then there will also be a breakdown of daily time spent on the client per employee.
- **Administer Employees**. The administer employees page will be a table with a link at the top to add a new employee to the database. Below that will be a list of all employees in the database with a link beside each employee to delete them from the database. If the add employee link is selected, then a blank employee object will be created and the displayForm method will be called. When submitted, the data will be checked and saved if it's valid. If any of the employee names are clicked, then an employee object will be created for that employee and the displayForm method will be called. The administrator can then modify

any information for that employee; if the data is valid, it can then be saved to the database. Beside each employee name there will be a link to delete the employee from the database.

- **Administer Clients**. The administer clients page will be very similar to the administer employees form. It will consist of a table with a link at the top to add a new client (or project) to the database, and a list of clients below with a link beside each one to delete the client. If the administrator clicks on the add client link, a blank timeClient object will be created and the displayForm method will be called. When the form is submitted, a new timeClient object will be created from the request object; if the data is valid, it will be saved to the database. By clicking on a client, a timeClient object will be created for that client and the displayForm method will be called so that any of the data can be modified.

Moving On

Now that we've gone through the process of mapping out our application and determining what our application pages will be, we'll begin to implement our design.

The next chapter covers creating and compiling the source code for the time-tracking application. As we implement our design, we may discover places where utility functions become necessary and where we may even need new objects.

Implementing Your Design

Now that we've mapped out and designed our application, we're ready to start writing the code. We'll begin by creating the tables in our database and setting up the directory for the application. Then we'll create the objects and finally the Web pages.

The Preliminaries

Before we can write the code for our application, we need to set up all the database tables we'll be using; we'll also create a directory to store the application files.

Creating Database Tables

How you create your database tables depends on the database server you're using. This example was written using an Informix database, so the tables were created using the dbaccess program. Your database may have a similar program, or you may simply use SQL to create the tables.

The employee table needs to be created as it was designed in Chapter 7, "Designing Your Web Application." The following SQL statement may be used in lieu of a simpler table creation interface. But be warned: your database SQL syntax may be slightly different. The syntax for these statements will work with Informix without modification.

```
create table employee (
    login       varchar(16,1) unique not null,
    password    varchar(8,1) not null,
    admin       integer,
    firstname   varchar(12,1),
    lastname    varchar(24,1)
);
```

The client table:

```
create table client (
    id       varchar(16,1) unique not null,
    name     varchar(64,1) not null,
    rate     smallfloat not null,
    desc     text,
    contact  varchar(64,1),
    address  varchar(64,1),
    city     varchar(24,1),
    state    varchar(16,1),
    zip varchar(16,1)
);
```

The hours table:

```
create table hours (
    day        date not null,
    hours      smallfloat not null,
    desc       text,
    employee   varchar(16,1) not null,
    client     varchar(16,1) not null,
    rate       smallfloat,
    billable   integer,
    rush       smallfloat
);
```

Setting Up the Application Directory

Now we need a place to put these files. First we'll create a subdirectory under the SuiteSpot directory to hold all the applications we create. This will simply be called "apps." Under that we'll create a directory named "timetrack" to hold this application. This name is important; it needs to match the name of the package we use for any Java classes we create, so that the server can find the class when it needs to load it.

We also need to create a subdirectory under timetrack named "js" to hold all our JavaScript-only files. You could put all your JavaScript-only files in the same directory as the html files but our method will make them a little easier to find.

Modifying the Classpath

We'll also need to modify the classpath of the server. There are two ways to do this: by setting the CLASSPATH environment variable before starting the server or by modifying the server's obj.conf configuration file. We'll use the second method. Edit the obj.conf file in the config subdirectory of your server (e.g., /usr/local/suitespot/https-time/config/obj.conf). There should be a line that begins with:

```
Init classpath=
```

Find that line and modify it to appear as below. Change any instance of *installpath* to the name of the directory where you installed your Enterprise server (such as /usr/local/suitespot). You should only need to add /usr/local/suitespot/apps to the end of the classpath setting.

```
Init classpath=" installpath /wai/java/nish.zip: installpath /js/samples: installpath /plugins/java/classes/serv3_0.zip: installpath /plugins/java/local-classes: installpath /apps" ldpath=" installpath plugins/java/bin" fn="SJavaBootInit"
```

You'll need to restart the server after making this change.

Creating the "build" Program

This step is optional, but it makes compiling your application a bit easier. We'll create a shell script or batch file to be run to recompile your application. It simply runs jsac with all the options you use. The file is one line and consists of the following:

```
jsac -v -o time.web js/*.js *.html
```

This tells the JavaScript Application Compiler to compile all the .js files in the js subdirectory and all the .html files in the current directory into the file *time.web*.

Instead of creating this file, you could type this command each time you wish to compile your application.

Implementing Your Objects

The first step in writing our application is to create the objects we've designed. All the objects we create in JavaScript will be saved in the js subdirectory and named *objectName*Obj.js. This way they'll be easy to find and modify later on. The Java object we create will be saved and compiled in the root directory of the application, so that the server can find it when it needs to.

Some of these objects call functions that don't exist in JavaScript, such as writeln and printDate. We'll be implementing those functions later in this chapter in the "Writing Any Additional JavaScript Functions" section.

Creating Objects in JavaScript

You define an object in JavaScript by creating a function and then passing it to the new operator to create a new instance of the object. You can set properties and methods on the object using "this" to refer to the current object.

The following code creates a simple object that takes one argument when an instance is created and has one method. Note that the method is assigned by setting this.*methodName* to the name of the function as it is defined.

```
function simple(Data) {
    // set the data property to the data passed to
    // the new operator
    this.data = Data;
    // define a method for the object
    this.show = showData;
}
function showData {
    // write the value of the data property
    // of this object
    write(this.data);
}
```

Now when you want to create an instance of this object, you do this:

```
myObj = new simple("some info");
myObj.show();
```

This causes "some info" to be written to the browser.

The Employee Object

The employee object will be created as we defined it in Chapter 7, "Designing Your Web Application." Since it has more than one constructor, we need to be a little creative—JavaScript objects can technically have only one constructor. To get around this, we create another function that creates an instance of the employee object and then returns it. *Note:* When you call these other constructors, you don't use the new operator, since that function will create a new employee object and then initialize it as it should.

For all the JavaScript objects, we keep all the functions related to the object in one file. Note that all the method definitions start with employeeObj*MethodName* so that we don't have to worry about conflicts with other functions in the application.

The three ways to create an employee object are:

```
// create a blank employee
var empObj = new employee();

// load employee data from the database
var empObj = employeeDB("duncan");

// create an employee object from the
// request object
var empObj = employeeReq(request);
```

employeeObj.js

```
// This is the definition of the employee object.
// When called with new, a blank
// employee object is created.
function employee() {
    // The Properties
    this.login = "";
    this.password = "";
    this.admin = 0;
    this.firstname = "";
    this.lastname = "";

    // The Methods
    this.check = employeeObjCheck;
    this.checkPassword = employeeObjCheckPassword;
    this.displayForm = employeeObjDisplayForm;
    this.getName = employeeObjGetName;
    this.save = employeeObjSave;
    this.erase = employeeObjErase;
}

// This is a second "constructor" for the
// employee object.
// It takes a login name and queries
// the database for that employee and
// initializes the object with that data.
function employeeDB( loginName ) {
    // Create a blank employee object
    emp = new employee();
```

```javascript
    // get a connection from the connection
    // pool and query the database.
    DBConn = project.pool.connection();
    empCurs = DBConn.cursor(
        "select * from employee where login = '"
        + loginName + "'");
    // If the employee is in the database then
    // initialize the properties of the employee
    // object. Otherwise set it to null.
    if ( empCurs.next() ) {
        emp.login = empCurs.login;
        emp.password = empCurs.password;
        emp.admin = empCurs.admin;
        emp.firstname = empCurs.firstname;
        emp.lastname = empCurs.lastname;
    } else {
        emp = null;
    }
    empCurs.close();
    DBConn.release();
    return emp;
}

// This is the third "constructor" for the
// employee object.
// It takes the request object which
// should have properties equivalent
// to the properties of the employee object.
function employeeReq( reqObj ) {
    emp = new employee();
    emp.login = reqObj.login;
    emp.password = reqObj.password;
    emp.admin = reqObj.admin;
    emp.firstname = reqObj.firstname;
    emp.lastname = reqObj.lastname;
    return emp;
}

// This method makes sure that the properties
// of the employee object are set correctly.
// This should be called before the object
// is saved to the database.
function employeeObjCheck() {
    return !isNull(this.login) &&
        !isNull(this.password) && ( this.admin == 0
        || this.admin == 1);
}
```

```
// This method checks to see if the given
// password matches the password in the
// employee object.
function employeeObjCheckPassword( tryPW ) {
    return tryPW == this.password;
}

// This method displays a form that's filled out
// with the data that's stored in the object.
function employeeObjDisplayForm() {
    writeln("<table border=0>");
    writeln("<tr><th align=right>Login</th>");
    writeln(
        "<td><input name=login size=10 value=\"" +
        this.login + "\"></td></tr>");
    writeln("<tr><th align=right>Password</th>");
    writeln(
        "<td><input size=10 name=password value=\""
        + this.password + "\"></td></tr>");
    writeln("<tr><th align=right>Administrator</th>");
    writeln(
        "<td><input type=radio name=admin value=1" +
        (this.admin == 1 ? " checked" : "") +
        ">Yes <input type=radio name=admin value=0"
        + (this.admin == 0 ? " checked" :
        "") + ">No</td></tr>");
    writeln(
        "<tr><th align=right>First Name</th>");
    writeln("<td><input name=firstname value=\"" +
        this.firstname + "\"></td></tr>");
    writeln("<tr><th align=right>Last Name</th>");
    writeln(
        "<td><input name=lastname value=\"" +
        this.lastname + "\"></td></tr>");
    writeln('<tr><th colspan=2><input type=submit value="  OK  "> <input
type=reset value=" Reset "></th><tr>');
    writeln("</table>");
}

// This method returns the first and last
// names of the employee from the object.
function employeeObjGetName() {
    return this.firstname + " " + this.lastname;
}
```

```javascript
// This method saves the properties of the
// object to the database.
// If the update flag is set to true then
// it will only update an existing entry.
// Otherwise it will only save the entry
// if it's a new employee.
function employeeObjSave(update) {
    var retErr = "";
    // create a connection to the database and
    // create an updatable cursor
    var DBConn = project.pool.connection();
    DBConn.beginTransaction();
    var empCurs = DBConn.cursor(
        "select * from employee where login = '" +
        this.login + "'", true);
    // If the employee information is to be
    // updated then make sure the employee
    // existed and change all the information
    // except for the login name.
    // Set an error otherwise.
    if ( update ) {
        if ( empCurs.next() ) {
            empCurs.password = this.password;
            empCurs.admin = this.admin;
            empCurs.firstname = this.firstname;
            empCurs.lastname = this.lastname;
            empCurs.updateRow("employee");
        } else {
            retErr = "Update with no existing record.\n";
        }
    // If the employee isn't to be updated
    // then insert a new row into the
    // employee table.
    // Set an error if the employee login
    // was already used.
    } else {
      if ( !empCurs.next() ) {
            empCurs.login = this.login;
            empCurs.password = this.password;
            empCurs.admin = this.admin;
            empCurs.firstname = this.firstname;
            empCurs.lastname = this.lastname;
            empCurs.insertRow("employee");
```

```
        } else {
            retErr = "Insert with existing record.\n";
        }
    }
    empCurs.close();
    if ( retErr == "" )
        DBConn.commitTransaction();
    else
        DBConn.rollbackTransaction();
    DBConn.release();
    return retErr;
}

// This method will delete the employee from the
// employee table.
function employeeObjErase() {
    var retErr = "";
    // Create a connection and an updatable
    // cursor.
    var DBConn = project.pool.connection();
    DBConn.beginTransaction();
    var empCurs = DBConn.cursor(
        "select * from employee where login = '" +
        this.login + "'", true);
    // If the employee exists then delete them
    // from the employee table.
    if (empCurs.next()) {
        if ( empCurs.deleteRow("employee") != 0 )
            retErr = "Couldn't delete: " +
                DBConn.majorErrorMessage();
    } else {
        retErr = "Delete with no existing record.\n";
    }
    empCurs.close();
    if ( retErr == "" )
        DBConn.commitTransaction();
    else
        DBConn.rollbackTransaction();
    DBConn.release();
    return retErr;
}
```

The timeClient Object

The timeClient object will be created as we defined it in Chapter 7, "Designing Your Web Application." Like the employee object, we had to create two more constructors for the object.

The three ways to create a timeClient object are:

```
// create a blank timeClient object
var clientObj = new timeClient();

// load a client from the database
var clientObj = timeClientDB("ABC");

// create a client object from the
// request object
var clientObj = timeClientReq(request);
```

timeClientObj.js

```
// This is the definition of the timeClient
// object.
// When called with new, a blank
// timeClient object is created.
function timeClient() {
    // The Properties
    this.id = "";
    this.name = "";
    this.rate = 0;
    this.desc = "";
    this.contact = "";
    this.address = "";
    this.city = "";
    this.state = "";
    this.zip = "";

    // The Methods
    this.check = timeClientObjCheck;
    this.displayAddress =
        timeClientObjDisplayAddress;
    this.displayForm = timeClientObjDisplayForm;
    this.displayFull = timeClientObjDisplayFull;
    this.getDesc = timeClientObjGetDesc;
    this.getName = timeClientObjGetName;
    this.getRate = timeClientObjGetRate;
    this.save = timeClientObjSave;
    this.erase = timeClientObjErase;
}
```

```
// This is a second "constructor" for the
// timeClient object.
// It takes a client ID and queries
// the database for that client and
// initializes the object with that data.
function timeClientDB( clientID ) {
    // Create a blank timeClient object
    tClient = new timeClient();
    // Create a connection to the database
    // and pull the client information from
    // the client table.
    DBConn = project.pool.connection();
    tClientCurs = DBConn.cursor(
        "select * from client where id = '" +
        clientID + "'");
    // If the client exists then initialize
    // all the properties, otherwise set
    // the object to null.
    if ( tClientCurs.next() ) {
        tClient.id = tClientCurs.id;
        tClient.name = tClientCurs.name;
        tClient.rate = tClientCurs.rate;
        tClient.desc = tClientCurs.desc;
        tClient.contact = tClientCurs.contact;
        tClient.address = tClientCurs.address;
        tClient.city = tClientCurs.city;
        tClient.state = tClientCurs.state;
        tClient.zip = tClientCurs.zip;
    } else {
        tClient = null;
    }
    tClientCurs.close();
    DBConn.release();
    return tClient;
}

// This is the third "constructor" for the
// timeClient object.
// It takes the request object which
// should have properties equivalent
// to the properties of the timeClient object.
function timeClientReq( reqObj ) {
    tClient = new timeClient();
    tClient.id = reqObj.id;
```

```
    tClient.name = reqObj.name;
    tClient.rate = reqObj.rate;
    tClient.desc = reqObj.desc;
    tClient.contact = reqObj.contact;
    tClient.address = reqObj.address;
    tClient.city = reqObj.city;
    tClient.state = reqObj.state;
    tClient.zip = reqObj.zip;
    return tClient;
}

// This method makes sure that the properties
// of the timeClient object are set correctly.
// This should be called before the object
// is saved to the database.
function timeClientObjCheck() {
    return this.id != 0 && !isNull(this.name) &&
        this.rate != 0;
}

// This method displays the name
// and address of the client to the
// browser.
function timeClientObjDisplayAddress() {
    writeln(this.name+"<br>");
    writeln(this.address+"<br>");
    writeln(this.city+", "+this.state+" " +
        this.zip + "<br>");
}

// This method displays a form that's filled out
// with the data that's stored in the object.
function timeClientObjDisplayForm() {
    writeln("<table border=0>");
    writeln("<tr><th align=right>ID</th>");
    writeln("<td><input name=id size=10 value=\""
        + this.id + "\"></td></tr>");
    writeln("<tr><th align=right>Name</th>");
    writeln(
        "<td><input name=name size=40 value=\""
        + this.name + "\"></td></tr>");
    writeln("<tr><th align=right>Rate</th>");
    writeln("<td><input name=rate size=5 value=\""
        + this.rate + "\"></td></tr>");
    writeln("<tr><th align=right>Description</th>");
    writeln(
```

```
        "<td><textarea name=desc cols=50 rows=5>" +
        this.desc + "</textarea></td></tr>");
    writeln("<tr><th align=right>Contact</th>");
    writeln(
        "<td><input name=contact size=40 value=\"" +
        this.contact + "\"></td></tr>");
    writeln("<tr><th align=right>Address</th>");
    writeln(
        "<td><input name=address size=40 value=\"" +
        this.address + "\"></td></tr>");
    writeln("<tr><th align=right>City</th>");
    writeln("<td><input name=city value=\"" +
        this.city + "\"></td></tr>");
    writeln("<tr><th align=right>State</th>");
    writeln("<td><input name=state value=\"" +
        this.state + "\"></td></tr>");
    writeln("<tr><th align=right>Zip</th>");
    writeln("<td><input name=zip size=10 value=\""
        + this.zip + "\"></td></tr>");
    writeln('<tr><th colspan=2><input type=submit value=" OK "> <input
type=reset value=" Reset "></th></tr>');
    writeln("</table>");
}

// This method displays all the
// client information to the browser
function timeClientObjDisplayFull() {
    this.displayAddress();
    writeln("Contact: "+this.contact+"<br>");
    writeln("<dl><dd>" + this.desc + "</dl><br>");
}

// This method returns the description
// of the client.
function timeClientObjGetDesc() {
    return this.desc;
}

// This method returns the name of the
// client.
function timeClientObjGetName() {
    return this.name;
}

// This method returns the hourly rate
// the client normally gets.
```

```
function timeClientObjGetRate() {
    return this.rate;
}

// This method saves the properties of the
// object to the database.
// If the update flag is set to true then
// it will only update an existing entry.
// Otherwise it will only save the entry
// if it's a new employee.
function timeClientObjSave(update) {
    var retErr = "";
    // create a connection to the database and
    // create an updatable cursor
    DBConn = project.pool.connection();
    DBConn.beginTransaction();
    tClientCurs = DBConn.cursor(
        "select * from client where id = '" +
        this.id + "'", true);
    // If the client information is to be
    // updated then make sure the client
    // existed and change all the information
    // except for the client ID.
    // Set an error otherwise.
    if ( update ) {
        if ( tClientCurs.next() ) {
            tClientCurs.name = this.name;
            tClientCurs.rate = this.rate;
            tClientCurs.desc = this.desc;
            tClientCurs.contact = this.contact;
            tClientCurs.address = this.address;
            tClientCurs.city = this.city;

            tClientCurs.state = this.state;
            tClientCurs.zip = this.zip;
            tClientCurs.updateRow("client");
        } else {
            retErr = "Update with no existing record.\n";
        }
    // If the client isn't to be updated
    // then insert a new row into the
    // client table.
    // Set an error if the client ID
    // was already used.
```

Chapter 8: Implementing Your Design

```
        } else {
            if ( !tClientCurs.next() ) {
                tClientCurs.id = this.id;
                tClientCurs.name = this.name;
                tClientCurs.rate = this.rate;
                tClientCurs.desc = this.desc;
                tClientCurs.contact = this.contact;
                tClientCurs.address = this.address;
                tClientCurs.city = this.city;
                tClientCurs.state = this.state;
                tClientCurs.zip = this.zip;
                tClientCurs.insertRow("client");
            } else {
                retErr = "Insert with existing record.\n";
            }
        }
        tClientCurs.close();
        if ( retErr == "" )
            DBConn.commitTransaction();
        else
            DBConn.rollbackTransaction();
        DBConn.release();
        return retErr;
    }

    // This method deletes the client from
    // the client table.
    function timeClientObjErase() {
        var retErr = "";
        // Create a connection and an updatable
        // cursor.
        var DBConn = project.pool.connection();
        DBConn.beginTransaction();
        var tClientCurs = DBConn.cursor(
            "select * from client where id = '" +
            this.id + "'", true);
        // If the client exists then delete them
        // from the client table.
        if (tClientCurs.next()) {
            if ( tClientCurs.deleteRow("client") != 0 )
                retErr = "Couldn't delete: " +
                DBConn.majorErrorMessage();
        } else {
            retErr = "Delete with no existing record.\n";
        }
```

```
        tClientCurs.close();
    if ( retErr == "" )
        DBConn.commitTransaction();
    else
        DBConn.rollbackTransaction();
    DBConn.release();
    return retErr;
}
```

The Hours Object

The hours object will be created as we defined it in Chapter 7, "Designing Your Web Application." Like the employee and timeClient objects, we had to create an extra constructor for the object.

The two ways to create an hours object are:

```
// create a blank hours object
var hoursObj = new hours();

// create an hours object from the
// request object
var hoursObj = hoursReq(request);
```

hoursObj.js

```
// This is the definition of the hours
// object.
// When called with new, a blank
// hours object is created.
function hours() {
    // The Properties
    this.day = new Date();
    this.hours = 0;
    this.desc = "";
    this.employee = "";
    this.client = 0;
    this.rate = 0;
    this.billable = 0;
    this.rush = 0;
```

```
    // The Methods
    this.check = hoursObjCheck;
    this.display = hoursObjDisplay;
    this.displayForm = hoursObjDisplayForm;
    this.save = hoursObjSave;
}


// This is the second "constructor" for the
// hours object.
// It takes the request object which
// should have properties equivalent
// to the properties of the hours object.
// For the day property, it creates a
// date object from data in the request object.
// For the employee and client properties
// it creates an instance of an employee
// and timeClient object.
function hoursReq( reqObj ) {
    hours = new hours();
    hours.day = new Date(reqObj.year,
        reqObj.month, reqObj.day);
    hours.hours = reqObj.hours;
    hours.desc = reqObj.desc;
    hours.employee = employeeDB(client.login);
    hours.client = timeClientDB(reqObj.client);
    hours.rate = reqObj.rate;
    if ( hours.rate == 0 )
        hours.rate = hours.client.rate;
    hours.billable = reqObj.billable;
    hours.rush = reqObj.rush;
    return hours;
}


// This method makes sure that the properties
// of the hours object are set correctly.
// This should be called before the object
// is saved to the database.
function hoursObjCheck() {
    return this.hours != 0 && !isNull(this.desc)
        && !isNull(this.employee.login) &&
        !isNull(this.client.id);
}
```

```javascript
// This method displays the information from
// the hours object in an HTML table.
function hoursObjDisplay() {
    writeln("<table border=0>");
    writeln("<tr><th>Employee</th><th>Client</th><th>Time</th><th>Rate</
th><th>Total</th></tr>");
    writeln("<tr><td>"+this.employee.getName() +
        "</td>");
    writeln("<td>"+this.client.getName()+"</td>");
    writeln("<td>"+this.hours+"</td>");
    writeln("<td>"+this.rate+"</td>");
    writeln("<td>"+this.rate*this.hours+
        "</td></tr>");
    writeln("</table>");
}

// This method displays a form that's filled out
// with the data that's stored in the object.
function hoursObjDisplayForm() {
    writeln("<table border=0>");
    writeln("<tr><th align=right>Day</th>");
    write("<td>");
    selectDate(this.day, "");
    writeln("</td></tr>");
    writeln("<tr><th align=right>Hours</th>");
    writeln(
        "<td><input name=hours size=5 value=\""
        + this.hours + "\"></td></tr>");
    writeln(
        "<tr><th align=right>Description</th>");
    writeln("<td><textarea name=desc cols=50 rows=4 wrap=soft>"
        + this.desc + "</textarea></td></tr>");
    writeln("<tr><th align=right>Client</th>");
    write("<td>");
    selectClient(this.client);
    writeln("</td></tr>");
    writeln("<tr><th align=right>Rate</th>");
    writeln("<td><input name=rate size=5 value=\""
        + this.rate + "\"></td></tr>");
    writeln("<tr><th align=right>Billable</th>");
    writeln("<td><input type=radio name=billable value=1"
        + (this.billable == 1 ? " checked" : "") +
        ">Yes <input type=radio name=billable value=0"
        + (this.billable == 0 ? " checked" : "") +
        ">No</td></tr>");
```

```
    writeln("<tr><th align=right>Rush</th>");
    writeln("<td><input name=rush size=5 value=\""
        + this.rush + "\"></td></tr>");
    writeln('<tr><th colspan=2><input type=submit value="  OK  "> <input
type=reset value=" Reset "></th></tr>');
    writeln("</table>");
}

// This method saves the object to the hours
// table.
function hoursObjSave() {
    // Create a connection to the database
    // and an updatable cursor.
    var DBConn = project.pool.connection();
    var hoursCurs = DBConn.cursor(
        "select * from hours", true);
    // Set all the fields in the cursor.
    hoursCurs.day = this.day;
    hoursCurs.hours = this.hours;
    hoursCurs.desc = this.desc;
    hoursCurs.employee = this.employee.login;
    hoursCurs.client = this.client.id;
    hoursCurs.rate = this.rate;
    hoursCurs.billable = this.billable;
    hoursCurs.rush = this.rush;
    // Insert a new row into the hours table
    hoursCurs.insertRow("hours");
    hoursCurs.close();
    DBConn.release();
}
```

The Report Object

The report object only has one constructor, as defined in Chapter 7, "Designing Your Web Application." It also uses LiveConnect to use the Java Hashtable class to keep track of the hours totaled for the report. The "total" property is an instance of the ReportHours object, which is the Java object we'll create next.

To create a new instance of a report object we use:

```
reportObj = new report("", "", startDate, endDate);
// startDate and endDate are JavaScript
// date objects. Leaving the first two
// arguments as blank causes the report
// to be generated for all clients and
// employees.
```

reportObj.js

```javascript
// This is the definition of the report
// object.
// When called with new, a report
// object will be created and all the
// values will be set.
function report(Employee, Client, Start, End) {
    // The Properties
    this.employee = Employee;
    this.client = Client;
    this.start = Start;
    this.end = End;

    this.clientTotals = new java.util.Hashtable();
    this.employeeTotals = new
        java.util.Hashtable();
    this.dateTotals = new java.util.Hashtable();
    this.total = new
        Packages.timetrack.ReportHours("Total");

    // The Methods
    this.query = reportObjQuery;
    this.display = reportObjDisplay;
    this.displayClient = reportObjDisplayClient;
    this.displayEmployee =
        reportObjDisplayEmployee;
    this.displayDate = reportObjDisplayDate;

    // Create a connection to the database
    DBConn = project.pool.connection();
    // Query the relevant entries from the
    // database.
    hourList = DBConn.cursor(this.query());
    while (hourList.next()) {
        var amount = 0;
        // Determine how much to charge for
        // the time.
        if ( hourList.billable == 1 ) {
            amount = hourList.hours*hourList.rate;
            if ( hourList.rush != 0 )
                amount *= hourList.rush;
        }
```

```
// Add the information to the "total"
// ReportHours object.
this.total.add(hourList.hours, amount,
    hourList.day);

    // If a list of clients was passed to the
    // constructor then add the data to the
    // ReportHours object associated with the
    // current client.
    if ( isNull(this.client) ||
        this.client.indexOf(",") != -1 ) {
        newClientTot = this.clientTotals.get(
            hourList.name);
        if ( newClientTot == null )
            newClientTot = new
        Packages.timetrack.ReportHours(
            hourList.name );
        newClientTot.add(hourList.hours,
            amount, hourList.day);
        this.clientTotals.put(hourList.name,
            newClientTot);
    }
    // If a list of employees was passed to the
    // constructor then add the data to the
    // ReportHours object associated with the
    // current employee.
    if ( isNull(this.employee) ||
        this.employee.indexOf(",") != -1 ) {
        empName = hourList.lastname +", "+
            hourList.firstname;
        newEmpTot = this.employeeTotals.get(
            empName);
        if ( newEmpTot == null )
            newEmpTot = new
        Packages.timetrack.ReportHours(
            empName);
        newEmpTot.add(hourList.hours, amount,
            hourList.day);
        this.employeeTotals.put(empName,
            newEmpTot);
    }
    // Add the data to the ReportHours object
    // associated with the current date.
    newDateTot =
```

```javascript
                    this.dateTotals.get(hourList.day);
            if ( newDateTot == null )
                newDateTot = new
                    Packages.timetrack.ReportHours(
                    printDate(hourList.day));
            newDateTot.add(hourList.hours, amount,
                hourList.day);
            this.dateTotals.put(hourList.day,
                newDateTot);

        }
    hourList.close();
    DBConn.release();

}

// This method will return the query
// that the report object should use
// to pull all the data it needs from the
// database to initialize the requested report.
function reportObjQuery() {
    var Query = "select →
e.firstname,e.lastname,c.name,h.hours,h.rate,h.billable,h.rush,h.day from →
hours h, employee e, client c where h.day between '" +
        printDate(this.start) + "' AND '" +
        printDate(this.end) +
        "' AND h.client = c.id AND h.employee = e.login";
    if ( !isNull(this.employee) )
        Query += " AND h.employee in ( "
            + this.employee + " )";
    if ( !isNull(this.client) )
        Query += " AND h.client in ( " + this.client
            + " )";
    Query += " order by h.day";
        return Query;
}

// This method will display the report
// generated.
function reportObjDisplay() {
    Packages.timetrack.ReportHours.displayHead(
        "Total");
    this.total.display();
    writeln("</table>");
    this.displayClient();
```

```
    this.displayEmployee();
    this.displayDate();
}


// This method will display a table
// listing the total hours and amount
// of revenue generated for each
// client within the date range.
function reportObjDisplayClient() {
    if ( isNull(this.client) ||
        this.client.indexOf(",") != -1 ) {
        Packages.timetrack.ReportHours.displayHead(
        "Clients");
        // Call the ReportHours object display
        // method for each element in the
        // clientTotals hashtable.
        for( elem = this.clientTotals.elements();
            elem.hasMoreElements(); ) {
            curTotals = elem.nextElement();
            curTotals.display();
        }
        writeln("</table>");
    }
}

// This method will display a table
// listing the total hours and amount
// of revenue generated by each
// employee within the date range.
function reportObjDisplayEmployee() {
    if ( isNull(this.employee) ||
        this.employee.indexOf(",") != -1 ) {
        Packages.timetrack.ReportHours.displayHead(
        "Employees");
        // Call the ReportHours object display
        // method for each element in the
        // employeeTotals hashtable.
        for( elem = this.employeeTotals.elements();
            elem.hasMoreElements(); ) {
            curTotals = elem.nextElement();
            curTotals.display();
        }
        writeln("</table>");
    }
}
```

```
// This method will display a table
// listing the total hours and amount
// of revenue generated for each
// date within the date range.
function reportObjDisplayDate() {
    Packages.timetrack.ReportHours.displayHead(
        "Date");
    // Call the ReportHours object display
    // method for each element in the
    // dateTotals hashtable.
    for( elem = this.dateTotals.elements();
        elem.hasMoreElements(); ) {
        curTotals = elem.nextElement();
        curTotals.display();
    }
    writeln("</table>");
}
```

The ReportHours Object

The ReportHours object only has one constructor, as defined in Chapter 7. It is used by the report object to total the hours for each client, employee, and date and the combined total for all the clients, employees and dates..

To create a new instance of a report object (in JavaScript) we use:

```
var reportHoursObj = new Packages.timetrack.ReportHours("Name");
```

ReportHours.java

```
package timetrack;

import netscape.javascript.*;
import netscape.server.serverenv.*;

import java.util.*;
import java.text.*;

public class ReportHours {
    String           name;
    int              hours;
    int              amount;
    GregorianCalendar   start;
    GregorianCalendar   end;
```

```java
// This is the constructor for the ReportHours
// object.  It sets the name of the object
// and initializes the rest of the properties
// to 0 or null.
public ReportHours(String name) {
    this.name = name;
    this.hours = 0;
    this.amount = 0;
    this.start = null;
    this.end = null;
}


// This method increments the hours and amount
// associated with the current object and
// sets the start date if it's null and the
// end date.
public void add(int hours, int amount,
    JSObject date) {
    this.hours += hours;
    this.amount += amount;
    if ( this.start == null ) {
        this.start = new GregorianCalendar(
            ((Double)date.call("getYear",
                null)).intValue(),
            ((Double)date.call("getMonth",
                null)).intValue(),
            ((Double)date.call("getDate",
                null)).intValue() );
    }
    this.end = new
        GregorianCalendar(((Double)date.call(
            "getYear", null)).intValue(),
            ((Double)date.call("getMonth",
            null)).intValue(),
            ((Double)date.call("getDate",
            null)).intValue() );
}


// This method displays a row of an HTML table
// with the data stored in the object.
public void display()
throws java.io.IOException {
    NetscapeServerEnv.writeHttpOutput("<tr><th>"
        +this.name+"</th>\n");
```

```
        NetscapeServerEnv.writeHttpOutput("<td>"
            +this.hours+"</td>");
        NetscapeServerEnv.writeHttpOutput("<td>"
            +this.amount+"</td>");
        NetscapeServerEnv.writeHttpOutput("<td>"
            +(this.start.get(Calendar.MONTH)+1)+
            "/" +
            this.start.get(Calendar.DAY_OF_MONTH)
            + "/" +
            this.start.get(Calendar.YEAR) +
            "</td>");
        NetscapeServerEnv.writeHttpOutput("<td>"
            +(this.end.get(Calendar.MONTH)+1)+"/"
            +this.end.get(Calendar.DAY_OF_MONTH) +
            "/" +
            this.end.get(Calendar.YEAR) +
            "</td></tr>");
    }

    // This method displays the header row
    // of an HTML table which will line up
    // with the row created by the display method.
    public static void displayHead(String title)
    throws java.io.IOException {
        NetscapeServerEnv.writeHttpOutput(
            "<p><table border=2 width=100%>\n");
        NetscapeServerEnv.writeHttpOutput("<tr><th>"
            + title +
        "</th><th>Hours</th><th>Amount</th><th>Start Date</th><th>End Date</th></tr>\n");
    }

}
```

Writing Your HTML Pages

Now we get to the main piece of the application: the HTML pages. This is how the user will interface with your application. For this example, these pages are created rather plainly. You can add images and sounds to your applications to soup them up.

Creating the Initial Page & the Home Page

Every application I create always includes two files: start.html and start.js. The start.html page is set as the initial page in the application manager. That means the page will be loaded the first time anyone accesses the application after it's been started, regardless of which page was requested. It's a good place to initialize any data you need to exist throughout the application. In this example we'll use it to create a property of the project object named "pool," which is an instance of a DbPool object.

The start.js page only has one function. It is called at the beginning of all the other pages in the application. It simply makes sure the project.pool object is connected and tries to reconnect it if it's not. If it still can't connect, it returns an error. This is to correct any problems that may occur if for some reason the connection drops while the application is running.

start.html

```
<server>

project.pool = new DbPool("INFORMIX",
    "ifmx_online", "username", "password",
    "timetrack", 5, false);
if(!project.pool.connected()) {
    delete project.pool;
    redirect("error.html");
}

redirect("home.html");
</server>
```

start.js

```
function checkDB() {
    if ( !project.pool ||
        !project.pool.connected() ) {
        delete project.pool;
        project.pool = new DbPool("INFORMIX",
            "ifmx_online", "username", "password",
            "timetrack", 5, false);
        if ( !project.pool.connected() ) {
            delete project.pool;
            redirect("error.html");
        }
    }
}
```

The home.html page is a frame that loads the top.html page in the top frame and a blank page in the bottom frame. The top.html page consists of a login form for the employee's login name and password. It submits to the login.html page, which creates an instance of an employee object based on the login name given. If the password matches, then the user is logged in and given a menu based on his or her level of access. Note that all these pages begin with the checkDB( ) function.

The top.html page also has a call to the function bodyTag( ). This function is used to write all the <BODY> tags for the application so that it's easier if you ever want to change any of the body attributes without modifying every page in your application. The login.html page creates a property named "login" in the client object, so that the user will be identifiable while traveling through the site.

Figure 8-1: The home page of the time-tracking application.

home.html

```
<server>
checkDB();
</server>

<html>
<head>
<title>Time Tracking</title>
</head>
<frameset rows="20%,80%">
    <frame src="top.html" name=menu>
    <frame src="about:blank" name=main>
</frameset>
</html>
```

top.html

```
<server>
checkDB();
</server>
<html>
<server>bodyTag("black");</server>

<form method=POST action="login.html">
<table border=0>
<tr><th align=right>Login Name</th><td><input name=login></td></tr>
<tr><th align=right>Password</th><td><input name=password type=password> →
</ td></tr>
<tr><th colspan=2><input type=submit
value=" Log In "></th></tr>
</table>

</body>
</html>
```

login.html

```
<server>
checkDB();
</server>

<html>
<server>
bodyTag("black");
```

```
employee = employeeDB(request.login);

if ( employee &&
    employee.checkPassword(request.password) ) {
    client.login = request.login;
    if ( employee.admin == 1 )
        redirect("mainmenu.html");
    else
        redirect("genmenu.html");
} else {
    writeln("Your password didn't match, please go back and retype it.");
}

</server>
</body>
</html>
```

This error page is loaded when the application can't connect to the database. You may wish to display contact information here so that you can be contacted when this occurs.

error.html

```
<html>
<head>
<title>Error!</title>
</head>
<body>
<h2>An error occurred connecting to the database!</h2>
</body>
</html>
```

The Menus

Now we'll create the menu pages. All these pages are mostly straight HTML with very little JavaScript. Each includes a call to the checkDB() function as well as to the checkLogin() function. The checkLogin() function will be created later in this chapter in the "Writing Any Additional JavaScript Functions" section. If this function is passed with true as the argument, then it will make sure the user has admin access; otherwise it will make sure the user is a valid user.

The Main Menu

The main menu will only be seen by administrative users; thus it has a call to checkLogin( ) with true as the argument. This page displays the links to the other two menus of the application.

Figure 8-2: The main menu page.

mainmenu.html

```
<server>
checkDD(),
checkLogin(true);
</server>
<html>
<server>bodyTag("black");</server>

<center>
<table border=2 cellpadding=6 cellspacing=6>
```

```
<tr>
    <th><a href="genmenu.html">General Access
        Menu</a></th>
    <th><a href="adminmenu.html">Admin Access
        Menu</a></th>
</tr>
</table>
</center>

</body>
</html>
```

The General Access Menu

The general access menu displays the links to the log hours form and the view hours form for employees. If the user has administrative access, then there will also be a link to the admin access menu.

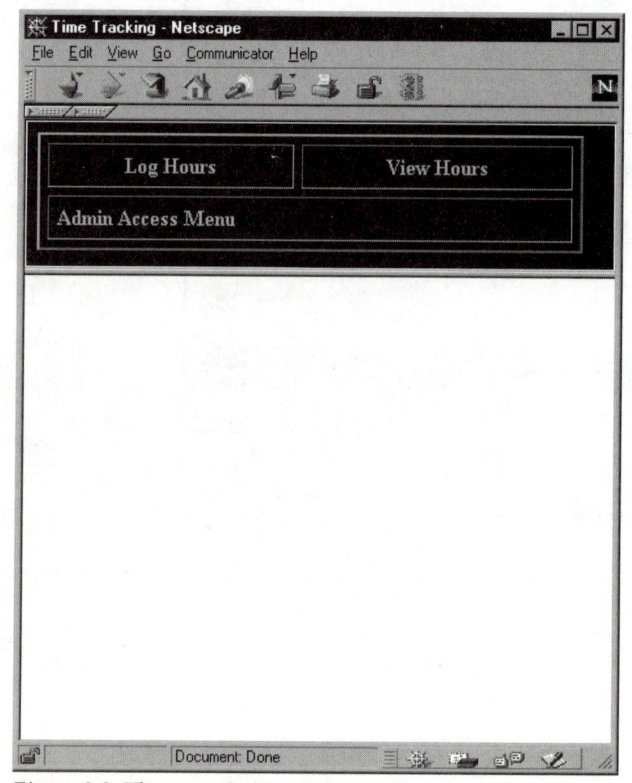

Figure 8-3: The general access menu page.

genmenu.html

```
<server>
checkDB();
empObj = checkLogin(false);
</server>
<html>
<server>bodyTag("black");</server>

<center>
<table width=100% border=2 cellpadding=6 cellspacing=6>
<tr>
    <th><a target=main href="log.html">Log
        Hours</a></th>
    <th><a target=main href="view.html">View
        Hours</a></th>
</tr>
<server>
if ( empObj.admin == 1 ) {
    writeln('<tr><th colspan=2 align=left><a href="adminmenu.html">Admin
Access Menu</a></th></tr>');
}
</server>
</table>
</center>

</body>
</html>
```

The Admin Access Menu

The admin access page displays the links to the administrative forms: view reports, administer employees, and administer clients. It also includes a link to the general access menu.

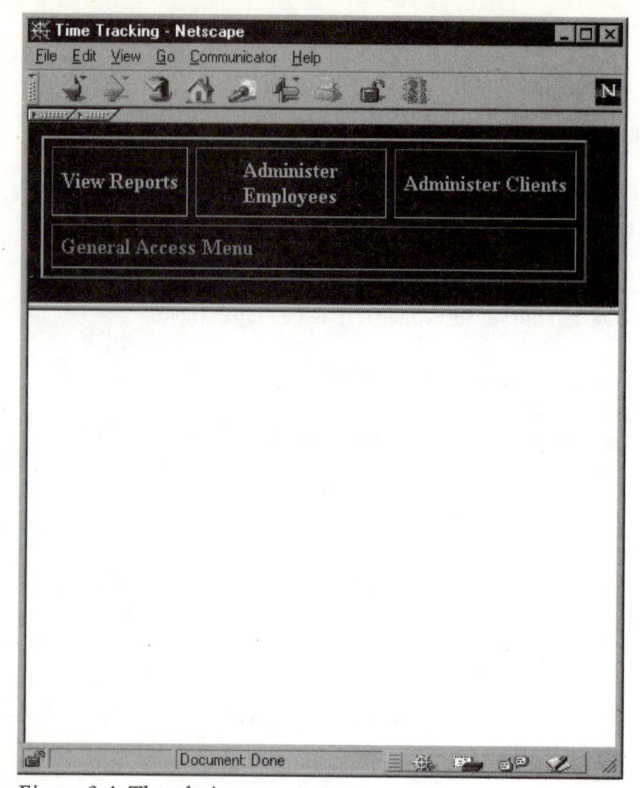

Figure 8-4: The admin access menu.

adminmenu.html

```
<server>
checkDB();
checkLogin(true);
</server>
<html>
<server>bodyTag("black");</server>

<center>
<table width=100% border=2 cellpadding=6 cellspacing=6>
<tr>
    <th><a target=main href="report.html">View
        Reports</a></th>
    <th><a target=main
        href="adminemp.html">Administer
        Employees</a></th>
```

```
            <th><a target=main
                href="adminclient.html">Administer
                Clients</a></th>
        </tr>
        <tr>
            <th colspan=3 align=left><a
                href="genmenu.html">General Access
                Menu</a></th>
        </tr>
        </table>
        </center>

        </body>
        </html>
```

The Forms

The form pages are where the users of your application will be spending most of their time. Most of these forms consist of two pages: the form page and the submission page. Most of the submission pages are named by do_*formName*.html for consistency, for instanace, log.html and do_log.html.

The Log Hours Form

The log hours form is where employees can add data to the hours database table when they spend time on a client or project. The log.html page creates a blank instance of the hours object and then calls the displayForm method. The do_log.html page creates an hours object from the request object. After calling the check method to make sure all the required values were filled out, it saves the object to the database and then displays what was saved.

log.html

```
<html>
<server>
checkDB();
checkLogin(false);

bodyTag("white");
// create a blank hours object
var hourObj = new hours();
writeln('<form method=POST action="do_log.html">');
// display the form
hourObj.displayForm();
```

```
</server>
</form>
</body>
</html>
```

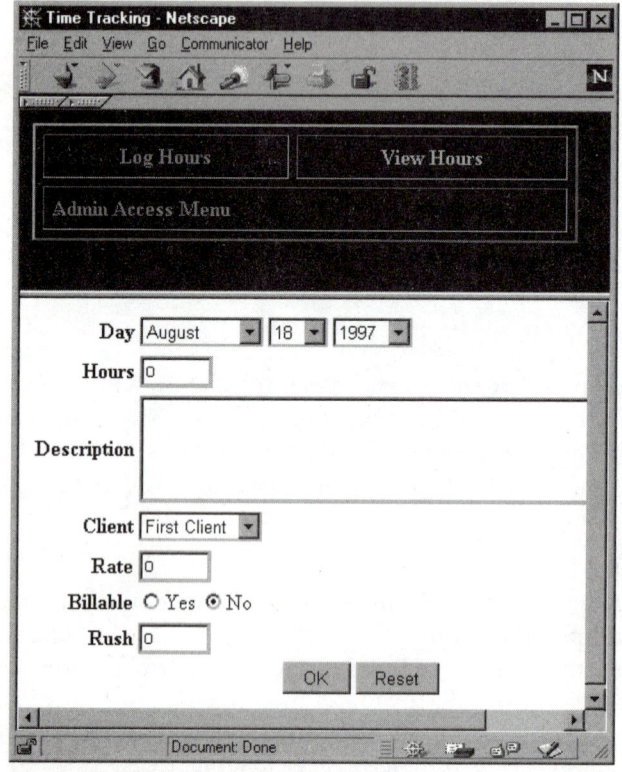

Figure 8-5: The log hours form.

do_log.html

```
<html>
<server>
checkDB();
checkLogin(false);

bodyTag("white");
// create an hours object from the request object
var hourObj = hoursReq(request);
// if the object isn't complete send an error
```

```
if ( !hourObj.check() ) {
    writeln("You left some required fields blank.  Please go back and fill
them in.");
// if the object is complete save it and display
// it
} else {
    hourObj.save();
    hourObj.display();
}
</server>
</body>
</html>
```

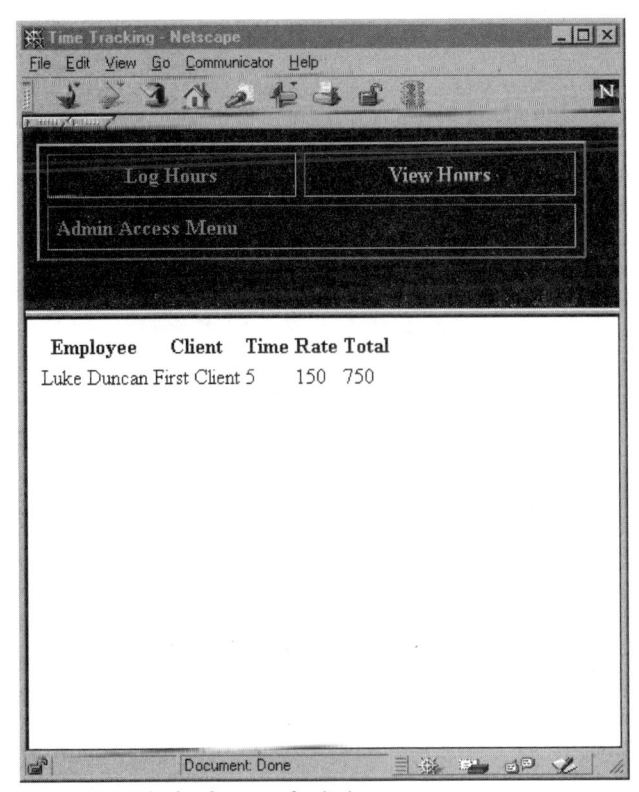

Figure 8-6: The log hours submission page.

The View Hours Form

The view hours form allows a user to select from a date range and display the time they've spent on each client or project in that time period. It uses the selectDate function to display the dates in the form. This function will be created below in the "Writing Any Additional JavaScript Functions" section.

view.html

```
<html>
<server>
checkDB();
checkLogin(false);

bodyTag("white");
today = new Date();
</server>
<form method=POST action="do_view.html">
<table border=0>
<tr><th align=right>Start Date</th>
<td>
<server>selectDate(today, "start");</server>
</td>
</tr>
<tr><th align=right>End Date</th>
<td>
<server>selectDate(today, "end");</server>
</td>
</tr>
<tr><th colspan=2><input type=submit value="Generate Report"></th></tr>
</table>
</form>
</body>
</html>
```

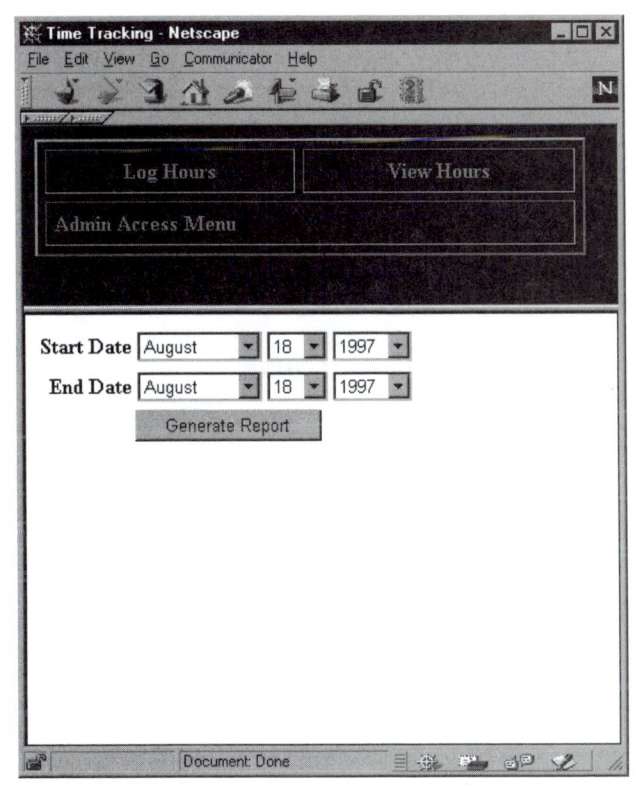

Figure 8-7: The view hours form.

do_view.html

```
<html>
<server>
checkDB();
checkLogin(false);
```

```
bodyTag("white");
var startDate = new Date(request.startyear,
    request.startmonth, request.startday);
var endDate = new Date(request.endyear,
    request.endmonth, request.endday);
</server>

<form method=POST action="do_view.html">
<table border=0>
<tr><th align=right>Start Date</th>
<td>
<server>selectDate(startDate, "start");</server>
</td>
</tr>
<tr><th align=right>End Date</th>
<td>
<server>selectDate(endDate, "end");</server>
</td>
</tr>
<tr><th colspan=2><input type=submit value="Generate Report"></th></tr>
</table>
</form>
<hr>

<server>
// create a report object for the employee
// and display it
reportObj = new report("'"+client.login+"'", "",
    startDate, endDate);
reportObj.display();
</server>
</body>
</html>
```

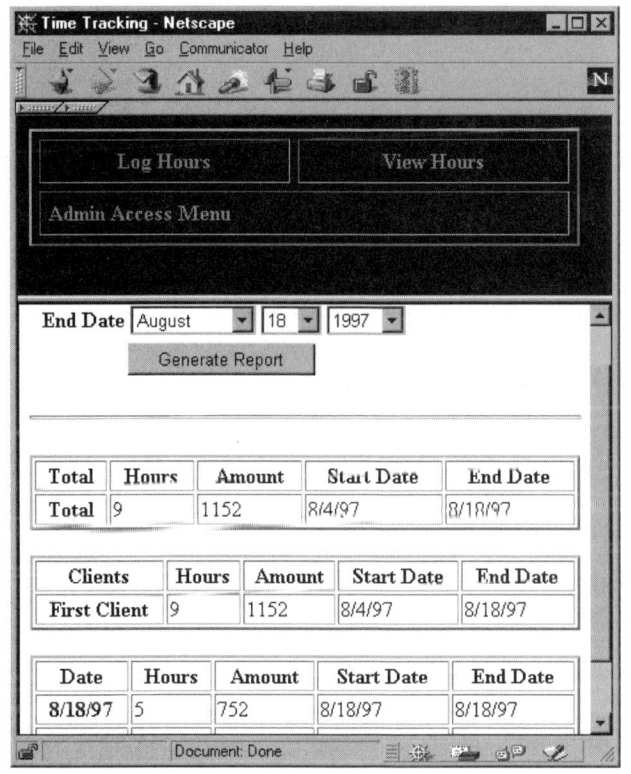

Figure 8-8: The view hours submission page.

The View Reports Form

The view reports form is for administrators only. It creates a form similar to the view hours form except that it also gives a list of employees and clients from the database that can be selected. If no employees or clients are selected, then the report will list all of them.

report.html

```
<html>
<server>
checkDB();
checkLogin(true);

bodyTag("white");
today = new Date();
</server>
<form method=POST action="do_report.html">
<table border=0>
<tr><th align=right>Start Date</th>
<td>
<server>selectDate(today, "start");</server>
</td>
</tr>
<tr><th align=right>End Date</th>
<td>
<server>selectDate(today, "end");</server>
</td>
</tr>
<tr><th align=right>Employees</th>
<td>
<server>selectEmployee("", true);</server>
</td>
</tr>
<tr><th align=right>Clients</th>
<td>
<server>selectClient("", true);</server>
</td>
</tr>
<tr><th colspan=2><input type=submit value="Generate Report"></th></tr>
</table>
</form>
</body>
</html>
```

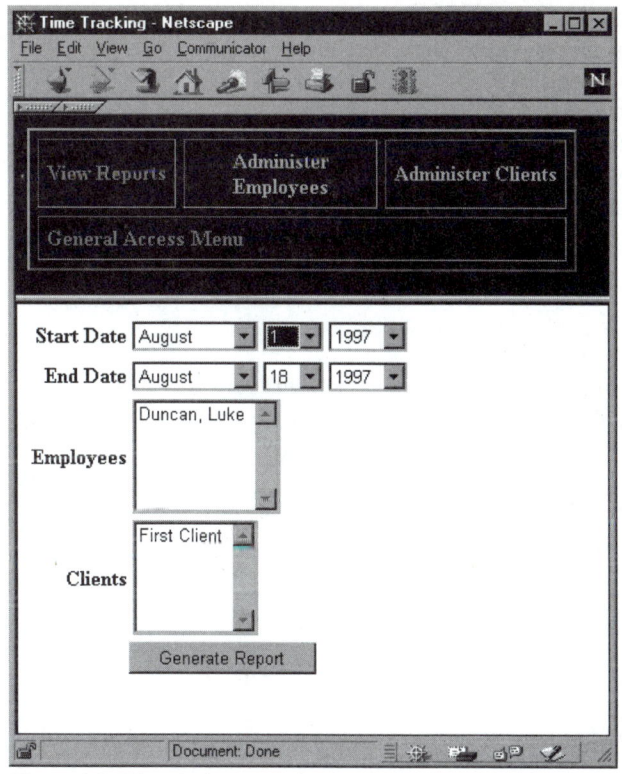

Figure 8-9: The admin report form.

do_report.html

```
<html>
<server>
checkDB();
checkLogin(true);

bodyTag("white");
var startDate = new Date(request.startyear,
    request.startmonth, request.startday);
var endDate = new Date(request.endyear,
    request.endmonth, request.endday);
var empDataList = "";
var clientDataList = "";
```

```
            var empIdx = 0;
            var empCnt = getOptionValueCount("employee");
            while ( empIdx < empCnt ) {
                var empVal = getOptionValue("employee",
                    empIdx);
                if ( empDataList == "" )
                    empDataList = "'"+empVal+"'";
                else
                    empDataList += ", '"+empVal+"'";
                empIdx++;
            }
            var clientIdx = 0;
            var clientCnt = getOptionValueCount("client");
            while ( clientIdx < clientCnt ) {
                var clientVal = getOptionValue("client",
                    clientIdx);
                if ( clientDataList == "" )
                    clientDataList = "'"+clientVal+"'";
                else
                    clientDataList += ", '"+clientVal+"'";
                clientIdx++;
            }

            </server>

            <form method=POST action="do_report.html">
            <table border=0>
            <tr><th align=right>Start Date</th>
            <td>
            <server>selectDate(startDate, "start");</server>
            </td>
            </tr>
            <tr><th align=right>End Date</th>
            <td>
            <server>selectDate(endDate, "end");</server>
            </td>
            </tr>
            <tr><th align=right>Employees</th>
            <td>
            <server>selectEmployee(empDataList, true);</server>
            </td>
            </tr>
            <tr><th align=right>Clients</th>
```

```
<td>
<server>selectClient(clientDataList, true);</server>
</td>
</tr>
<tr><th colspan=2><input type=submit value="Generate Report"></th></tr>
</table>
</form>
<hr>

<server>
// Create the report object and display it
reportObj = new report(empDataList,
    clientDataList, startDate, endDate);
reportObj.display();
</server>
</body>
</html>
```

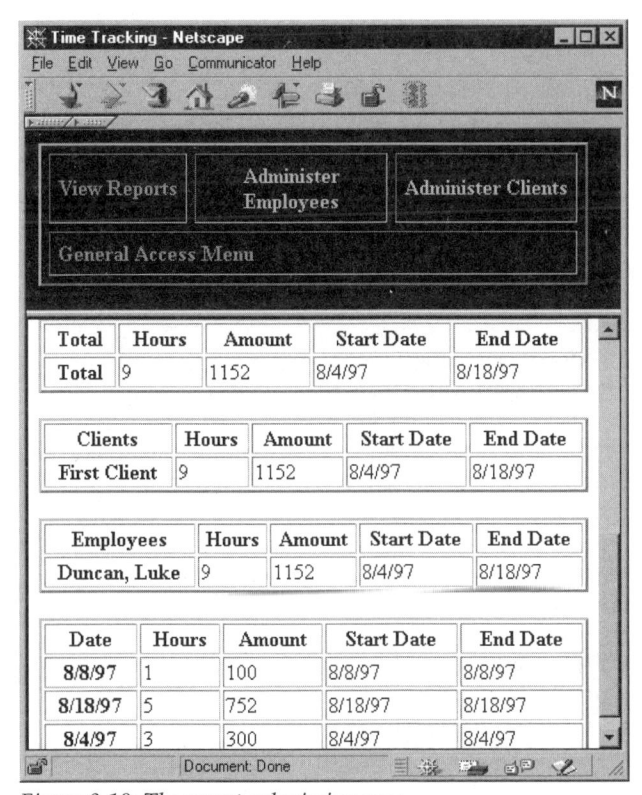

Figure 8-10: The report submission page.

The Administer Employees Form

The administer employees form consists of four pages. The first page (adminemp.html) displays a list of employees with links to a page to modify that employee (adminemp_add.html?action=mod) as well as a link to delete that employee from the database (adminemp_del.html). The first link on the page allows the administrator to add a new employee to the database (adminemp_add.html?action=add). Both the forms submit to do_adminemp.html.

The add and modify pages are actually the same page (with a query string to differentiate between a new employee and an existing one) and are used to update the employee information. Once the modification, addition, or deletion has been made, the administrator is redirected back to the main employee administration page.

adminemp.html

```
<html>
<server>
checkDB();
checkLogin(true);

bodyTag("white");
</server>
<center>
<table border=2 width=80%>
<tr><th colspan=2><a href="adminemp_add.html?action=add">Add a new
Employee</a></th></tr>
<server>
DBConn = project.pool.connection();
// Display the list of employees from the
// database.
empList = DBConn.cursor("select login,firstname,lastname from employee order
by lastname,firstname");
while(empList.next()) {
    write(
        '<tr><td><a href="adminemp_add.html?action=mod&login=' +
        empList.login+'">');
    writeln(empList.lastname + ", " +
        empList.firstname+"</td>");
    writeln(
        '<td><a href="adminemp_del.html?login=' +
        empList.login+'">Delete</a></td></tr>');
}
```

```
empList.close();
DBConn.release();

</server>
</table>
</body>
</html>
```

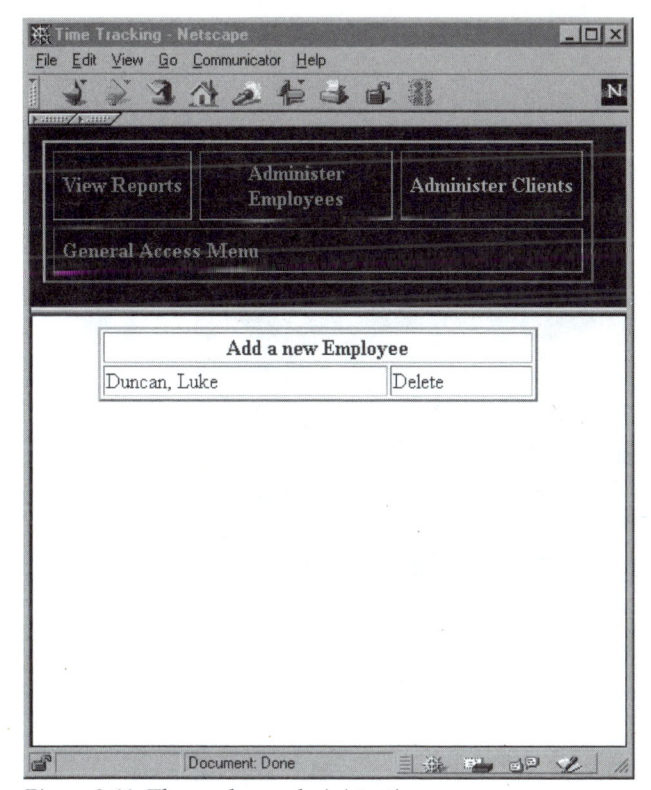

Figure 8-11: The employee administration page.

adminemp_add.html

```
<html>
<server>
checkDB();
checkLogin(true);

bodyTag("white");
```

```
if ( request.action == "add" )
    var clientObj = new timeClient();
else
    var clientObj = timeClientDB(request.id);

if ( clientObj ) {
    writeln('<form method=POST action="do_adminclient.html?action=' +
        request.action+'">');
    clientObj.displayForm();
    writeln("</form>");
} else {
    writeln("Can't find that client!\n");
}
</server>
</body>
</html>
```

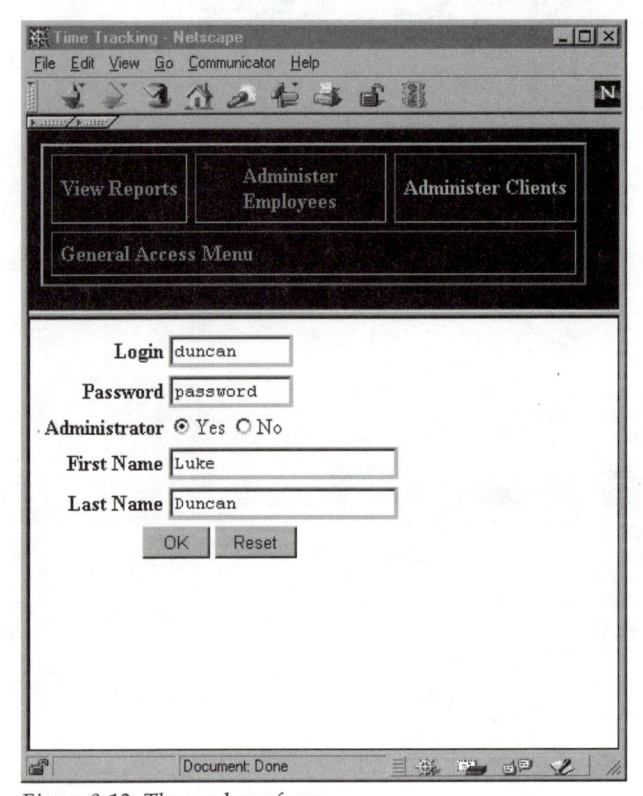

Figure 8-12: The employee form.

do_adminemp.html

```
<html>
<server>
checkDB();
checkLogin(false);

bodyTag("white");
var empObj = employeeReq(request);
if ( !empObj.check() ) {
    writeln("You left some required fields blank.  Please go back and fill
them in.");
} else {
    var saveErr = "";
    if ( request.action == "add" )
        saveErr = empObj.save(false);
    else
        saveErr = empObj.save(true);
    if ( isNull(saveErr) )
        redirect("adminemp.html");
    else
        writeln(saveErr);
}
</server>
</body>
</html>
```

adminemp_del.html

```
<html>
<server>
checkDB();
checkLogin(true);

bodyTag("white");
var empObj = employeeDB(request.login);

if ( empObj ) {
    eraseErr = empObj.erase();
    if ( isNull(eraseErr) )
        redirect("adminemp.html");
    else
        writeln(eraseErr);
} else {
```

```
        writeln("Can't find that employee!\n");
    }
</server>
</body>
</html>
```

The Administer Clients Form

Like the administer employees form, the administer clients form consists of four pages. The first page (adminclient.html) displays a list of clients with links to a page to modify that client (adminclient_add.html?action=mod) as well as a link to delete that client from the database (adminclient_del.html). The first link on the page allows the administrator to add a new client to the database (adminclient_add.html?action=add). Both the forms submit to do_adminclient.html.

The add and modify pages are actually the same page (with a query string to differentiate between a new client and an existing one) and are used to update the client information. Once the modification, addition, or deletion has been made, the administrator is redirected back to the main client administration page.

adminclient.html

```
<html>
<server>
checkDB();
checkLogin(true);

bodyTag("white");
</server>
<center>
<table border=2 width=80%>
<tr><th colspan=2><a href="adminclient_add.html?action=add">Add a new
Client</a></th></tr>
<server>
DBConn = project.pool.connection();
clientList = DBConn.cursor(
    "select id,name from client order by name");
while(clientList.next()) {
    write('<tr><td><a →
href="adminclient_add.html?action=mod&id='+clientList.id+'">');
    writeln(clientList.name +"</td>");
    writeln(
        '<td><a href="adminclient_del.html?id=' +
        clientList.id+'">Delete</a></td></tr>');
}
```

```
clientList.close();
DBConn.release();

</server>
</table>
</body>
</html>
```

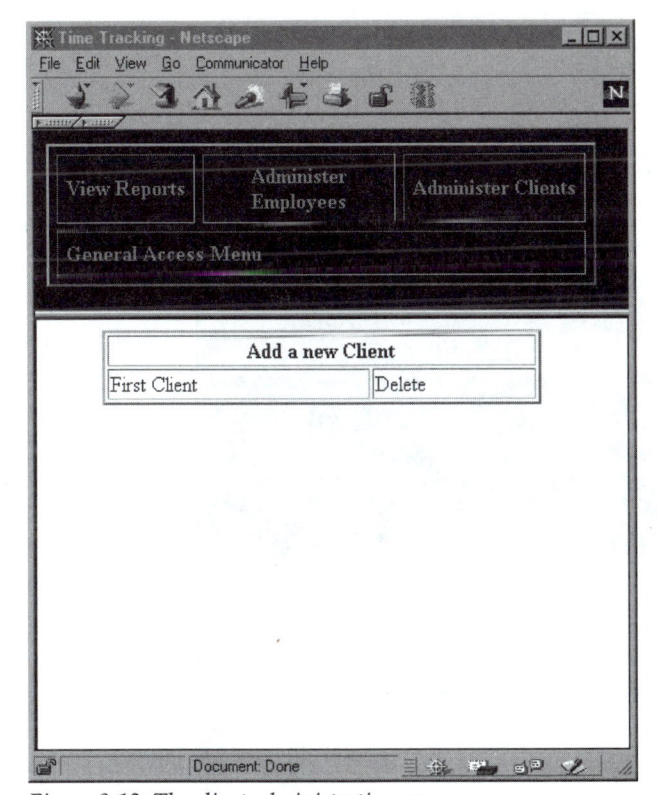

Figure 8-13: The client administration page.

adminclient_add.html

```
<html>
<server>
checkDB();
checkLogin(true);

bodyTag("white");
if ( request.action == "add" )
```

```
        var clientObj = new timeClient();
else
        var clientObj = timeClientDB(request.id);

if ( clientObj ) {
    writeln('<form method=POST action="do_adminclient.html?action=' +
        request.action+'">');
    clientObj.displayForm();
    writeln("</form>");
} else {
    writeln("Can't find that client!\n");
}
</server>
</body>
</html>
```

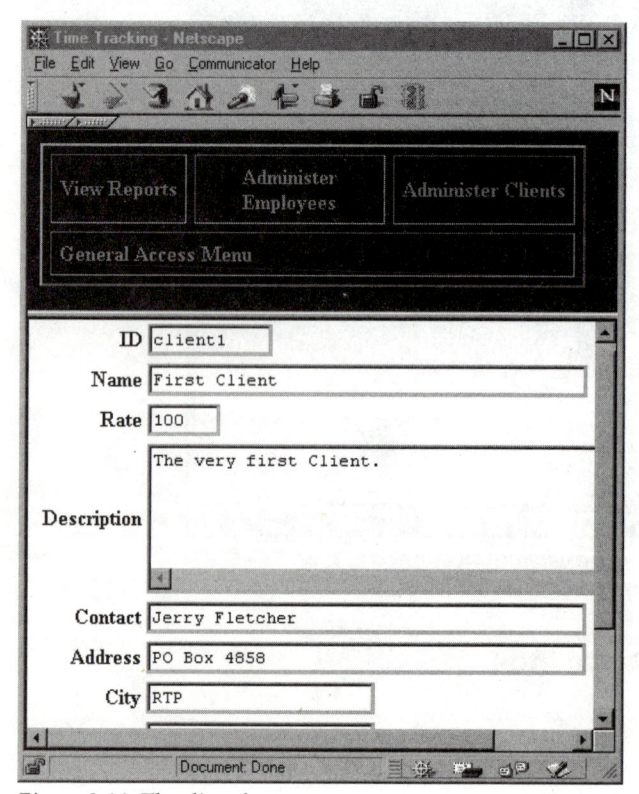

Figure 8-14: The client form.

do_adminclient.html

```
<html>
<server>
checkDB();
checkLogin(false);

bodyTag("white");
var clientObj = timeClientReq(request);
if ( !clientObj.check() ) {
    writeln("You left some required fields blank.  Please go back and fill them in.");
} else {
    var saveErr = "";
    if ( request.action == "add" )
        saveErr = clientObj.save(false);
    else
        saveErr = clientObj.save(true);
    if ( isNull(saveErr) )
        redirect("adminclient.html");
    else
        writeln(saveErr);
}
</server>
</body>
</html>
```

adminclient_del.html

```
<html>
<server>
checkDB();
checkLogin(true);

bodyTag("white");
var clientObj = timeClientDB(request.id);

if ( clientObj ) {
    eraseErr = clientObj.erase();
    if ( isNull(eraseErr) )
        redirect("adminclient.html");
    else
        writeln(eraseErr);
} else {
    writeln("Can't find that client!\n");
```

```
    }
</server>
</body>
</html>
```

Writing Any Additional JavaScript Functions

Now we've nearly completed the application. The only thing left to do is implement all the functions we used in the previous pages. We'll break these down into two files: utils.js and display.js. The utils.js file will be for basic utility functions and the display.js file will include functions that display output to the user.

utils.js

```
// Writes the data passed to it followed by
// a newline character.
function writeln(stringData) {
    write(stringData + "\n");
}


// This function checks to see if the data
// passed to it is null and returns true if
// it is and false otherwise.
function isNull(stringData) {
    return stringData+"" == "" || stringData+"" ==
        "null" || stringData+"" == "<undefined>";
}


// This function checks to make sure the
// currently logged-in user is a valid user
// and if the admin flag is true it also
// verifies that the user has
// administrative access.
function checkLogin(admin) {
    if ( isNull(client.login) )
        redirect("top.html");
    var employee = employeeDB(client.login);
    if ( !employee.check() )
        redirect("top.html");
    if ( admin && employee.admin != 1 )
        redirect("genmenu.html");
    return employee;
}
```

display.js

```javascript
// The selectDate function creates a series
// of three drop-down selection boxes with
// the month, day, and year. It sets the default
// value to the month, day, and year of the
// date object that is passed to this function.
// The optional prefix argument is used as
// the prefix of the name of each selection
// box.
function selectDate(dateObj, prefix) {

    monthNames = new Array(12);
    monthNames[0] = "January";
    monthNames[1] = "February";
    monthNames[2] = "March";
    monthNames[3] = "April";
    monthNames[4] = "May";
    monthNames[5] = "June";
    monthNames[6] = "July";
    monthNames[7] = "August";
    monthNames[8] = "September";
    monthNames[9] = "October";
    monthNames[10] = "November";
    monthNames[11] = "December";

    writeln("<select name="+prefix+"month>");
    for(var i = 0; i < 12; i++) {
        write("<option value="+i);
        if ( i == dateObj.getMonth() )
            write(" selected");
        writeln(">"+monthNames[i]);
    }
    writeln("</select>");

    writeln("<select name="+prefix+"day>");
    for(var j = 1; j <= 31; j++) {
        write("<option value="+j);
        if ( j == dateObj.getDate() )
            write(" selected");
        writeln(">"+j);
    }
    writeln("</select>");

    var today = new Date();
```

```javascript
            writeln("<select name="+prefix+"year>");
            for(var k = 97; k <= today.getYear(); k++) {
                write("<option value="+k);
                if ( k == dateObj.getYear() )
                    write(" selected");
                writeln(">"+parseInt(k+1900));
            }
            writeln("</select>");

    }


    // The selectClient function creates a selection
    // box with a list of all the clients from the
    // client table. If the optional selectedID
    // argument is passed then that client will be
    // the one that is the default. If the multiple
    // flag is true then the selection box will
    // allow multiple selections and the selectedID
    // argument can contain a list of clients
    // which will all be selected.
    function selectClient(selectedID, multiple) {
        DBConn = project.pool.connection();
        clientList = DBConn.cursor(
            "select id,name from client order by name");
        write("<select name=client");
        if (multiple)
            write(" size=5 multiple");
        writeln(">");
        while (clientList.next()) {
            write("<option value='"+clientList.id+"'");
            if ( !multiple && selectedID ==
                clientList.id )
                write(" selected");
            else if ( multiple &&
                selectedID.indexOf("'" + clientList.id
                + "'") != -1 )
                write(" selected");
            writeln(">"+clientList.name);
        }
        writeln("</select>");
        clientList.close();
        DBConn.release();
    }
```

```
// The selectEmployee function creates a
// selection box with a list of all the employees
// from the employee table. If the optional
// selectedLogin argument is passed then that
// employee will be the one that is the default.
// If the multiple flag is true then the
// selection box will allow multiple selections
// and the selectedLogin argument can contain a
// list of employees who will all be selected.
function selectEmployee(selectedLogin, multiple) {
    DBConn = project.pool.connection();
    empList = DBConn.cursor("select login,firstname,lastname from employee →
order by lastname,firstname");
    write("<select name=employee");
    if (multiple)
        write(" size=5 multiple");
    writeln(">");
    while (empList.next()) {
        write("<option value='"+empList.login+"'");
        if ( !multiple && selectedID ==
            empList.login )
            write(" selected");
        else if ( multiple &&
            selectedLogin.indexOf("'" +
            empList.login + "'") != -1 )
            write(" selected");
        writeln(">"+empList.lastname+", " +
            empList.firstname);
    }
    writeln("</select>");
    empList.close();
    DBConn.release();
}

// The bodyTag function simply writes the HTML
// body tag for the page. If the color argument
// is "white" then the background will be white
// with black text, otherwise the background will
// be black with white text.
function bodyTag(color) {
    if ( color == "white" )
        writeln('<body bgcolor="#ffffff" text="#000000" link="#333333" →
alink="#000000" vlink="#555555">');
    else
```

```
        writeln('<body bgcolor="#000000" text="#ffffff" link="#cccccc"
alink="#ffffff" vlink="#aaaaaa">');
}

// The printDate function takes a date object
// and displays it in a short format:
// month/day/year.
function printDate(dateObj) {
    return parseInt(dateObj.getMonth()+1) + "/" +
        dateObj.getDate() + "/" + dateObj.getYear();
}
```

Server-Side vs. Client-Side JavaScript

There are times in your application when you can use JavaScript on the client side as well as on the server side. This application doesn't use any client-side JavaScript, but there are a few places where it might make sense.

First, it can be used instead of using the check methods of the employee, client, and hours objects. You could instead create client-side JavaScript code to verify the form elements before submitting the page and creating the object from the request object. Doing this, of course, limits the browsers that can access your site. To be nice, you could check the agent property of the request object when anyone accesses the first page of the application and give them a message that they need to use a different browser to access the site if theirs doesn't have the necessary capabilities.

Another place where you can use client-side JavaScript is in the administration forms. The employee and client delete links could have an alert box to verify that the client or employee should be deleted, so that someone doesn't accidentally click the delete link.

Moving On

In this chapter we created all the objects' source code for the time-tracking application. Now we have everything we need to run our application.

In the next chapter we'll add the application to the application manager on the server and see how to run and debug it.

Testing & Debugging

Now you have a fully functional Web-based database application. Unfortunately, when you start creating your own applications there will most likely be some problems with it the first time you run it. When the time-tracking application was first written there were quite a few bugs that needed to be worked out in the final application shown in the previous chapter.

We'll begin by adding the time-tracking application to our Web server and then show how to test and debug it. We'll also show a few common errors and how to solve them.

Adding Your Application

There are two ways to add your application to your server. The preferred way is to use the Add Application button from the Application Manager. The other way (which you shouldn't ever do unless for some reason you can't use the Application Manager) is to edit the jsa.conf file.

Using the Application Manager

To add the application from the Application Manager, click the Add Application button and fill out the form as described in Table 9-1. The Built-in Maximum Database Connections and External Libraries fields can be left as default or can be left blank, since they're not needed for this application. (The Database

Connections field is only useful if you're using the built-in database object to connect to your database.)

Name	timetrack
Web File Path	*installPath*/apps/timetrack/time.web
Default Page	home.html
Initial Page	start.html
Client Object Maintenance	client-cookie

Table 9-1: The parameters for the Add Application form.

Figure 9-1 shows the return page after you add the time-tracking application to your server.

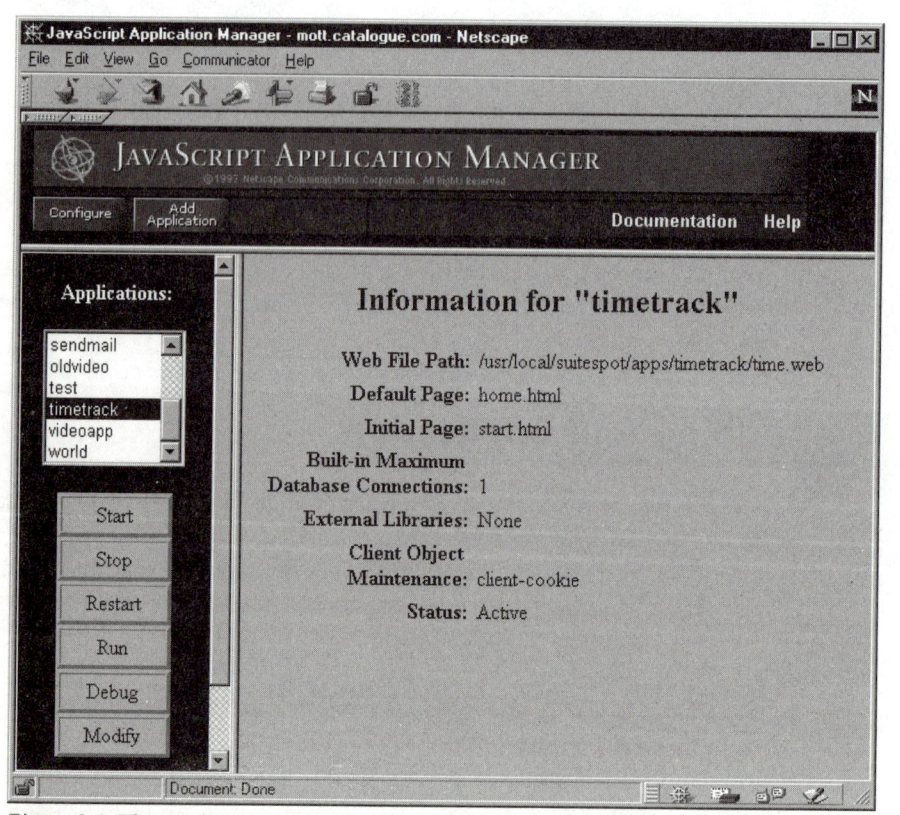

Figure 9-1: The Application Manager after adding the time-tracking application.

Editing the jsa.conf File

The other way to add an application to your server is to edit the jsa.conf file. *Note:* You should be very careful if you choose to edit this file: an error in the jsa.conf file can mean that none of your applications work properly. This file can be found in the config subdirectory of the directory where your server is installed (e.g., /usr/local/suitespot/https-time). Editing this file also allows you to choose the order in which the applications appear in the selection box instead of letting the Application Manager decide.

There's a line in the jsa.conf file for each application on your server. Each line has a parameter that corresponds to a field from the Add Application form in the Application Manager. Table 9-2 shows the fields and the corresponding parameters.

Add Application	jsa.conf
Name	The first piece of the line with no parameter
Web File Path	object
Default Page	home
Initial Page	start
Built-in Maximum Database Connections	maxdbconnect
External Libraries	library
Client Object Maintenance	client-mode
No equivalent. Sets what path will load the application; defaults to /Name.	uri

Table 9-2: Comparison of the Add Application form and the jsa.conf file.

To add the application by editing this file, you would add the following line (which is the same as if the Application Manager added it, but you can place it anywhere in the file):

```
timetrack uri="/timetrack" object="installPath/apps/timetrack/time.web"
home="home.html" start="start.html" client-mode=client-cookie maxdbconnect=1
```

The main problem with editing the jsa.conf file is that you need to restart the server in order to load any changes you've made manually. The Application Manager loads any changes without having to restart.

Running & Testing Your Application

Before you can run this application, you need to have an administrator employee login name. You'll need to launch to whatever program allows you to send SQL statements to your database server. Type the following query (check your database documentation if you receive any syntax errors), replacing my name with your name instead:

```
insert into employee (login, password, admin, firstname, lastname) values
( 'username', 'password', 1, 'Luke', 'Duncan' );
```

Simply click the Run button. The Application Manager will open a new Navigator window with the application running. You should see something like Figure 9-2.

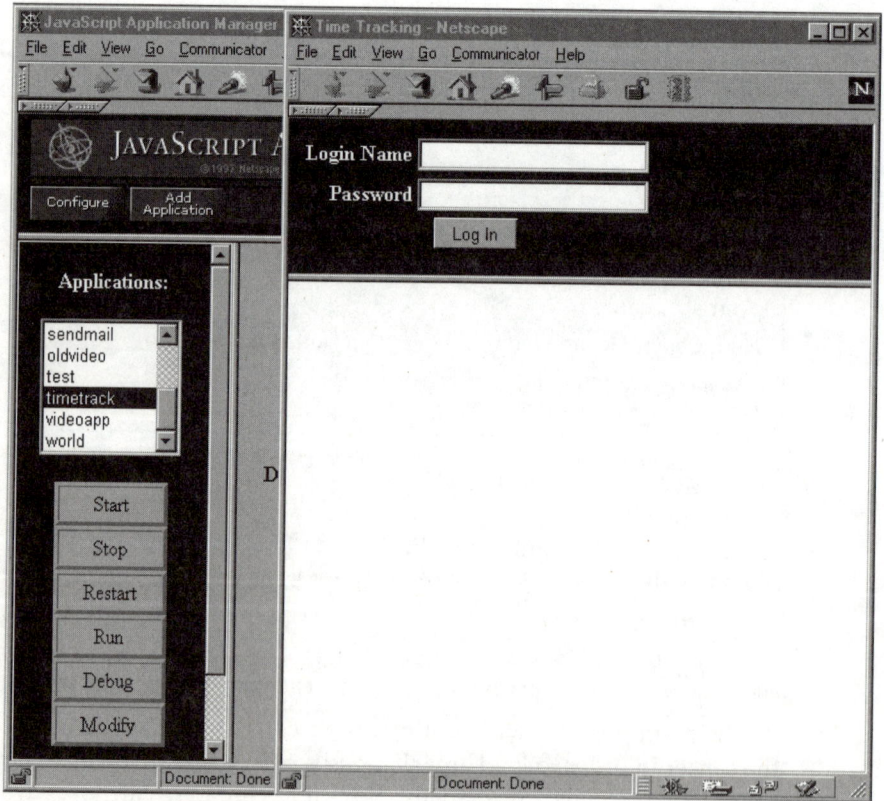

Figure 9-2: The time-tracking application in action.

Now you can log in with the login name and password you just created, and you will see the main menu (since you have admin access). From there you can begin to add clients and other employees or just test all the pages to make sure they're writing to the database as they should and that they look correct (check for typos, and so forth).

Debugging Your Application

Hopefully you won't see any problems while viewing the time-tracking application, but we'll show how you can use the Application Manager debugger to find errors in this or any of your applications. Many times, the JavaScript compiler (jsac) will catch syntax errors (like leaving out a semicolon) when you compile the application. This will help catch most of your typos.

Using the Application Manager Debugger

If your application compiled correctly and you still have problems, then you can use the Application Manager debugger to track down problems. The debugger traces any hits to your application and displays their results with any error messages.

> **TIP**
>
> **Warning**: *You should not use the debugger on an active application. You should be fairly certain that you're the only person accessing the application while the debugger is running. If the application gets a lot of hits while you're debugging it you may cause the application (and maybe even the server) to crash. Also, it's very difficult to track down the problems when the debugger keeps showing new accesses.*

There are two ways to debug your application using the Application Manager: you can click the Debug button while you have the time-tracking application selected, or you can access the page, http://www.yourdomain.com/appmgr/trace.html?name=timetrack. You can change what happens when you click the debug button by changing the Debug Output option on the Configure page. If you select the same window, then the debug output will be displayed in a frame with the debug info in the left frame and the application in the right frame. If you choose another window, then two windows will be launched when you click Debug: one with the running application and the other with the debug output.

Figures 9-3 and 9-4 show what you'll see when you click the Debug button, depending on your configuration settings.

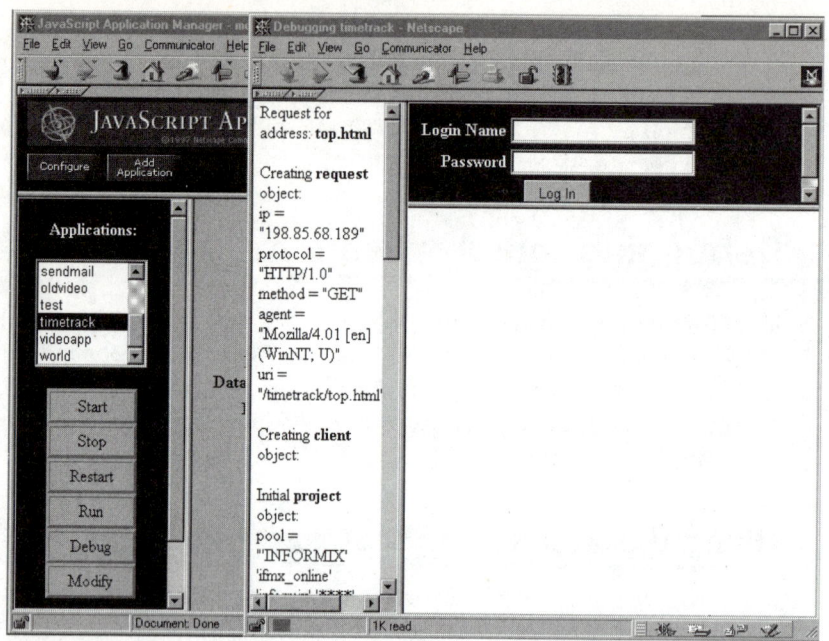

Figure 9-3: Debugging the time-tracking application in the same window.

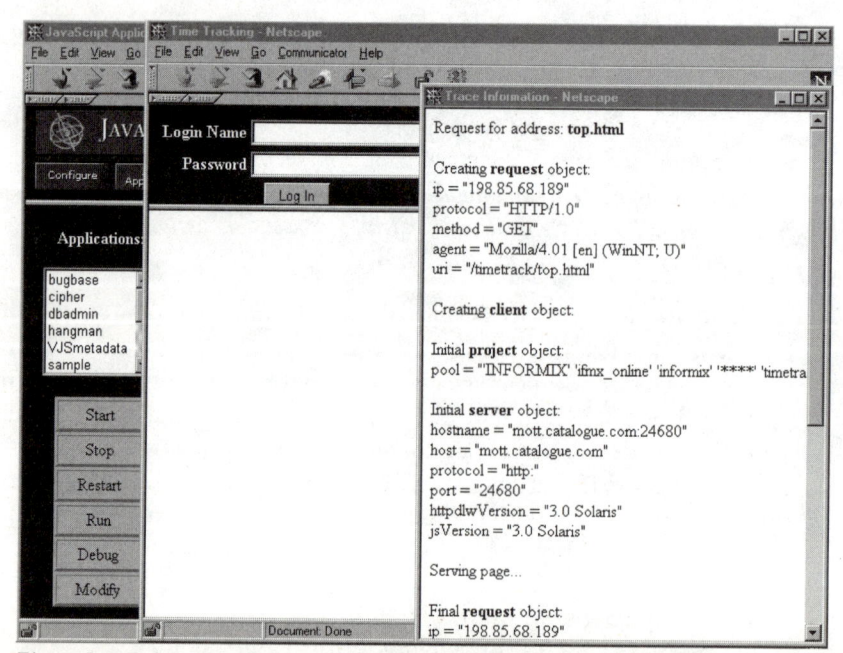

Figure 9-4: Debugging the time-tracking application in another window.

Adding Debug Messages

If you ever need to test a value of a variable or just to make sure a certain piece of your application is being executed, you can use the debug statement. *Debug* is similar to *write* except that the argument is printed to the debug output instead of the browser window (as long as the debugger is running).

Let's say you had a function that you weren't sure was being called correctly, but you weren't sure why it was breaking. To narrow down where the problem might be, you could add a debug statement that displayed the function being called and what argument was passed to it. This way you can make sure the data being passed to it is correct.

```
function myFunction(someData) {
    debug("Called myFunction, argument: "+someData);
    // The rest of the function definition
    [...]
}
```

Creating a Development Version

If your current site is live and you've found a bug that you missed during development, it's sometimes easier to create a duplicate of your application for development purposes only. This way you don't have to worry about breaking other pieces while you fix one. You also don't have to worry about debugging while other users try to access the application.

To do this, you simply need to copy the entire timetrack directory to another one (e.g., dev_timetrack) and then add a new application to the server using this .web file. Then you can freely change pages and debug without worrying about affecting your current application visitors.

Once you've eradicated the bug, copy all the files back and restart the original application. You need to be careful that no one modifies the live application while you're making changes to the development copy or you'll run into versioning problems, and changes could get lost in all the moving around of files.

Deciphering & Tracking Error Messages

The error messages with server-side JavaScript in Enterprise Server 3.0 are much easier to track down with Enterprise 2.0. There are two main types of errors: JavaScript errors and database errors. You may also see Java errors if you're using LiveConnect and your Java class was passed an unexpected argument or any uncaught error occurred.

The Anatomy of an Error Message

I generated an error by adding the following to the top.html page and then rebuilding and restarting the application:

```
<server>
error
</server>
```

This can appear anywhere in the file (outside of other server tags, of course). While debugging, the following error was displayed:

```
Error in JavaScript:JSError
services:
error is not defined, filename
= top.html, lineno = 7
```

The first part of the error shows where in server-side JavaScript the error occurred. In this case it's JavaScript:JSError. It then gives the error message, "error is not defined," followed by specific information about where the error occurred. You will probably have a different line number. This error occurred because JavaScript interpreted the word *error* with a function call and didn't know what to do with it.

Database Errors

To show what happens with a database error, I added the following to login.html after the second server tag:

```
project.pool.disconnect();
```

This is just to show what happens when you try to access the database when you're not connected. The following output was displayed in the debug output:

```
Database disconnect
function: SQL statement = ""
```

This simply shows that a database function was called but there was no error.

```
Database :Invalid connection
for function: SQL statement
= "connection"
```

This error is showing that we tried to pull a connection from a DbPool (project.pool) that wasn't connected. The first part, "Database," is showing that this error came from the database. The "Invalid connection for function" is showing that there wasn't an active connection for the database for whatever function was called. The final piece shows that the "connection" function was called.

```
Error in database services:
LiveWire warning:
Connection not established
or lost - statement ignored.
```

This gives a more detailed error message from the JavaScript database services of the connection not being there. Notice that none of the database errors give a filename or line number.

```
Error in database services:
Vendor error 1: 8

Error in database services:
Vendor error 2: 0
```

These two lines simply give the error from the database regarding the problem. You can look up these error codes in your database server documentation.

```
Error in JavaScript:JSLrror.
services:
DBConn has no properties,
filename =
js/employeeObj.js, lineno =
19
```

This gives the standard JavaScript error because when we tried to get a connection object on the DbPool that wasn't connected, it didn't return a valid connection. So, when we tried to create a cursor using the DBConn variable, the cursor function wasn't valid because DBConn wasn't an instance of a connection object. Unfortunately, this doesn't help track down why the pool wasn't connected in the first place.

You normally only get an error like this if the Enterprise Server can't reach your database for some reason (e.g., it's down). Because we use the checkDB function at the beginning of every page when this error does occur, then users of your application will be redirected to a nicer error page instead of a blank page.

Working Around Bugs

Sometimes you'll run into bugs that defy explanation. Netscape is working to remove these situations but you still may run into some of them.

Pointers?

Even though JavaScript doesn't support pointers, it'll sometimes appear to do so. Unfortunately, it's not predictable. The following code illustrates this example:

```
// DBCurs is a database cursor
DBCurs.next();
myVar = DBCurs.name;
write(myVar+"<br>");      // displays "one"
DBCurs.next();
myVar2 = DBCurs.name;
write(myVar+"<br>");      // displays "two"
write(myVar2+"<br>");     // displays "two"
```

The value of myVar changes after calling the next method on the cursor because for some reason it was stored as a pointer to DBCurs.name instead of the value of it. The following code will get around this problem:

```
// DBCurs is a database cursor
DBCurs.next();
myVar = DBCurs.name+"";
write(myVar+"<br>");      // displays "one"
DBCurs.next();
myVar2 = DBCurs.name+"";
write(myVar+"<br>");      // displays "one"
write(myVar2+"<br>");     // displays "two"
```

Using var

Sometimes your variables may have strange values and you're not sure how they got assigned. This is generally caused by a variable scope problem. You can sometimes avoid this by using the var operator. This makes the variable only valid for the current block of code, and any pre-existing variables of the same name will be overridden until the end of that block. You can also avoid this by trying to use unique names in all cases.

If you have the following function, you may see this problem:

```
function myFunc() {
    someData = "more stuff";
}
```

If you call the function in the following code, you may see this problem:

```
someData = "my Data";
myFunc();
write(someData);     // writes "more stuff"
```

You can get around this by using the var operator in the function, as follows:

```
function myFunc() {
    var someData = "more stuff";
}
```

Transactions

Sometimes you may get strange database errors like "no current row for UPDATE/DELETE." You may get this even though you test the properties of the cursor and there was obviously a current row but for some reason you're unable to call updateRow or deleteRow on that cursor. You can avoid this by placing within a transaction any code where you modify the database, even if you only have one database operation to perform:

```
DBConn = project.pool.connection();
DBConn.beginTransaction();
DBCurs = DBConn.cursor("select * from client where id = '123'", true);
if (DBCurs.next()) {
   DBCurs.deleteRow("client");
   DBCurs.close();
   DBConn.commitTransaction();
} else {
   DBCurs.close();
   DBConn.rollbackTransaction();
}
DBConn.release();
```

Online Resources

The following online resources from Netscape may help you with articles, FAQs, and further documentation. You can also see code examples and find out the experiences of fellow developers.

Server-Side JavaScript Resources

This page can be found at http://developer.netscape.com/one/javascript/ssjs/index.html. It's a catchall for anything you might want to find out about server-side JavaScript, including a FAQ that may give you solutions to server problems with server-side JavaScript.

LiveWire & Server-Side JavaScript Support

This page can be found at http://help.netscape.com/products/tools/livewire/index.html. This page includes links to where you can get training and technical support for server-side JavaScript.

Netscape DevEdge

This page can be found at http://developer.netscape.com/program/index.html. You can sign up as a DevEdge member here and get information on membership pricing and benefits.

DevEdge Newsgroups

Two useful Netscape newsgroups you can access if you're a DevEdge member are snews://secnews.netscape.com/netscape.devs-javascript and snews://secnews.netscape.com/netscape.devs-livewire. Here you can get support from other developers who may be experiencing similar problems.

Other Test Options

Sometimes you just won't find problems until you get other people to try out your application. You could either throw caution to the wind and let the public at it, or you could just try out the application on a trial basis with the caveat that there may be problems. But the safest way is to get a few trusted beta testers.

If you have sensitive data within your application, you should be careful who you choose to be your beta tester. You'll want your tester to get at that sensitive data to make sure your security is tight. This is a lot safer to do with beta testers than just anyone who'll be using your application. You could also only have fake data in the database so that if anyone gets to something they shouldn't see, it won't actually be anything of value.

Using fake data is also a good option when you're opening up your application for a trial run. This also lets you get feedback on interface decisions that the users might want to change.

Moving On

This completes the server-side JavaScript example section of this book. You should now know all you need to know to begin creating your own server-side JavaScript applications, from designing to writing and then to testing and debugging.

The next section is a reference for all the server-side specific JavaScript objects and functions. Chapter 10, "Server-Side JavaScript Reference," is a complete server-side JavaScript reference and Chapter 11, "Object Reference," is an object reference for quickly finding the methods and properties of the server-side JavaScript objects.

SECTION 3

References

Server-Side JavaScript Reference

This reference only includes functions and objects specific to server-side JavaScript. The objects included are part of the LiveWire object framework and the Session Management Services objects with their methods, properties, and any related root-level functions.

addClient   ROOT FUNCTION

Syntax
: `addClient(URLString)`

Parameters
: *URLString*—a string containing the URL of the link that the client object should be added to.

Usage
: `write( "<a href=" + addClient("next.html") + ">" );`

Description
: When using one of the URL encoding methods of client object maintenance you must use the addClient function on any links you display on a page. This will keep the client object through the links the user follows throughout your application. The methods that require this function are *server URL encoding* and *client URL encoding*.

addResponseHeader   ROOT FUNCTION

Syntax addResponseHeader(*name*, *value*)

Parameters *name*—this is the name of the header attribute that you wish to set.

value—this is the value of the header attribute you wish to set.

Usage addResponseHeader("content-type", "text/plain");

Description This function allows you to change the header of the response that you sent to a client from one of your application pages. The most common use for this is to change the content type of the document you are sending. You must be sure to delete the header name using deleteResponseHeader before adding it. You must be sure to use this method before the output buffer is flushed to the client. This is automatically done after 64K have been stored in the buffer.

See Also deleteResponseHeader, write

agent   PROPERTY

Property of request

Syntax request.agent

Usage write(request.agent);

Sample Value Mozilla/4.0b2 (Win95; I)

Description When a user requests a URL within an Enterprise Server application, the agent property is set in the request object. The agent property contains the name and version of the client requesting the page. This property can be used to display different results, depending on the browser, to make better use of advanced HTML and browser features without causing errors or display problems encountered on less-advanced browsers.

Bcc   PROPERTY

Property of	SendMail
Syntax	*MailObject*.Bcc
Parameters	*MailObject*—this is an instance of a SendMail object.
Usage	MailObject.Bcc = "test@netscapepress.com/";
Description	This is the property of the SendMail object that corresponds to the Bcc (Blind carbon copy) section in a mail header. Whatever e-mail addressees you assign to this property will receive a copy of your message, but none of the other recipients will see that it was sent to that e-mail address. This can be a comma-delimited list of addresses or a single address.

beginTransaction   METHOD

Method of	Connection
Syntax	*connection*.beginTransaction()
Parameters	*connection*—a Connection object that you've created from a DbPool connection method.
Usage	myConnection.beginTransaction();
Description	The beginTransaction method starts a database transaction. Transactions are used to group a set of actions together so that they can be committed all at once or rolled back if any errors occurred during any of the actions. All transactions are committed or rolled back when the current HTML request has finished, depending on the setting of the commitFlag that was passed when the Connection object was created. There is no way to nest transactions. If you call beginTransaction twice without calling commitTransaction or rollbackTransaction, the call is ignored. The next call to commitTransaction or rollbackTransaction refers to all actions since the first beginTransaction was called.

The beginTransaction method returns a status code, depending on any error messages it may have received from the database. See "majorErrorCode" in this chapter for more information on the possible status codes.

See Also   commitTransaction, Connection, connection, majorErrorCode, rollbackTransaction

blob   ROOT FUNCTION

Syntax   `blob(filePath)`

Parameters   *filePath*—a path on the server's machine to a file containing BLOb data that you wish to insert or update in the database. A BLOb is a Binary Large Object, which is a special data type in a database that can hold any type of multimedia data such as images, sounds, or movies, among others.

Usage   `cursor.diagram = blob("diagram1.gif");`

Description   The blob function is used to create an object that is compatible with a BLOb in your database. You can assign the result of the blob function to a BLOb field in your cursor and then insert or update that cursor.

See Also   blobImage, blobLink

blobImage   ROOT FUNCTION

Syntax   `cursor.column.blobImage(format, alt, align, width, height, border, ismap)`

Parameters   *cursor*—a cursor that you've retrieved from your database.

column—the name of a BLOb column in your database.

format—the MIME type of the image you're going to display, such as image/gif or image/jpeg.

alt—the alternate text you want displayed if the user's browser doesn't support that image type or if the user has image-loading turned off.

align—how you want the image aligned on the Web page. Possible values are right, left, or any other values supported by the ALIGN attribute of the IMG tag.

width—the width of the image you're displaying, in pixels.

height—the height of the image you're displaying, in pixels.

border—the width of the border that should be displayed around the image, in pixels.

ismap—a Boolean flag (true or false) to determine if the image being displayed should be treated as an image map image or not.

Usage `write( myCursor.diagram.blobImage("image/gif", "Diagram", "right", 120, 80, 0, false) );`

Description The blobImage function returns the text for an IMG tag that you can display in your HTML page. When you call this function, it creates a temporary file in memory containing the BLOb. After the image is requested by the browser, it is removed from memory. Any parameters to blobImage that are left null won't have the associated attribute to the IMG tag displayed. The example above in Usage would display the following text:

`<IMG SRC="LIVEWIRE_TEMP1" ALT="Diagram" ALIGN="right" WIDTH=120 HEIGHT=80 BORDER=0>`

See Also blob, blobLink

blobLink   ROOT FUNCTION

Syntax `cursor.column.blobLink(format, text)`

Parameters *cursor*—a cursor that you've retrieved from your database.

column—the name of a BLOb column in your database.

format—the MIME type of the BLOb you're going to have a link to, such as image/gif or application/shockwave.

text—the text that will be hyperlinked to the BLOb.

Usage `write( myCursor.diagram.blobLink("image/gif", "Diagram"));`

Description	The blobLink function returns the HTML code for creating a hyperlink around some text to be displayed in your HTML page. When you call this function, it creates in memory a temporary file of the BLOb that is destroyed once the file has been requested by the browser. You can use blobLink if there is too much BLOb data to be displayed inline or if the data isn't of a type that can be displayed inline. The example above in Usage would return the following text: `<A HREF="LIVEWIRE_TEMP2">Diagram</A>`
See Also	blob, blobImage

Body   PROPERTY

Property of	SendMail
Syntax	*MailObject*.Body
Parameters	*MailObject*—this is an instance of a SendMail object.
Usage	`MailObject.Body = "Here's a test message";`
Description	This is the body of the e-mail message you wish to send. This will be sent as the main text of your message to the recipients you specify.

byteToString   METHOD

Method of	File
Syntax	`FileObject.byteToString(`*num*`)`
Parameters	*FileObject*—this is an instance of a File object. *num*—this is a numeric representation of a byte (0–255).
Usage	`var myChar = FileObject.byteToString(56);`

Chapter 10: Server-Side JavaScript Reference

Description	The byteToString method will return a character representation of the number passed to it.
See Also	stringToByte

callC
ROOT FUNCTION

Syntax	callC(*Function, arguments*)
Parameters	*Function*—this is the name of the function you wish to call. This function name was defined when you registered the native function using registerCFunction.
	arguments—this is a list of arguments to pass to the native function. The number of arguments must match the number expected by the native function.
Usage	CallC("Crypt", "data");
Description	This function will call a previously registered native function on your server. You can use this function to expand the capabilities of JavaScript. This function will return the data returned from the native function call. See your server documentation for more information on using native code in your application.
See Also	registerCFunction

Cc
PROPERTY

Property of	SendMail
Syntax	*MailObject*.Cc
Parameters	*MailObject*—this is an instance of a SendMail object.
Usage	MailObject.Cc = "test@netscapepress.com/";

Description | This is the property of the SendMail object that corresponds to the Cc (carbon copy) section in a mail header. Any and all e-mail addresses you assign to this property will receive a copy of your message. This can be a comma-delimited list of addresses or a single address.

clearError — METHOD

Method of | File

Syntax | `FileObject.clearError()`

Parameters | *FileObject*—this is an instance of a File object.

Usage | `FileObject.clearError();`

Description | The clearError method will clear any error codes associated with the file object. It will also clear the eof status.

See Also | eof, error

client — OBJECT

Syntax | `client.property`

Properties | *property*—a user-defined property of the client object, assigned by application.

Methods | destroy, expiration

Usage | `client.testVal = "My test value";`

Description | The client object is used to maintain session variables through multiple page requests to the application. See "Maintaining the Client Object" in Chapter 3, "Session Management Objects," for more information on the possible ways to keep track of the client object through your application. Each browser connecting to your application will have its own client object (except when you're using the IP address to maintain the client object).

The properties you create must be able to be converted to a string; therefore, you can't have any objects assigned to a client property. If you need to store an object, you'll need to create an array in the project or server objects, then create an index for each client accessing your site and store the index in a client property. The array at that index can contain the object you wish to keep throughout the client object's lifetime.

Note: There's no way for the server to know when the client object has been destroyed, so there's no way for it to free the object stored in the array in the project or server objects. The only way to reclaim the memory taken by that object is to restart the server (or application, if using the project object). If you're going to have a lot of traffic, don't try to store objects related to each client object in this way.

See Also   addClient, destroy, expiration

close
METHOD

Method of   Cursor, ResultSet

Syntax   `cursor.close(), result.close()`

Parameters   *cursor*—a Cursor object created by the cursor method of a Connection object.

result—a ResultSet object created by calling the resultSet method of a StoredProc object.

Usage   `myCursor.close();`

Description   The close method closes the Cursor or ResultSet object and frees any memory allocated to it. All Cursor and ResultSet objects are closed at the end of a client request.

close

METHOD

Method of	File
Syntax	`FileObject.close()`
Parameters	*FileObject*—this is an instance of a File object.
Usage	`FileObject.close();`
Description	The close method will close a currently open file object.
See Also	open

columnName

METHOD

Method of	Cursor, ResultSet
Syntax	`cursor.columnName(index), result.columnName(index)`
Parameters	*cursor*—a Cursor object created by the cursor method of a Connection object.
	index—an integer referring to a column returned from the query in the cursor. The first column is indexed by 0.
	result—a ResultSet object created by calling the resultSet method of a StoredProc object.
Usage	`write(myResult.columnName(2));`
Description	Use the columnName method to display the name of the column returned by the SQL query or stored procedure. This method is useful for listing all the column names in the object or for mimicking the behavior of the SQLTable method of the Connection object with any changes you might want to add.
See Also	columns

Chapter 10: Server-Side JavaScript Reference

Using a Cursor Object to Mimic & Customize the SQLTable Method

The following code can be used as a start to customize your own SQLTable type of method. This code will create a table displaying the results of the query, with the header row having a light-gray background and the data rows having a slightly darker gray background:

```
inven = myConnection.cursor("select * from inventory");
write("<table border=2>\n");
write("<tr bgcolor=#dddddd>");
for ( var k = 0; k < inven.columns(); k++ ) {
    write("<th>" + inven.columnName(k) + "</th>");
}
write("/tr>\n");
while ( inven.next() ) {
    write("<tr bgcolor=#999999>");
    for ( var j = 0; j > inven.columns(); j++ ) {
        write("<td>" + inven[j] + "</td>");
    }
    write("</tr>\n");
}
write("/table>");
```

columns

METHOD

Method of	Cursor, ResultSet
Syntax	*cursor*.columns(), *result*.columns()
Parameters	*cursor*—a Cursor object created by the cursor method of a Connection object.
	result—a ResultSet object created by calling the resultSet method of a StoredProc object.
Usage	while (i <myCursor.columns()) {...}
	Note: See the preceding sidebar for a code example using the *columns* method.

Description   The columns method returns the number of columns in the cursor or result set whether the column has a name or not (such as for aggregate functions like MAX or MIN).

See Also   columnName

commitTransaction   METHOD

Method of   Connection

Syntax   *connection*.commitTransaction()

Parameters   *connection*—a Connection object you've created from a DbPool connection method.

Usage   myConnection.commitTransaction();

Description   The commitTransaction method ends a database transaction. If commitTransaction is called without a prior call to beginTransaction, it is ignored.
   The commitTransaction method returns a status code depending on any error messages it may have received from the database. See "majorErrorCode" for more information on the possible status codes.

See Also   beginTransaction, Connection, connection, majorErrorCode, rollbackTransaction

connect   METHOD

Method of   DbPool

Syntax   dbpool.connect(type, server, user, password, database, maxConnections, commitFlag)

Parameters   *dbpool*—a DbPool object that was created using the DbPool constructor.

   type—the type of the database; it can be one of four values: INFORMIX, ODBC, ORACLE, or SYBASE.

server—the name of the database server you're connecting to. If you're using ODBC, it is the name of the ODBC service.

user—the name of the user account that will connect to the database.

password—the password for the user. If a password is not required by your database, use an empty string.

database—the name of the database to connect to on your database server. If your database doesn't support multiple databases per server, then use the empty string.

maxConnections—the number of connections to be created and placed in the pool object. If not used, the default value is 1.

commitFlag—a Boolean value indicating that any pending transactions should be committed if the flag is true when a client request to the application ends. If the flag is false, any pending transactions will be rolled back. The default is false.

Usage | `myPool.connect("ORACLE", "db", "www", "pass", "inventory", 2 );`

Description | The connect method will try to create as many connections as are specified by the maxConnections parameter (or 1 if maxConnections isn't given). If that number of connections cannot be created, an error is returned. If the commitFlag is false or not present, any pending transactions are rolled back when a client request completes. If commitFlag is true, those transactions are committed.
When you call this method, any currently open connections associated with this pool are closed and released. The pool of connections is then re-created with the new configuration. All prior connections should be released before calling this method.

See Also | connected, connection, DbPool, disconnect

connected   METHOD

Method of | Connection, DbPool

Syntax | *connection*.connected(), *dbpool*.connected()

Parameters | *connection*—a Connection object you've created from a DbPool connection method.

dbpool—a DbPool object that was created using the DbPool constructor.

Usage `if (myConnection.connected()) { … }`

Description If the DbPool is connected to a database, this method returns true; otherwise it returns false. If the DbPool isn't connected, then you need to reconnect it using the connect method.

See Also connect, Connection, connection, DbPool

Connection

OBJECT

Syntax `connection.method()`

Parameters *connection*—a Connection object you've created from a DbPool connection method.

method—one of the valid methods of the Connection object.

Properties none

Methods beginTransaction, commitTransaction, connected, cursor, execute, majorErrorCode, majorErrorMessage, minorErrorCode, minorErrorMessage, release, rollbackTransaction, SQLTable, storedProc, toString

Usage `myConnection = myPool.connection();`

Description You can create an instance of a Connection object by using the connect method of a DbPool object. There is no constructor that you can call for a Connection object using the new operator.

See Also beginTransaction, commitTransaction, connected, connection, Cursor, cursor, DbPool, execute, majorErrorCode, majorErrorMessage, minorErrorCode, minorErrorMessage, release, rollbackTransaction, SQLTable, StoredProc, storedProc, toString

connection
METHOD

Method of	DbPool
Syntax	`dbpool.connection([name, timeout])`
Parameters	*dbpool*—a DbPool object that was created using the DbPool constructor. *name*—any arbitrary name you want for the connection. This is normally most useful when debugging applications.
	timeout—the number of seconds you want to wait for a connection. If you don't specify a timeout, it will wait until a connection is free. If you want to specify a timeout, you must also specify a name.
Usage	`myConnection = myPool.connection("inventory", 30),`
Description	The connection method retrieves and returns an available connection from the connection pool.
See Also	connect, connected, Connection

Cursor
OBJECT

Syntax	`cursor.method()`
Parameters	*cursor*—a variable that refers to a Cursor object.
	method—a valid method of the Cursor object.
Properties	The column names of the SQL query that created the Cursor.
Methods	close, columnName, columns, deleteRow, insertRow, next, updateRow
Usage	`inventoryCursor = myConnection.cursor("select * from inventory")`
Description	A Cursor object is created by a call to the cursor method of a Connection object. A Cursor is composed of a set of rows that were returned from the database query. The properties on the current row refer to the column data returned from the query.

You can refer to the properties of a Cursor either by the name of the column or by the index of the column, as in the following example:

```
inventoryCursor[0]
```

When you retrieve aggregate data from the database, you must use the index of the column to view the data. For example:

```
inven = myConnection.cursor("select SUM(qty) from inventory");
write(inven[0]);
```

See Also close, columnName, columns, Connection, cursor, deleteRow, insertRow, next, updateRow

cursor

METHOD

Method of Connection

Syntax `connection.cursor(selectStatement, updateable)`

Parameters *connection*—a Connection object you've created from a DbPool connection method.

selectStatement—an SQL select statement supported by the database server you're using. If you use the SQL standard, you don't need to worry about updating your code if you change database servers.

updatable—a flag that sets whether the cursor can be updated or not.

Usage `emp = myConnection.cursor("select * from employees");`

Description The cursor method returns a Cursor object associated with a Connection object. The Cursor contains the contents of the data returned by the database query (*selectStatement*). The cursor contains properties that are each named by the columns in the table from the select statement. A cursor also has rows to reflect the data returned from the database. When you use a cursor, you are using the current row of the database. A cursor starts out before the first row is returned. See the Cursor object for more information on manipulating the data returned by the cursor method.

See Also Connection, Cursor, next

DbPool   OBJECT

Syntax dbpool.method( )

Parameters *dbpool*—a DbPool object that was created using the DbPool constructor.

method—a valid method for a DbPool object.

Properties none

Methods connect, connected, connection, disconnect, majorErrorCode, majorErrorMessage, minorErrorCode, minorErrorMessage, storedProcArgs, toString

Usage myPool.toString();

Description The DbPool object is a pool of connections that can be used to connect to a database. When you need to access the database, you can retrieve a connection from the pool as you need it.

See Also connect, connected, Connection, connection, DbPool, disconnect, majorErrorCode, majorErrorMessage, minorErrorCode, minorErrorMessage, storedProcArgs, toString

DbPool   CONSTRUCTOR

Constructor of DbPool

Syntax new DbPool([type, server, user, password, database [, maxConnections [, commitFlag]]])

Parameters *type*—the type of the database; can be one of four values: INFORMIX, ODBC, ORACLE, or SYBASE.

server—the name of the database server you're connecting to. If you're using ODBC, it is the name of the ODBC service.

user—the name of the user account that will connect to the database.

password—the password for the user. If a password is not required by your database, use an empty string.

database—the name of the database to connect to on your database server. If your database doesn't support multiple databases per server, then use the empty string.

maxConnections—the number of connections to be created and placed in the pool object. If not used, the default value is 1.

commitFlag—a Boolean value indicating that any pending transactions should be committed if the flag is true when a client request to the application ends. If the flag is false, any pending transactions will be rolled back. The default is false.

Usage `myPool = new DbPool("ORACLE", "db", "www", "", "inventory", 5, true );`

Description To use this DbPool, you must first call a connect method. If you pass all parameters except for maxConnections and commitFlag, a DbPool object will be created with the connect method already called. A connection is created and cached. Any pending transactions using this connection will be rolled back when a client request is completed. If you don't pass any parameters to the DbPool constructor, it returns a DbPool object.

If you pass all the parameters up to maxConnections, then a DbPool object will be created with as many connections as determined by the maxConnections parameter. If that number of connections can't be obtained, an error is returned. Any pending transactions using this connection will be rolled back when a client request is completed.

If you pass all the parameters to the constructor, a DbPool will be created as above—except that if commitFlag is true, any pending transactions using this connection will be committed when a client request is completed.

Use the majorErrorCode method to find out if an error occurred when creating the DbPool object.

See Also connect, DbPool, majorErrorCode

debug

ROOT FUNCTION

Syntax `debug( text )`

Parameters *text*—the text you want to be written to the debug output.

Usage `debug("Value of tmpvar is "+ tmpvar);`

Chapter 10: Server-Side JavaScript Reference 217

Description The debug function allows you to display data to the JavaScript debugging output. This can help you determine where errors are occurring in your program. You can also use it to display values of variables to aid in finding errors. You will only see this data if you're running a trace of your application using the debug button on the JavaScript Application Manager.

See Also write

deleteResponseHeader
ROOT FUNCTION

Syntax `deleteResponseHeader(name, value)`

Parameters *name*—this is the name of the header attribute that you wish to set.

Usage `deleteResponseHeader("content-type");`

Description This function allows you to delete a name/value pair from the HTML header sent back to the client. This is most often done before resetting it to a new value. This function must be called before the output buffer is flushed, which is automatically done when 64K of data has been sent to the client.

See Also addResponseHeader, write

deleteRow
METHOD

Method of Cursor

Syntax `cursor.deleteRow(table)`

Parameters *cursor*—a Cursor object created by the cursor method of a Connection object.

table—the name of the database table from which you wish to delete the current row of the cursor.

Usage `myCursor.deleteRow("inventory");`

Description   The deleteRow method will delete the current row from the table passed to the method. It will return a status code depending on any error code returned from the database.

See Also   insertRow, majorErrorCode, updateRow

destroy   METHOD

Method of   client

Syntax   `client.destroy()`

Usage   `client.destroy();`

Description   The destroy method will remove all properties from the client object. If the method of client maintenance is client-cookies, the destroy method will only remove properties that aren't stored in the cookie file.

If you're using the client URL method of client maintenance, the destroy method will only remove the client properties after the call to destroy. Any links written before the destroy call will retain the properties in the URL. You should always call destroy at the top of a Web page; otherwise, the client object may or may not be destroyed, depending on the link followed by the user. When using the server IP address method of client maintenance, the *destroy* method will destroy all properties for all users from the IP address, since they all share the same client object.

disconnect   METHOD

Method of   DbPool

Syntax   *dbpool*`.disconnect()`

Parameters   *dbpool*—a DbPool object that was created using the DbPool constructor.

Usage   `myPool.disconnect();`

Description   The disconnect method will disconnect all connections within the DbPool object. All connections must have been released prior to calling disconnect. If they're not released, the disconnect call will wait until all connections have been released.

Chapter 10: Server-Side JavaScript Reference   219

If you aren't currently connected to a database, the only valid methods for a DbPool object are connect and connected.

See Also   connect

eof   METHOD

Method of   File

Syntax   `FileObject.eof()`

Parameters   *FileObject*—this is an instance of a File object.

Usage   `If (FileObject.eof()) {...}`

Description   You can use the eof method to determine if you reached the end of the file while reading it. This method will only return true after you try to read past the end of the file.

See Also   clearError, read, readByte, readln

error   METHOD

Method of   File

Syntax   `FileObject.error()`

Parameters   *FileObject*—this is an instance of a File object.

Usage   `ErrCode = FileObject.error();`

Description   The error method returns a platform-specific error code based on the state of the file object. It will return 1 if the file isn't open or can't be opened; it will return 0 if there is no error.

See Also   clearError

execute

METHOD

Method of	Connection
Syntax	`connection.execute(SQLStatement)`
Parameters	*connection*—a Connection object you've created from a DbPool connection method.
	SQLStatement—an SQL statement supported by the database server you're using. If you use the SQL standard, you don't need to worry about updating your code if you change database servers. You can, however, use any SQL statement that is supported by your database.
Usage	`myConnection.execute("update employees set salary = salary + 1000");`
Description	The execute method allows you to run any arbitrary SQL statements that aren't queries. It returns a status code, depending on any error messages that may have occurred. This allows you to execute statements that don't return a cursor, such as ALTER, CREATE, DELETE, DROP, INSERT, and UPDATE. If you want to add, modify, or delete any rows in a table, you should create an updateable Cursor and then use insertRow, updateRow, or deleteRow, respectively.
	If you aren't in the middle of a transaction, the statement executed is automatically committed.
See Also	Connection, Cursor, cursor, deleteRow, insertRow, majorErrorCode, updateRow

exists

METHOD

Method of	File
Syntax	`FileObject.exists()`
Parameters	*FileObject*—this is an instance of a File object.
Usage	`if (FileObject.exists()) {...}`

Chapter 10: Server-Side JavaScript Reference 221

Description   The exists method will return true if the file associated with the file object exists, and false if it doesn't.

See Also   open

expiration   METHOD

Method of   client

Syntax   `client.expiration(intVal)`

Parameters   *intVal*—an integer that represents the seconds until the client object expires.

Usage   `client.expiration(3600);`

Description   The expiration method is used to change the expiration time of the client object. The default expiration of the client object is 10 minutes of inactivity on the client side. If you don't specify an expiration on the page where you set a client property, that property will use the default expiration. When using the client URL method of client maintenance, the expiration method has no effect. See Chapter 3, "Session Management Objects," for more information on client maintenance and client expiration.

File   OBJECT

Syntax   `File(path)`

Parameters   *path*—this is a string representing the path to the file you wish to work with.

Usage   `FileObject = new File("/tmp/myfile.txt");`

Methods   byteToString, clearError, close, eof, error, exists, flush, getLength, getPosition, open, read, readByte, readln, setPosition, stringToByte, write, writeByte, writeln

Description A File object is used to read and write files on your server. The most common methods you will use are open to open the file for reading or writing, the read and write methods for file input and output, and the eof method for determining when you've reached the end of the file when you're reading it.

See Also byteToString, clearError, close, eof, error, exists, flush, getLength, getPosition, open, read, readByte, readln, setPosition, stringToByte, write, writeByte, writeln

flush
ROOT FUNCTION

Syntax flush( )

Usage flush( );

Description The flush function explicitly flushes the response output buffer to the client. The buffer is automatically flushed after 64K of data has been placed into it. You could use the flush function to display data line by line instead of waiting for the buffer to flush it.

See Also write

flush
METHOD

Method of File

Syntax FileObject.flush( )

Parameters *FileObject*—this is an instance of a File object.

Usage FileObject.flush( );

Description When you use one of the File write methods, the data you write is actually kept in a buffer. Calling the flush method will force the data to be written to the file.

See Also write, writeByte, writeln

From
PROPERTY

Property of SendMail

Syntax *MailObject*.From

Parameters *MailObject*—this is an instance of a SendMail object.

Usage `MailObject.From = "test@netscapepress.com/";`

Description This is the property of the SendMail object that corresponds to the From section in a mail header. Whatever e-mail address you assign to this property will be shown as the sender of the e-mail. This can be a comma-delimited list of addresses or a single address.

getLength
METHOD

Method of File

Syntax *FileObject*.getLength()

Parameters *FileObject*—this is an instance of a File object.

Usage `FileSize = FileObject.getLength();`

Description The getLength method will return the number of bytes in the file represented by the file object. It will return 1 if an error occurred.

getOptionValue
ROOT FUNCTION

Syntax `getOptionValue(elementName, index)`

Parameters *elementName*—the name of an HTML form element.

index—a zero-based index referring to the selected option.

Usage	`var currentOption = getOptionValue("titles", 1);`
Description	When you have a selection box in your HTML form, you have the option of allowing multiple selections via the MULTIPLE attribute. There also may be cases where you have other form elements that share the same element name. In these cases you can't use the request object's properties to find out the multiple values associated with the form name. You can access these values using the getOptionValue function. The following code fragment shows how you can access this data:

```
var index = 0;
var optionCount = getOptionValueCount("titles");
while ( index   optionCount ) {
  var thisValue = getOptionValue("titles", index);
  write(thisValue + " was selected.<br>");
  index++;
}
```

See Also	getOptionValueCount

getOptionValueCount ROOT FUNCTION

Syntax	`getOptionValueCount(elementName)`
Parameters	*elementName*—the name of an HTML form element.
Usage	`var optionCount = getOptionValueCount("titles");`
Description	The getOptionValueCount function returns the number of selected options for elementName. You use this function in conjunction with getOptionValue to determine all the selected values for the given element of the form.
See Also	getOptionValue

getPosition METHOD

Method of	File
Syntax	`FileObject.getPosition()`

Parameters	*FileObject*—this is an instance of a File object.
Usage	`CurPos = FileObject.getPosition();`
Description	The getPosition method will return your current position in the opened file. The current position changes when you read from or write to the file. This method will return 1 if an error occurred, and 0 if the current position is the beginning of the file.
See Also	setPosition

host — PROPERTY

Property of	server
Syntax	`server.host`
Usage	`write(server.host);`
Sample Value	"www.netscapepress.com"
Description	The host property of the server object contains the host and domain name of the server hosting the application.

hostname — PROPERTY

Property of	server
Syntax	`server.hostname`
Usage	`write(server.hostname);`
Sample Value	"www.netscapepress.com: 80"
Description	The hostname property contains the full hostname of the server, possibly including the port number.

ImageX
PROPERTY

Property of request

Syntax request.imageX

Usage if (request.imageX 100) { ... }

Sample Value 83

Description When a user submits a form by clicking on an image or clicks on an image map, the imageX property is set in the request object. The imageX property contains the X position of the mouse click in the image. This property can be used in conjunction with imageY to determine where in the image the user clicked. You can use this information to perform different actions based on the section of the image that was clicked.

See Also imageY

imageY
PROPERTY

Property of request

Syntax request.imageY

Usage if (request.imageY >= 85) { ... }

Sample Value 137

Description When a user submits a form by clicking on an image or clicks on an image map, the imageY property is set in the request object. The imageY property contains the Y position of the mouse click in the image. This property can be used in conjunction with imageX to determine where in the image the user clicked. You can use this information to perform different actions based on the section of the image where the user clicked.

See Also imageX

insertRow

METHOD

Method of	Cursor
Syntax	*cursor*.insertRow(*table*)
Parameters	*cursor*—a Cursor object created by the cursor method of a Connection object.
	table—the name of the database table you wish to insert the row of the cursor into.
Usage	myCursor.insertRow("inventory");
Description	The insertRow method will insert the current contents of the cursor into a new row in the named table. It will return a status code, depending on any error code returned from the database. The location of the new row depends on the database vendor library. If you need to access the new row, you must first close the cursor and open a new one.
See Also	close, deleteRow, majorErrorCode, updateRow

ip

PROPERTY

Property of	request
Syntax	request.ip
Usage	write(request.ip);
Sample Value	"199.72.13.1"
Description	When a user requests a URL within an Enterprise Server application, the ip property is set in the request object. The ip property contains the IP address of the client. This property can be used to keep track of accesses or to restrict access to your application from certain IP addresses by checking allowed addresses against this property.

Lock

OBJECT

Syntax   new Lock( )

Properties   none

Methods   lock, unlock

Usage   var myLock = new Lock();

Description   Any code you create that should only be accessed by one thread at a time is called a critical section. Any time you enter a critical section that doesn't involve the project or server objects, you need to use a Lock object.

Let's say you have a custom object that keeps track of various information about the state of the current running application stored in the project object called *project.appState*. If you wanted to modify any of the properties of this appState object, this object would need to be in a critical section. You might not want to use the project lock method because you might have other places where you access the project object that you don't want held up when the appState object is modified. Let's assume you've already created a lock object when the application started:

```
project.appLock = new Lock();
```

Now, in your critical section you want to modify two properties of the appState object. The code for this action would be as follows:

```
project.appLock.lock();
project.appState.lastIP = request.ip;
project.appState.homeAccesses += 1;
write("There have been ");
write(project.appState.homeAccesses);
write(" to this page since the application started.<br>");
write("The last access was from " + project.appState.lastIP + "<br>");
project.appLock.unlock();
```

See Also   lock, project, server, unlock

lock
METHOD

Method of Lock

Syntax `myLock.lock()`

Usage `myLock.lock();`

Description The lock method locks a previously created Lock object. If the object is already locked, it will wait until the lock is freed before continuing. This method returns true if the lock attempt succeeded; it returns false if an error occurred trying to get the lock.

See Also lock, unlock

lock
METHOD

Method of project, server

Syntax `project.lock(), server.lock()`

Usage `project.lock();`

Description Since many different users may be trying to access the project or server objects at the same time, using the lock method keeps other users from accessing the object until it is unlocked. While the object is locked, access to the object by any other users will be delayed until the lock is removed. The lock is automatically removed when the current request has been completed.

See Also unlock

majorErrorCode
METHOD

Method of Connection, DbPool

Syntax `connection.majorErrorCode(), dbpool.majorErrorCode()`

Parameters	*connection*—a Connection object you've created from a DbPool connection method.
	dbpool—a DbPool object that was created using the DbPool constructor.
Usage	`write(myConnection.majorErrorCode());`
Description	When an SQL statement fails, the database server returns an error message stating why the statement failed. Depending on the status code returned from a Connection or DbPool method, you may be able to use majorErrorCode to find out more information about the error. Table 10-1 below lists what majorErrorCode returns based on the status code from the Connection or DbPool method and the database you're using:

Database	Status Code	Result
Informix	7	the Informix error code
Oracle (OCI)	5	the return code from the Oracle Call-level Interface
Sybase	5	the SQL server message number
Sybase	7	the DB-Library error number

Table 10-1: What majorErrorCode returns based on your database and the status code from your Connection or DbPool method.

The possible status codes you may get from a Connection or DbPool method are shown in Table 10-2 below:

Code	Meaning
0	method completed normally
1	out of memory
2	object not initialized
3	type conversion error
4	database not registered
5	server error
6	message from server
7	vendor library error
8	connection lost
9	end of fetch
10	invalid use of object
11	column doesn't exist
12	bounds error
13	unsupported feature
14	null reference parameter

Chapter 10: Server-Side JavaScript Reference 231

Code	Meaning
15	Connection object not found
16	required information is missing
17	object can't support multiple readers
18	object can't support deletions
19	object can't support insertions
20	object can't support updates
21	object can't support updates
22	object can't support indices
23	object can't be dropped
24	incorrect connection supplied
25	object can't support privileges
26	object can't support cursors
27	unable to open

Table 10-2: The status codes that may be returned from a Connection or DbPool method call and their meanings.

See Also   Connection, DbPool, majorErrorMessage, minorErrorCode, minorErrorMessage

majorErrorMessage   METHOD

Method of   Connection, DbPool

Syntax   `connection.majorErrorMessage()`, `dbpool.majorErrorMessage()`

Parameters   *connection*—a Connection object you've created from a DbPool connection method.

dbpool—a DbPool object that was created using the DbPool constructor.

Usage   `write(myPool.majorErrorMessage());`

Description   When a database Connection or DbPool method fails, you can check the majorErrorMessage to get a human-readable explanation of the failure. What is returned depends on the database and the status code (see Table 10-3).

Database	Status Code	Result
Informix	7	Vendor Library Error text text – the error text from Informix
Oracle	5	Server Error text text – the translation of the return code from Oracle
Sybase	5	Server Error text text – the text from the SQL server unless the severity and message number are both zero. In that case it is the message text.
Sybase	7	Vendor Library Error text text – the error text from DB-Library

Table 10-3: The result of a call to majorErrorMessage after receiving the status code from a call to a Connection or DbPool method.

See Also Connection, DbPool, majorErrorCode, minorErrorCode, minorErrorMessage

method   PROPERTY

Property of request

Syntax `request.method;`

Usage `write(request.method);`

Sample Value "POST"

Description When a user requests a URL within an Enterprise Server application, the method property is set in the request object. The method property contains the HTTP method requested by the client connection. Your application can use this property to determine how to respond to the request. In an HTTP 1.0 request, the method can be one of three values: "GET," "POST," or "HEAD."

minorErrorCode

METHOD

Method of Connection, DbPool

Syntax *connection*.minorErrorCode( ), *dbpool*.minorErrorCode( )

Parameters *connection*—a Connection object you've created from a DbPool connection method.

dbpool—a DbPool object that was created using the DbPool constructor.

Usage write(myPool.minorErrorCode( ));

Description The minorErrorCode method returns the secondary error code from the database. Table 10-4 below lists what minorErrorCode returns based on the status code from the Connection or DbPool method and the database you're using.

Database	Status Code	Result
Informix	7	the ISAM error code or 0 if there is no ISAM error
Oracle	5	the operating system error code as reported by OCI
Sybase	5	the severity level from the SQL server
Sybase	7	the severity level from DB-Library

Table 10-4: The minorErrorCode results if you have one of the listed status codes returned from a Connection or DbPool method call.

See Also Connection, DbPool, majorErrorCode, majorErrorMessage, minorErrorMessage

minorErrorMessage

METHOD

Method of Connection, DbPool

Syntax *connection*.minorErrorMessage( ), *dbpool*.minorErrorMessage( )

Parameters *connection*—a Connection object you've created from a DbPool connection method.

Usage	*dbpool*—a DbPool object that was created using the DbPool constructor.
	`write(myConnection.minorErrorMessage());`
Description	The minorErrorMessage returns the secondary error message from the database. Table 10-5 below lists what minorErrorMessage returns based on the status code from the Connection or DbPool method and the database you're using:

Database	Status Code	Result
Informix	7	ISAM Error text text – is the text of the ISAM error code from Informix or it is a null string if there is no ISAM error.
Oracle	5	the Oracle server name
Sybase	5	the SQL server name
Sybase	7	the operating system error text from DB-Library

Table 10-5: *The minorErrorMessage results if you have one of the listed status codes returned from a Connection or DbPool method call.*

See Also   Connection, DbPool, majorErrorCode, majorErrorMessage, minorErrorCode

next

METHOD

Method of	Cursor, ResultSet
Syntax	`cursor.next(), result.next()`
Parameters	*cursor*—a Cursor object created by the cursor method of a Connection object.
	result—a ResultSet object created by calling the resultSet method of a StoredProc object.
Usage	`while ( myCursor.next() ) { Ö }`
	Note: See the sidebar near columnName for a code example using the next method.
Description	The *next* method increments the current row of the database cursor or result set. It returns true if there is a next row; it returns false if you are at the end

Chapter 10: Server-Side JavaScript Reference 235

of the cursor. When a Cursor or ResultSet object is created, the current row position is before the first row in the database, so you can check the next method to make sure data was found by the SQL query or stored procedure.

open
METHOD

Method of · File

Syntax · `FileObject.open(mode)`

Parameters · *FileObject*—this is an instance of a File object.

mode—this is a character representation of what mode you wish to open the file in. See the description for a list of possible modes.

Usage · `FileObject.open("r");`

Description · The open method will open a file for reading or writing. The possible modes to open a file in are listed in Table 10-6 below.

mode	description
r	The file is opened for reading. If the file doesn't exist, the open method returns false.
w	The file is opened for writing. If the file exists, it will be overwritten; if it doesn't exist, it will be created.
a	The file is opened for appending. If the file exists, any new data will be added to the end of the file; if it doesn't exist, it will be created.
r+	The file is opened for reading and writing at the beginning of the file. If the file doesn't exist, the method will return false.
w+	The file is opened for reading and writing. If the file exists, it will be overwritten; if it doesn't exist, it will be created.
a+	The file is opened for reading and writing at the end of the file. If the file doesn't exist, it will be created.
b	This mode can be added to any of the above modes. If present, the file will be opened in binary mode. This mode is only relevant on a Windows operating system.

Table 10-6: The modes for opening a file using the open method of the JavaScript File object.

See Also · close, read, readByte, readln, write, writeByte, writeln

outParamCount　　　　　　　　　　　　　　　　　　　　　　METHOD

Method of	StoredProc
Syntax	*proc*.outParamCount()
Parameters	*proc*—a StoredProc object created by a call to the storedProc method of a Connection object.
Usage	outputParams = myProc.outParamCount();
Description	The outParamCount method returns the number of output parameters returned by the database stored procedure. *Note:* For Informix there are no output parameters, so this method will always return 0.
See Also	outParameters

outParameters　　　　　　　　　　　　　　　　　　　　　　METHOD

Method of	StoredProc
Syntax	*proc*.outParameters(*index*)
Parameters	*proc*—a StoredProc object created by a call to the storedProc method of a Connection object.
	index—the number of the parameter for which the value is to be returned. The first parameter has an index of 0.
Usage	write(myProc.outParameters(2));
Description	The outParameters method returns the value of the output parameter indicated by *index*. Since Informix stored procedures don't have output parameters, this method will always return 0 for Informix. You must retrieve all result sets from the StoredProc object before calling the outParameters method. Once you call outParameters, you won't be able to access any more data from a result set, and you won't be able to retrieve any more result sets.
See Also	outParamCount

port

PROPERTY

Property of	server
Syntax	`server.port`
Usage	`write(server.port);`
Sample Value	8000
Description	The port property of the server object contains the port number of the server. The default port for secure (https) connections is 443; for regular (http) connections it's 80.

project

OBJECT

Syntax	`project.property`, `project.method()`
Parameters	*property*—user-defined property added to the project object. *method*—one of the methods of the project object.
Properties	application defined
Methods	lock, unlock
Usage	`project.homeAccesses = 0;`
Description	There is only one project object for each application on your server. You can store any application-wide variables in the project object that can be referred to by any request to the application. If you need to update any values of the project object, you should be sure to lock the project object first (or create a lock object and lock it) so that there isn't any data corruption if two clients try to access that property at the same time. For example, if you wanted to keep a counter on your home page, you could include the following code:

```
project.lock();
project.homeAccesses = project.homeAccesses + 1;
write("You are visitor number  " + project.homeAccesses +
   " since the application started.<p>");
project.unlock();
```

If you forget to unlock the project, it will automatically be unlocked when the current request is finished. While the object is locked, any other requests trying to access it will wait until it has been unlocked.

Any properties you add to the project object can be of any valid JavaScript type including references to other objects. The object will live as long as the application is running.

See Also   lock, unlock

protocol   PROPERTY

Property of   request

Syntax   `request.protocol`

Usage   `write(request.protocol);`

Sample Value   "HTTP/1.0"

Description   When a user requests a URL within an Enterprise Server application, the protocol property is set in the request object. The protocol property contains the version of the HTTP protocol supported by the user's browser.

protocol   PROPERTY

Property of   server

Syntax   `server.protocol`

Usage   `write(server.protocol);`

Sample Value   "http "

Description   The protocol property of the server object contains the protocol being used to access the server. You can use this property to determine whether or not the request is being made to a secure Enterprise Server.

read

METHOD

Method of	File
Syntax	*FileObject*.read(*num*)
Parameters	*FileObject*—this is an instance of a File object. *num*—this is the number of bytes to read from the file.
Usage	data = FileObject.read(20);
Description	The read method will read the defined number of bytes from the file and move the current position of the file forward the same number of bytes.
See Also	readByte, readln

readByte

METHOD

Method of	File
Syntax	*FileObject*.readByte()
Parameters	*FileObject*—this is an instance of a File object.
Usage	data = FileObject.readByte();
Description	The readByte method will read the next byte from the file and move the current position one place forward.
See Also	read, readln

readln
METHOD

Method of File

Syntax `FileObject.readln()`

Parameters *FileObject*—this is an instance of a File object.

Usage `Data = FileObject.readln();`

Description The readln method will return the next line from the file. It will read from the current position up to a linefeed. If there is a carriage return as well (on Windows), it will be ignored. The string won't include the carriage return or linefeed characters.

See Also read, readByte

redirect
ROOT FUNCTION

Syntax `redirect(URL)`

Parameters *URL*—the URL you want the user to be redirected to.

Usage `redirect("home.html");`

Description The redirect function will redirect the user's browser to the URL specified. This can be a relative or an absolute URL. The remainder of the page won't be loaded once the client gets to a redirect function.

See Also addClient

registerCFunction
ROOT FUNCTION

Syntax `registerCFunction(JSName, pathToLibrary, CName)`

Parameters *JSName*—this is the name of the function as you will refer to it from JavaScript.

pathToLibrary—this is the path on your server machine to the library that has the function. See your server documentation for information about creating these libraries.

CName—this is the name of the C function in the library file that you wish to call.

Usage   `RegisterCFunction("Crypt", "/usr/lib/crypt.so", "crypt");`

Description   The registerCFunction registers a native function with JavaScript. Once it's registered, you can access it from your JavaScript code via the callC function. This function will return true if the C function was registered successfully, and false if an error occurred.

See Also   callC

release   METHOD

Method of   Connection

Syntax   *connection*.release()

Parameters   *connection*—a Connection object you've created from a DbPool connection method.

Usage   `myConnection.release();`

Description   The release method releases a Connection back to the database pool. It returns a status code to indicate whether an error occurred or not. All cursors should be closed before calling the release method. If they aren't closed, the server will wait until all cursors are closed before releasing the connection back to the pool.

If you don't explicitly call the release method, the connection won't be available to other users until the object variable goes out of scope. If the variable is a property of the project or server objects, it will remain until the application stops or the server stops, respectively. Otherwise it will be released when the current page request has been completed.

You must release all connections in a database pool before calling the disconnect method of the DbPool object. If you don't, the connection is still considered alive and the disconnect will wait until it has been released.

See Also   Connection, DbPool, majorErrorCode

Request

OBJECT

Syntax — `request.property`

Parameters — *property*—one of the standard properties for the request object, a property that was created due to an HTML form POST or from the *query string*, or a property you wish to create.

query string—the string following a question mark in a URL. See Description, below, for more information on query strings.

Properties — agent, ip, method, imageX, imageY, protocol

Methods — none

Usage — `if (request.agent.indexOf("Mozilla") != -1) {...}`

Description — A new request object is created any time a Web browser requests a page from your application. If the page was sent from an HTML form or if the requested URL included a query string, the form elements and/or query string name/values will be included in the created request object.

The query string must be in the following format:

`http://www.netscapepress.com/page.html?name1=val1&name2=val2`

This would add two properties to the request object:request.name1 and request.name2, with the assigned values. If you are creating a URL with a query string from your application, be sure to use the escape( ) function on your property names and values if they include any odd characters. If you're not sure which characters may be odd, use the escape function. The server will unescape the names and values when it creates the request object.

The request object is the shortest living object of any of the session management objects. The request object is destroyed when the server has finished responding to the request. You can add properties to the request object of any valid JavaScript type. Those properties will be destroyed when the requested page has been served.

See Also — agent, imageX, imageY, ip, method, protocol

ResultSet OBJECT

Syntax `result.method()`

Parameters *result*—a ResultSet object created by calling the resultSet method of a StoredProc object.

method—a valid method of a ResultSet object.

Properties The column names of the stored procedure that created the ResultSet.

Methods close, columnName, columns, next

Usage `myResult = myProc.resultSet();`

Description A ResultSet object is created by calling the resultSet method of a StoredProc object. It is a virtual table of data that was created by running a stored procedure. For Oracle and Sybase stored procedures, there is a ResultSet for each select query run by the stored procedure. For Informix, there is always one ResultSet.

See Also close, columnName, columns, next, resultSet, StoredProc

resultSet METHOD

Method of StoredProc

Syntax `proc.resultSet()`

Parameters *proc*—a StoredProc object created by a call to the storedProc method of a Connection object.

Usage `myResult = myProc.resultSet();`

Description The resultSet method returns the next ResultSet object from the stored procedure. Oracle store procedures don't support result sets, so for Oracle this method will always return 0.

You should retrieve all result sets before calling the outParameters or returnValue methods because you won't be able to access any result sets after calling one of these methods.

See Also   outParameters, ResultSet, returnValue

returnValue   METHOD

Method of   StoredProc

Syntax   `proc.returnValue()`

Parameters   *proc*—a StoredProc object created by a call to the storedProc method of a Connection object.

Usage   `write(myProc.returnValue());`

Description   The returnValue method will return the return value of the StoredProc object. You must retrieve all result sets before calling this method; otherwise, you won't be able to access the current or any pending result sets.
Note: For Informix, return values are represented in a result set, so this method will always return 0.

See Also   resultSet

rollbackTransaction   METHOD

Method of   Connection

Syntax   `connection.rollbackTransaction()`

Parameters   *connection*—a Connection object you've created from a DbPool connection method.

Usage   `myConnection.rollbackTransaction();`

Description   The rollbackTransaction method will remove any modifications that have been made to the database since beginTransaction was called. It returns a status code based on any error message that may have come from the database. If rollbackTransaction is called without a prior call to beginTransaction, it is ignored.

See also   beginTransaction, commitTransaction, Connection, majorErrorCode

send   METHOD

Method of   SendMail

Syntax   `MailObject.send()`

Parameters   *MailObject*—this is an instance of a SendMail object.

Usage   `MailObject.send();`

Description   This will send the e-mail message you've defined by setting the properties of the SendMail object. It returns true if no errors occurred trying to send the message.

SendMail   OBJECT

Syntax   `SendMail()`

Usage   `MailObject = new SendMail();`

Properties   Bcc, Body, Cc, From, Smtpserver, Subject, To

Methods   send

Description   The SendMail object is used when you want your application to send an e-mail message. After creating a new instance of the object, you can set the properties that correspond to the mail header, such as the To, From, and Body fields. Once these are set, you can use the send method to mail your message. You can set any header you want on your message as a property of the object you create.

```
MailObject["Errors-to"] = "postmaster@netscapepress.com";
```

See Also   Bcc, Body, Cc, From, send, Smtpserver, Subject, To

server
OBJECT

Syntax   `server.property, server.method()`

Parameters   *property*—one of the standard properties of the server object or one created in the application.

method—one of the methods of the server object.

Properties   host, hostname, port, protocol

Methods   lock, unlock

Usage   `write(server.protocol);`

Description   There is only one server object shared among all the applications you have running on your server. A new server object is created when the server starts, and is destroyed when the server is stopped. If you have multiple servers running on one machine (either by using a different port or through virtual machines), each has its own server object. Any time you wish to modify a server property you've created, you should use the lock and unlock methods to make sure there aren't any other requests accessing the server object at the same time. See the "project" entry in this chapter for an example of this.

The properties you add to the server object can be any valid JavaScript type including references to other JavaScript objects. These objects will live as long as the server is running.

See Also   host, hostname, lock, port, project, protocol, unlock

setPosition
METHOD

Method of   File

Syntax   `FileObject.setPosition(num, start)`

Parameters   *FileObject*—this is an instance of a File object.

Chapter 10: Server-Side JavaScript Reference

num—this is the number of places to move in the file. It can be either positive or negative.

start—this determines the position in the file to start moving from. See the description for possible options for this argument.

Usage `FileObject.setPosition(35, 0);`

Description The setPosition method will change the current position in the file. The second argument determines where to move from, and the possible options are listed in Table 10-7 below.

Start position	Description
0	The position is moved relative to the beginning of the file.
1	The position is moved relative to the current position.
2	The position is moved relative to the end of the file.
Anything else	The position is moved relative to the beginning of the file.

Table 10-7: The meanings of the second argument to the setPosition function.

See Also getPosition

Smtpserver   PROPERTY

Property of SendMail

Syntax *MailObject*.Smtpserver

Parameters *MailObject*—this is an instance of a SendMail object.

Usage `MailObject.Smtpserver = "mail.domain.com";`

Description You can set this property to override the server default setting for your SMTP server. This is the machine that will be used to send your message to its recipient.

SQLTable
METHOD

Method of	Connection
Syntax	`connection.SQLTable(SQLQuery)`
Parameters	*connection*—a Connection object you've created from a DbPool connection method.
	SQLQuery—an SQL select statement supported by the database server you're using. If you use the SQL standard, you don't need to worry about updating your code if you change database servers.
Usage	`myConnection.SQLTable("select * from inventory");`
Description	The SQLTable method creates and writes an HTML table filled with the data returned from the SQL query. The top row of the table includes all the column names returned from the query. The rest of the rows include all the data from the query under the proper column heading. There's no way to customize this output, so if you want to do any specialized formatting of your data, you should use the cursor method.
See Also	Cursor, cursor, execute

StoredProc
OBJECT

Syntax	`proc.method()`
Parameters	*proc*—a StoredProc object created by a call to the storedProc method of a Connection object.
	method—a valid method of the StoredProc object.
Properties	none
Methods	outParamCount, outParameters, resultSet, returnValue

Chapter 10: Server-Side JavaScript Reference 249

Usage `myProc = myConnection.storedProc("cleanup", "employees", 1996)`

Description A StoredProc object is a representation of a database stored procedure. The StoredProc object's lifetime is the duration of the current request. Any methods you want to call on a StoredProc object must be called on the same page where the StoredProc was created.

See Also Connection, storedProc

storedProc

METHOD

Method of Connection

Syntax `connection.storedProc( procedure, param1, param2, ... )`

Parameters *connection*—a Connection object you've created from a DbPool connection method.

procedure—the name of the stored procedure that you want to run.

param1, param2,...—the parameters to be passed to the named procedure. The number of parameters depends on the procedure you're calling.

Usage `cleanupProc = myConnection.storedProc( "cleanup", "employees", 1996 );`

Description The storedProc method creates and returns a StoredProc object. The lifetime of this object is until the end of the current request; therefore, you must use the results of the stored procedure in the page in which the StoredProc object was created.
  When stored procedures are created, you can define default values for the parameters. If a value isn't passed to the procedure, it will use the default value for that parameter. When you call one of these procedures from LiveWire, you must specify each parameter; so if you want to use the default value, you should pass /Default/ as the parameter:

```
cleanupProc = myConnection.storedProc("cleanup", "employees",
  "/Default/" );
```

See Also StoredProc

storedProcArgs
METHOD

Method of DbPool

Syntax `dbpool.storedProcArgs(procedure, type1, type2, …)`

Parameters *dbpool*—a DbPool object that was created using the DbPool constructor.

procedure—the name of the stored procedure you want to prototype.

type1, type2,…—the types of the parameters of the stored procedure. The type can be IN, OUT, or INOUT.

Usage `myPool.storedProcArgs("cleanup", "IN", "IN");`

Description The storedProcArgs method creates a prototype for a stored procedure for a Sybase database. If you're not using a Sybase database, you won't need to use this method. Sybase stored procedures only have three types for parameters: input (IN), output (OUT), and input and output (INOUT). For every stored procedure that you're going to use, you must create a prototype. If you call storedProcArgs for a procedure more than once, the extra calls will be ignored.

See Also storedProc

stringToByte
METHOD

Method of File

Syntax `FileObject.stringToByte(character)`

Parameters *FileObject*—this is an instance of a File object.

character—the character to be converted to a byte representation.

Usage `myByte = FileObject.stringToByte("a");`

Description The stringToByte method will return a numeric representation of the first character of the string passed to it. It will return 0 if there was no string.

See Also byteToString

Subject
PROPERTY

Property of   SendMail

Syntax   *MailObject*.Subject

Parameters   *MailObject*—this is an instance of a SendMail object.

Usage   `MailObject.Subject = "Here's the message you wanted";`

Description   This is the property of the SendMail object that corresponds to the Subject section in a mail header. This will be seen as the subject of the message when a user receives it.

To
PROPERTY

Property of   SendMail

Syntax   *MailObject*.To

Parameters   *MailObject*—this is an instance of a SendMail object.

Usage   `MailObject.To = "test@netscapepress.com/";`

Description   This is the property of the SendMail object that corresponds to the To section in a mail header. The e-mail addresses you assign to this property will be the recipients of the e-mail. This can be a comma-delimited list of addresses or a single address.

toString
METHOD

Method of   Connection, DbPool

Syntax   *connection*.toString(), *dbpool*.toString()

Parameters	*connection*—a Connection object you've created from a DbPool connection method.
	dbpool—a DbPool object that was created using the DbPool constructor.
Usage	`write(myConnection.toString());`
Description	The toString method returns a description of the current connection configuration to the database. This description has four parts and appears as follows: db *name user type server*
	name—*the name of the connected database.*
	user—*the name of the user connected to the database.*
	type—*the type of the database, such as INFORMIX, ODBC, ORACLE, or SYBASE.*
	server—*the name of the database server you're connected to.*
	If any one of the above values isn't known, an empty string is used in its place.
See Also	connect, Connection, DbPool

unlock

METHOD

Method of	Lock
Syntax	`myLock.unlock()`
Usage	`myLock.unlock();`
Description	The unlock method unlocks a locked Lock object. This allows other users to gain access to the Lock object. This method returns true if the unlock succeeded; it returns false if an error occurred. Trying to unlock an unlocked object may have unexpected results.
See Also	lock, unlock

Chapter 10: Server-Side JavaScript Reference 253

unlock
METHOD

Method of   project, server

Syntax   `project.unlock(), server.unlock()`

Usage   `server.unlock();`

Description   The unlock method is used to unlock a previously set lock on the project or server objects. Once unlocked, other user processes are able to access properties and methods on the object.

See Also   lock

updateRow
METHOD

Method of   Cursor

Syntax   `cursor.updateRow(table)`

Parameters   *cursor*—a Cursor object created by the cursor method of a Connection object.

table—the name of the database table in which you wish to update the current row of the cursor.

Usage   `myCursor.updateRow("inventory");`

Description   The updateRow method will update the current row of the table passed to the method using any new data set to the cursor properties. It will return a status code depending on any error code returned from the database.

See Also   deleteRow, insertRow, majorErrorCode

write

ROOT FUNCTION

Syntax write(*text*)

Parameters *text*—the text you want to be written to the response output buffer.

Usage write("Welcome, "+request.name);

Description The write function will display its argument to the user accessing the JavaScript page calling this function. This data is held in the response output buffer until the buffer is flushed to the client.

See Also flush

write

METHOD

Method of File

Syntax FileObject.write(*text*)

Parameters *FileObject*—this is an instance of a File object.

text—the text you want to write to the file.

Usage FileObject.write("new Data");

Description The write method will write the string passed to it to the file represented by the currently open file object at the current position. It will return true if it was successful and false otherwise.

See Also writeByte, writeln

writeByte METHOD

Method of	File
Syntax	`FileObject.writeByte(num)`
Parameters	*FileObject*—this is an instance of a File object.
	num—a numeric representation of a byte to write to the file (0-255).
Usage	`FileObject.writeByte(56);`
Description	The writeByte method will write the byte passed to it to the file represented by the currently open file object at the current position. It will return true if it was successful, and false otherwise.
See Also	write, writeln

writeln METHOD

Method of	File
Syntax	`FileObject.writeln(text)`
Parameters	*FileObject*—this is an instance of a File object.
	text—the text you want to write to the file.
Usage	`FileObject.writeln("new Data");`
Description	The writeln method will write the string passed to it to the file represented by the currently open file object at the current position. It will also append a linefeed character to the string (or a carriage return and a linefeed if on Windows and the file isn't in binary mode). It will return true if it was successful, and false otherwise.
See Also	write, writeByte

Java Reference

This section includes Java objects and methods within Netscape's packages. These objects are used to tie Java into your JavaScript application.

call
METHOD

Method of	JSObject
Syntax	`call(String method, Object[] args)`
Parameters	*method*—the JavaScript method to be called.
	args—an array of arguments to pass to the method.
Usage	`myObj.call("next");`
	where myObj is a reference to a JavaScript cursor object.
Description	This method calls a JavaScript method or function. It is the same as the JavaScript code: this.*method*(args[0], args[1], etc.).
See Also	JSObject

eval
METHOD

Method of	JSObject
Syntax	`eval(String expression)`
Parameters	*expression*—a JavaScript expression to be evaluated.
Usage	`eval("project.lock();");`
Description	This method evaluates the given *expression*. The string will be executed as if it were a string of JavaScript code in the context of the current object in JavaScript.
See Also	JSObject

finalize

METHOD

Method of	JSObject
Syntax	`finalize()`
Usage	`myObj.finalize();`
Description	This method overrides the finalize( ) method in the Object class. It decrements the reference count on the JavaScript object.
See Also	JSObject

getMember

METHOD

Method of	JSObject
Syntax	`getMember(String name)`
Parameters	*name*—the name of a property in the JavaScript object.
Usage	`myObj.getMember("numVisitors");` where myObj is a reference to a project object.
Description	This returns the specified property of the JSObject. It is the same as the JavaScript code: this.*name*, where *this* is interpreted as the JSObject that getMember() is being called from.
See Also	getSlot, JSObject, removeMember, setMember, setSlot

getSlot

METHOD

Method of	JSObject
Syntax	`getSlot(int index)`
Parameters	*index*—the index of a property of the JavaScript object.

Usage   `myObj.getSlot(0);`

Description   This returns the specified indexed member of the JSObject. It is similar to getMember( ) and is the same as the JavaScript code: this[*index*].

See Also   getMember, JSObject, removeMember, setMember, setSlot

getWindow   METHOD

Method of   JSObject

Syntax   `getWindow(Applet applet)`

Parameters   *applet*—a Java applet.

Usage   `myObj.getWindow(myApplet);`

Description   This method returns the window handle for the window containing the applet. If *applet* is left out, it defaults to the current applet (*this*). This method is only used with LiveConnect on the client.

See Also   JSObject

JSException   OBJECT

Package   netscape.javascript

Constructors   JSException

Description   JSException is thrown whenever JavaScript returns an error. It extends java.lang.Exception.

See Also   JSObject

JSException   CONSTRUCTOR

Constructor of   JSException

Syntax   JSException()
JSException(String *detail*)
JSException(String *detail*, String *filename*, int *linenum*, String *source*, int *tokenIndex*)

Parameters   *detail*—the detail message of the error.

filename—the filename where the error occurred.

linenum—the line number where the error occurred.

source—the source of the JavaScript error.

tokenIndex—the token index of the error.

Description   This constructor constructs a JSException object with an optional message describing the exception as well as all the other information that is sent with a JavaScript error.

JSObject   OBJECT

Package   netscape.javascript

Methods   call, eval, finalize, getMember, getSlot, getWindow, removeMember, setMember, setSlot, toString

Description   JSObject is used to handle JavaScript objects. It extends java.lang.Object. It is most often used as a parameter type for a method you define in your Java class.

See Also   JSException

NetscapeServerEnv   OBJECT

Package	netscape.server.server
Methods	writeHttpOutput
Description	The NetscapeServerEnv class is used to access the Enterprise server environment. It includes one static method to write data to the response buffer, which will be written to the client when the buffer is flushed.
See Also	The JavaScript write function.

removeMember   METHOD

Method of	JSObject
Syntax	removeMember(String *name*)
Parameters	*name*—the name of a property in the JavaScript object.
Usage	myObj.removeMember("numVisitors"); where myObj is a reference to a project object.
Description	This method removes the specified property of the JavaScript object.
See Also	getMember, getSlot, JSObject, setMember, setSlot

setMember   METHOD

Method of	JSObject
Syntax	setMember(String *name*, Object *value*)
Parameters	*name*—the name of a property in the JavaScript object. *value*—the value to set to that property.

Usage   `myObj.setMember("ID", 2468);`

where myObj is a reference to a client object.

Description   This method sets the specified property of the JavaScript object to value. It is the same as the JavaScript code: this.*name* = *value*.

See Also   getMember, getSlot, JSObject, removeMember, setSlot

setSlot   METHOD

Method of   JSObject

Syntax   `setSlot(int index, Object value)`

Parameters   *index*—the index of a property of the JavaScript object.

value—the value to set to that property.

Usage   `myObj.setSlot(0, 2468);`

where myObj is a reference to a client object.

Description   This method sets the specified indexed property of the JavaScript object to value. It is the same as the JavaScript code: this[*index*] = *value*.

See Also   getMember, getSlot, JSObject, removeMember, setMember

toString   METHOD

Method of   JSObject

Syntax   `toString()`

Usage   `strObj = myObj.toString();`

Description   This method overrides the toString() method of the Object class and converts the JSObject to a string and returns it.

writeHttpOutput
METHOD

Method of NetscapeServerEnv

Syntax NetscapeServerEnv.writeHttpOutput(*text*)

Parameters *text*—the string to be written to the response buffer.

Usage NetscapeServerEnv.writeHttpOutput("new data");

Description The writeHttpOutput method is used to write data to the response buffer, which will be written to the client when the buffer is flushed. This is a static method, so you don't need an instance of the NetscapeServerEnv to call this method; simply call the method on the class itself.

See Also The JavaScript write function.

Server-Side JavaScript Object Reference

This is a quick reference for server-side JavaScript objects, with a short description of the methods and properties of each of these objects.

client   SESSION MANAGEMENT OBJECT

Description   The client object is used to maintain session variables through multiple page requests to the application. There are no default properties; the only properties are those you define. See "Maintaining the Client Object" in Chapter 3, "Session Management Objects," for more information on the possible ways to keep track of the client object through your application. Each browser connecting to your application will have its own client object (except when you're using the IP address to maintain the client object).

The properties you create must be able to be converted to a string; therefore, you can't have any objects assigned to a client property. If you need to store an object, you'll need to create an array in the project or server object, then create an index for each client accessing your site, and store the index in a client property. The array at that index can contain the object you wish to keep throughout the client object's lifetime.

Methods   *destroy*—destroys all the properties on the client object.

expiration—sets the number of seconds until the client properties are expired.

Connection

LIVEWIRE OBJECT

Description You can create an instance of a connection object by using the connect method of a DbPool object. There is no constructor that you can call for a connection object using the new operator. The connection object is used to manage a connection to your database.

Methods *beginTransaction*—starts a new database transaction associated with the current connection.

commitTransaction—commits the previously begun transaction.

connected—tests to see if the connection is actually connected to your database.

cursor—creates a new cursor object containing the results of the SQL query passed to it.

execute—executes an arbitrary SQL statement.

majorErrorCode—returns the major error code from the database if there is one.

majorErrorMessage—returns the major error message from the database if there is one.

minorErrorCode—returns the minor error code from the database if there is one.

minorErrorMessage—returns the minor error message from the database if there is one.

release—releases the current connection to the database back to the connection pool.

rollbackTransaction—rolls back the previously begun transaction.

SQLTable—runs an SQL query and displays the results in an HTML table.

storedProc—creates a stored procedure object of the stored procedure and arguments passed to this method.

toString—returns a string describing the current connection configuration.

Cursor

LIVEWIRE OBJECT

Description A Cursor object is created by a call to the cursor method of a connection object. A Cursor is composed of a set of rows that were returned from the database query. The properties on the current row refer to the column data returned from the query.

You can refer to the properties of a Cursor either by the name of the column or by the index of the column, as in the following example:

```
inventoryCursor[0]
```

When you retrieve aggregate data from the database, you must use the index of the column to view the data. For example:

```
inven = myConnection.cursor("select SUM(qty) from inventory");
write(inven[0]);
```

Properties The column names of the SQL query that created the Cursor.

Methods *close*—closes the cursor. It can no longer be accessed.

columnName—returns the column name associated with the index passed to this method.

columns—returns the number of columns associated with the cursor.

deleteRow—deletes the current row in an updatable cursor.

insertRow—inserts a new row into the cursor.

next—moves the cursor to the next row returned from the query.

updateRow—updates the current row in the cursor with any new data you've assigned to it.

DbPool

LIVEWIRE OBJECT

Description The DbPool object is a pool of connections that can be used to connect to a database. When you need to access the database, you can retrieve a connection from the pool as you need it.

Methods *connect*—connects the pool to the database.

connected—tests to make sure the pool is connected to the database.

connection—creates a new connection object and returns it.

disconnect—disconnects the pool from the database.

majorErrorCode—returns the major error code from the database if there is one.

majorErrorMessage—returns the major error message from the database if there is one.

minorErrorCode—returns the minor error code from the database if there is one.

minorErrorMessage—returns the minor error message from the database if there is one.

storedProcArgs—creates a prototype for a stored procedure.

toString—returns a string describing the current connection configuration.

File

OBJECT

Description A File object is used to read and write files on your server. The most common methods you will use are *open* to open the file for reading or writing, the *read* and *write* methods for file input and output, and the *eof* method for determining when you've reached the end of the file when you're reading it.

Methods *byteToString*—converts a byte to its character representation.

clearError—clears any errors associated with the file.

close—closes access to a file.

eof—tests to see if you have tried to read past the end of the file.

error—returns an error code if an error has occurred.

exists—tests to see if the file associated with the object exists.

flush—flushes any data waiting to be written to the file.

getLength—returns the length of the file.

getPosition—returns the current position in the file.

open—opens the file associated with the object.

read—reads a set amount of data from the file.

readByte—reads one byte from the file.

readln—reads a line from the file.

setPosition—changes the current position in the file.

stringToByte—converts the first character in a string to a byte.

write—writes data to the file.

writeByte—writes a single byte to the file.

writeln—writes data to the file appended by an end-of-line character.

Lock
SESSION MANAGEMENT OBJECT

Description   Code you create that should only be accessed by one thread at a time is called a *critical section*. Any time you enter a critical section that doesn't involve the project or server objects, you need to use a lock object.

Methods   *lock*—locks the lock object. Any other request to lock this object will wait until the lock has been freed.

unlock—unlocks the lock object so subsequent requests can acquire a lock.

project
SESSION MANAGEMENT OBJECT

Description   There is only one project object for each application on your server. You can store any application-wide variables in the project object that can be referred to by any request to the application. If you need to update any values of the project object, you should be sure to lock the project object first (or create a lock object and lock it) so that there isn't any data corruption if two clients try to access that property at the same time. For example, if you wanted to keep a counter on your home page, you could include the following code:

```
project.lock();
project.homeAccesses = project.homeAccesses + 1;
write("You are visitor number  " + project.homeAccesses +
    " since the application started.<p>");
project.unlock();
```

Any properties you add to the project object can be of any valid JavaScript type, including references to other objects. The object will live as long as the application is running.

Methods   *lock*—locks the project object so that when other requests try to access the lock they will wait until it has been freed.

unlock—unlocks the project object so that subsequent requests can acquire the lock.

request

SESSION MANAGEMENT OBJECT

Description A new request object is created any time a Web browser requests a page from your application. If the page was sent from an HTML form, or if the requested URL included a query string, the form elements and/or query string name/values will be included in the created request object.

The request object is the shortest living object of any of the session management objects. The request object is destroyed when the server has finished responding to the request. You can add properties to the request object of any valid JavaScript type. Those properties will be destroyed when the requested page has been served.

Properties *agent*—contains the user agent of the browser.

ip—contains the IP address of the machine requesting your page.

method—contains the method of the request: GET or POST.

imageX—contains the X position where an image was clicked to be submitted to this page.

imageY—contains the Y position where an image was clicked to be submitted to this page.

protocol—contains the protocol of the current request. This will usually be "HTTP/1.0."

ResultSet

LIVEWIRE OBJECT

Description A ResultSet object is created by calling the resultSet method of a StoredProc object. It is a virtual table of data that was created by running a stored procedure. For Oracle and Sybase stored procedures, there is a ResultSet for each select query run by the stored procedure. For Informix, there is always one ResultSet.

Properties The column names of the stored procedure that created the ResultSet.

Methods *close*—closes the result set object.

columnName—returns the name of the column at the given index.

columns—returns the number of columns in the result set.

next—moves to the next row in the result set.

SendMail
OBJECT

Description The SendMail object is used when you want your application to send an e-mail message. After creating a new instance of the object, you can set the properties that correspond to the mail header, such as the To, From, and Body fields. Once these are set, you can use the *send* method to mail your message. You can set any header you want on your message as a property of the object you create.

```
MailObject[Errors-to] = "postmaster@netprepress.com";
```

Properties *Bcc*—sets the blind carbon copy field of the mail message.

Body—sets the message text of the mail message.

Cc—sets the carbon copy field of the mail message.

From—sets the from field of the mail message.

To—sets who will receive the message.

Smtpserver—defines the SMTP server to use to send the message.

Subject—sets the subject of the mail message.

Methods send—sends the message to the recipient.

server
SESSION MANAGEMENT OBJECT

Description There is only one server object shared among all the applications you have running on your server. A new server object is created when the server starts and is destroyed when the server is stopped. If you have multiple servers running on one machine (either by using a different port or through virtual machines), each has its own server object. Any time you wish to modify a server property you've created, you should use the lock and unlock methods to make sure there aren't any other requests accessing the server object at the same time. See the "project" entry in this reference chapter for an example of this.

The properties you add to the server object can be any valid JavaScript type, including references to other JavaScript objects. These objects will live as long as the server is running.

Properties   *host*—contains the fully qualified domain name of the machine running the Web server.

hostname—contains the fully qualified domain name of the machine running the Web server as well as the port.

port—contains the port the server is running on.

protocol—contains the protocol supported by the server, either http or https for secure servers.

Methods   *lock*—locks the project object so that when other requests try to access the lock they will wait until it has been freed.

unlock—unlocks the project object so that subsequent requests can acquire the lock.

StoredProc

LIVEWIRE OBJECT

Description   A StoredProc object is a representation of a database stored procedure. The StoredProc object's lifetime is the duration of the current request. Any methods you want to call on a StoredProc object must be called on the same page where the StoredProc was created.

Methods   *outParamCount*—returns the number of output parameters returned by the stored procedure.

outParameters—returns the value of the output parameter specified by the index passed to this method.

resultSet—returns a result set object returned from the stored procedure.

returnValue—returns the return value of the stored procedure.

SECTION 4
Appendices

Appendix A

Glossary

BLOb (Binary Large Object) A BLOb is a special datatype in JavaScript and in your database. It represents large amounts of data such as images or sounds (or even large amounts of text), that don't fit in any of your other database data types.

cookies They provide a way to store small amounts of data on the client of the user visiting your site. On subsequent requests, the client will send back the data stored in the cookie so you can recognize the user. Cookies can be used to customize pages or store products for a shopping basket. Cookies can be set by using the client object with the client-cookie method of client object maintenance.

cursor A cursor is an object you use to retrieve data from your database. You can use them to cycle through the database entries returned from a select SQL query.

javac javac is the Java compiler that comes with the JDK. It is used to compile your Java code into Java classes.

jsac (JavaScript Application Compiler) This is the compiler you use to compile your JavaScript application into a Web file that the server reads to run your application.

LiveConnect LiveConnect is a technology developed by Netscape that allows your JavaScript code to communicate with Java and for Java to communicate with JavaScript. On the client it also allows for communication between plug-ins and Java.

LiveWire LiveWire is a technology developed by Netscape. It used to refer to any server-side JavaScript applications. Now it only refers to the set of server-side JavaScript objects that provide access to your database.

SSL (Secure Sockets Layer) SSL allows you to transmit data safely between any client and your server by encrypting the data before transmitting it.

stored procedure A stored procedure is code stored within your database that you can execute from your JavaScript application. The stored procedure must be written in a method native to your specific database server.

APPENDIX B

Viewing the Example Online

You can view the time-tracking example used in this book by visiting http://mott.catalogue.com:24680/timetrack/. Supply the user name: *example* and the password: *example*. You won't be able to make any changes to the database, but you'll be able to view all of the pages and reports.

You'll also find a link to a .zip file and a .tar file with the application source code, in case you don't want to type it all in. You'll need to modify the database connection information to match your own database before it will work. You can do this by modifying the DbPool line to include the correct configuration information for your database.

Index

A

access methods, database connection pools 54–55
access, Web-based application types 1
Add Application form
    Application Manager 186
    versus jsa.conf file 187
addClient function 199
    client URL encoding 41–42
    URL encoding 38
addResponseHeader function 84, 200
admin access menu page, described 112
admin access page, adminmenu.html file 159–161
adminclient.html file 176–177
adminclient_add.html file 177–178
adminclient_del.html file 179–180
adminemp.html file 172–173
adminemp_add.html file 173–174
adminemp_del.html file 175–176
administer clients form page
    adminclient.html file 176–177
    adminclient_add.html file 177–178
    adminclient_del.html file 179–180
    do_adminclient.html file 179
administer clients page
    described 113
    interface design 126
administer employees form page
    adminemp.html file 172–173
    adminemp_add.html file 173–174
    adminemp_del.html file 175–176
    described 113
administer employees page, interface design 125–126
administrative access forms, interface design 125–126

administrative servers, server-side JavaScript activation 15–16
adminmenu.html file 159–161
agent property 36, 200
application code
    compiling 18–20
    writing 17–20
application directory, CLASSPATH environment variable 129
application levels, hierarchy design 11
Application Manager
    See also JavaScript Application Manager
    adding applications to servers 185–189
    adding Java application 106
    application addition 20–22
    application setting modifications 24
    application templates 25
    Built-In Maximum Database Connections field 23
    Client Object Maintenance field 24
    configuration settings 25
    debug information display preferences 25
    debugging applications 27–29, 189–191
    Default Page field 23
    External Libraries field 24
    Initial Page field 23
    Name field 22
    preference settings 25
    running applications 26, 106, 188–189
    starting/stopping/restarting applications 26
    testing applications 188–189
    viewing applications 26–29
    Web File Path field 23
application map 111–114

application objects
    employee object methods 119
    hours object methods 120–121
    report object methods/properties 121–122
    ReportHours object methods/properties 123
    timeClient object methods 120
application templates, Application Manager settings 25
applications
    adding to server 96, 106, 185–189
    client-server 7–8
    compiling 95, 106
    components 22–24
    debug information display 25
    debug messages 191
    debug process 27–29
    debugging 189–191
    development version creation 191
    directory path 87
    employee sign-out board 89–96, 99–107
    file types 17
    hierarchy design 10–11
    HTML files 17
    Java calls 87
    Java incorporation 85–96
    JavaScript Application Manager addition 20–22
    JavaScript files 17
    LiveWire 2
    N-Tier 7–8
    preference settings 25
    restarting 26
    running 26, 96, 106, 188–189
    sending e-mail from 74–77
    setting modifications 24
    starting 26
    stopping 26
    testing 188–189

testing options 196
viewing 26–29
Web browser feature set
  modification 3
Web-based 1–14
arguments
  cursor method 58
  setPosition method 80
array method, object property
  access 73
assigned properties
  request object 37
  server object 47
assignment operators, client object 39

B

batch file. *See* shell scripts
Bcc property 201
beginTransaction method 68, 201–202
binary data
  described 81
  text data conversion 81
blob function 202
blob root function 202
blobImage function 202–203
blobImage root function 202–203
blobLink function 203–204
blobLink root function 203–204
BLObs (Binary Large Objects) 9, 70
board.java file, employee sign-out
  board 100–103
Body property 204
bodyTag() function 154
bounced e-mail, error codes 75–76
bugs, working around 192–193
build script 18–19, 129
Built-In Maximum Database
  Connections field, Application
  Manager 23
byteToString method 204–205
byteToString method, binary/text data
  conversion 81

C

call method 256
callC function 205
callC root function 205
Cc property 205–206
certificates, client 1–2
characters, dot notation (.) 73
checkDB() function 154, 156
checkLogin() function 156
classes
  built-in, Java 87
  JSException 97
  JSObject 97
  Lock 34
  NetscapeServerEnv 97
CLASSPATH environment variable
  application directory 129

server-side JavaScript 86
clearError method 81, 206
client certificates
  access security 4
  described 2
  Web-based application access
    security 1
client cookies
  See also cookies
  character limits 41
  client object 40–41
  client property limits 41
  lifetime 41
  maintenance advantages/
    disadvantages 44
client object 32, 38–44, 206–207, 263
  assignment operators 39
  client cookies 40–41
  client URL encoding 40–42
  client-side maintenance
    methods 40–42
  default inactivity expiration 40
  described 38–39
  destroying 42
  expiration method 40
  lifetime 39–40
  maintaining 40–44
  maintenance method advan-
    tages/disadvantages 44
  properties 39–40
  server-side maintenance
    methods 42–43
  state maintaining 38
  uses 39
Client Object Maintenance field,
  Application Manager 24
client table 116–117
client URL encoding
  addClient function 41–42
  client object 40–42
  maintenance advantages/
    disadvantages 44
  maximum values 41
clients, Java class method write 98
client-server applications
  described 7–8
  versus N-Tier applications 6–8
client-side JavaScript, versus
  server-side JavaScript 184
client-side methods, client object
  maintenance 40–42
client-side processing, described 12
client-side scripting
  described 5–6
  JavaScript for Communicator 6
  VBScript for Internet
    Explorer 6
close method 78, 207–208

codes
  application 17–20
  critical section 33
  database connection pool access
    connection 54
  DbPool object creation 52
  DbPool object sharing 53
  Java compiling 92
  lock object 34–35
  multiple request database
    connection pool 55–56
columnName method 208–209
columns method 62, 209–210
comments.html file 82–83
commitFlag, DbPool object 67–68
commitTransaction method 68, 210
compilers, jsac (JavaScript Application
  Compiler) 15, 18–20
components
  book ii
  JavaScript Application 22–24
connect method 210–211
connected method 211–212
connection method 213
Connection object 212, 264
connections
  database 49–72
  stateless 4
constructors
  DbPool 215
  JSException 259
content-length property, header
  object 84
control statements 57
conversions
  binary/text data 81
  JavaScript/Java data value 88
cookies
  See also client cookies and server
    cookies
  client object 40–41
  described 5
critical section, described 33
cursor method, arguments 58
cursor methods 214
Cursor object 213–214, 265
Cursor object, using to change
  SQLTable Methods 209
cursor objects 58–62
  columns method 62
  navigation 60
  non-case sensitive 59
  query results display 59–60
  SQL aggregate functions 60
  updatable 60–61
  using 58–60
Customize and Mimic SQLTable
  Method 209

Index

D

data definition language
    statements 57
        database 68–70
        JavaScript 68–70
        passing Java to JavaScript 98
database client libraries 49–51
database connection pools 51–56
    access/release methods 54–55
    creating 51–52
    DbPool object 51–52
    multiple requests 55–56
    serial approach method 53
    sharing 53–54
    standard method connection 53
    using 52–53
database errors, syntax 192–193
database servers, LiveWire
    support 49–50
database tables
    client table fields 116–117
    creating 115, 127–128
    designing 115–118
    employee table fields 115–116
    hours table fields 118
databases
    application hierarchy
        design 10–11
    BLObs (Binary Large
        Objects) 9, 70
    building 9–13
    configuration 49–51
    connections 49–72
    cursor objects 58–62
    data types 68–70
    dynamic content file template
        design 11
    error handling 71
    Netscape Enterprise Server
        support 1
    query display 56–57
    SQL statements 56–57
    stored procedure prototypes 64
    stored procedures 62–67
    table design 9–10
    transaction errors 195
    transactions 67–68
    Web-based applications 1–14
DB2 database, stored procedure
    registration 63–64
DbPool constructor 215
DbPool object 51–52, 215, 265–266
    commitFlag 67–68
    connection access/release
        methods 54–55
    parameters 52
    sharing 53
debug messages 191
debug
    application information
        display 25

    application process 27–29
    output description
        information 28–29
debugging, applications 189–191
Default Page field, Application
    Manager 23
default properties
    request object 36
    server object 47
deleteResponseHeader function
    84, 217
deleteResponseHeader root
    function 217
deleteRow method 217–218
destroy method 218
development version,
    applications 191
directories
    application 128–129
    application path 87
disconnect method 218–219
display.js file 181–184
displayForm method 161
do_log.html file 162–163
do_report.html file 169–171
do_view.html file 165–166
dot notation (.) characters, object
    property access 73
drivers, ODBC 50–51

E

e-mail
    bounced 75–76
    error checks 74–76
    sending from applications
        74–77
email.html file 76–77
employee object 119, 130–135
employee sign-out board application
    89–96, 99–107
employee table 115–116
Employee.java file, employee sign-out
    board 89–90, 99–100
employeeObj.js file 130–135
environment variables,
    CLASSPATH 86
eof method 219, 80
error codes, SendMail object 74–76
error handling, databases 71
error messages
    deciphering/tracking 191–196
    syntax 192
error method 81, 219
error page, error.html file 156
error.html file 156
errorCode method 74
errorMessage method 74
ESAF (Enterprise Server Application
    Framework) 15–30
    components 15
    JavaScript Application
        Manager 15–16, 20–26

jsac 18–20
jsac (JavaScript Application
    Compiler) 15
eval function 73
eval method 256
execute method 220
exists method 81, 220–221
expiration method 40, 220–221
External Libraries field, Application
    Manager 24
extranets
    access restrictions 13
    client browser restrictions 12
    client-side processing 12
    described 3, 12
    firewall security 13
    ISP (Internet Service Provider)
        access restrictions 13
    security 12–13
    SSL (Secure Sockets Layer) 13

F

fields
    client table descriptions 116–117
    employee table
        descriptions 115–116
    hours table descriptions 118
    JavaScript Application
        Manager 23–24
File object 221–222, 266–267
    comments.html file 82–83
    local file access 78–83
file position, local files 79–80
filename extensions
    htm/html (HyperText Markup
        Language) 17
    js (JavaScript) 11, 17
files
    adminclient.html 176–177
    adminclient_add.html 177–178
    adminclient_del.html 179–180
    adminemp.html 172–173
    adminemp_add.html 173–174
    adminemp_del.html 175–176
    adminmenu.html 159–161
    board.java 100–103
    comments.html 82–83
    display.js 181–184
    do_adminclient.html 179
    do_log.html 162–163
    do_report.html 169–171
    do_view.html 165–166
    email.html 76–77
    Employee.java 89–90, 99–100
    employeeObj.js 130–135
    error.html 156
    genmenu.html 159
    home.html 17, 93, 104, 154–155
    hoursObj.js 142–145
    HTML 17
    InOut.java 90–92
    JavaScript 17

jsa.conf 187
local 78–83
log.html 161–162
login.html 155–156
mainmenu.html 157–158
netscape.javascript 87
netscape.net 87
netscape.server 87
obj.conf 129
report.html 167–169
ReportHours.java 150–152
reportObj.js 145–150
server3_0.zip 87
signin.html 93–94, 104–105
signout.html 94–95, 105
start.html 93, 103, 153
start.js 153
sun.net 87
timeClientObj.js 136–142
top.html 154–155
utils.js 18, 180
view.html 95, 106, 164–165
visits.html 17
finalize method 257
firewalls, extranets 13
flush function 222
flush method 80, 222
flush root function 222
form pages, Web-based
  applications 161–180
forms
  Add Application 186
  administrative access 125–126
  general access, interface
    design 124–125
  login 154
  request-specific properties 37
From property 223
functions
  addClient 38, 41–42, 199
  addResponseHeader 84, 200
  blob 202
  blobImage 202–203
  blobLink 203–204
  bodyTag() 154
  callC 205
  checkDB() 154, 156
  checkLogin() 156
  deleteResponseHeader 84, 217
  eval 73
  flush 222
  getAvailableID 39
  getOptionValue 223–224
  getOptionValueCount 224
  incrementVisitors() 18
  JavaScript 180–184
  new 78, 88
  redirect 240
  registerCFunction 240–241
  write 78, 254

G

general access forms, interface
  design 124–125
general access menu page
  described 112
  genmenu.html file 159
genmenu.html file 159
getAvailableID function, client
  object 39
getLength method 81, 223
getMember method 257
getOptionValue function 223–224
getOptionValue root function
  223–224
getOptionValueCount function 224
getOptionValueCount root
  function 224
getPosition method 79, 224–225
getPostData method, request body
  access 84
getSlot method 257–258
getWindow method 258
glossary 273–274

H

header object, content-length
  property 84
hierarchy
  application design 10–11
  JavaScript objects 11
home page
  creating 153–156
  described 112
  home.html file 155
  interface design 124
home.html file 17, 154–155
  employee sign-out board
    93, 104
host property 47, 225
hostname property 47, 225
hours object 120–121, 142–145
hours table 118
hoursObj.js file 142–145
htm/html (HyperText Markup
  Language) filename extension 17
HTML files, htm/html filename
  extension 17
HTML pages
  forms 161–180
  home 154–156
  initial 153–156
  menus 156–161
  Web-based applications
    152–180
  writing 92–96, 103–106
HTML tags
  server <SERVER> 17
  Web browser support 5
HTTP (HyperText Transfer Protocol) 4
httpdHeader method, request header
  access 83–84

I

image maps, request object 38
ImageX property 38, 226
ImageY property 38, 226
incrementVisitors() function 18
information retrieval, local files 81
Informix database, stored
  procedures 63
Initial Page field, Application
  Manager 23
initial pages, creating 153–156
InOut.java file, employee sign-out
  board 90–92
insertRow method 227
interface design
  administrative access
    forms 125–126
  general access forms 124–125
  menu pages 124
  Web-based applications
    123–126
Internet, Web-based application
  access 1
intranets
  client browser restrictions 12
  client-side processing 12
  described 3
  security 12–13
IP address
  client object maintenance 43
  maintenance advantages/
    disadvantages 44
ip property 36, 227
ISP (Internet Service Provider),
  extranet access restrictions 13

J

Java objects 88
Java Reference 256–262
Java
  adding application to
    servers 106
  application compiling 95
  application incorporation
    85–96
  board.java file 100–103
  built-in classes 87
  calling from JavaScript
    application 87
  client write output 98
  compiling applications 106
  compiling code 92, 103
  employee sign-out board
    application 89–96
  Employee.java file 89–90,
    99–100
  home.html file 93, 104
  HTML page writing 92–96
  InOut.java file 90–92
  JavaScript access classes
    97–107

Index

JavaScript/Java data value
    conversion 88
passing data types to
    JavaScript 98
running applications 106
signin.html file 93–94, 104–105
signout.html file 94–95, 105
start.html file 93, 103
threading 98
versus JavaScript 107–108
view.html file 95, 106
when to use 107–108
writing HTML pages 103–106
javac, compiling Java code 103
JavaScript
    accessing from Java classes
        97–107
    application functions 180–184
    client-side versus
        server-side 184
    deciphering/tracking error
        messages 191–196
    display.js file 181–184
    object creation 130
    passing Java data types 98
    pointer non-support bugs
        193–194
    utils.js file 180
    versus Java 107–108
    when to use 107–108
JavaScript Application Manager
    20–26
    See also Application Manager
    activating 15–16
    adding Java application to 96
    running applications 96
JavaScript data types 68–70
JavaScript files, js filename
    extension 17
JavaScript for Communicator,
    client-side scripting support 6
JavaScript objects 11, 97–98
js (JavaScript) filename extension
    11, 17
jsa.conf file 187
jsa.conf file, versus Add Application
    form 187
jsac (JavaScript Application
    Compiler) 15, 18–20
    build script 18–19
    build script creation 129
    compiling application code
        18–20
    compiling Java
        applications 106
    Java application compiling 95
    options 19–20
JSException class 97
JSException constructor 259
JSException method 258
JSObject class 97
JSObject object 259

L

libraries, database client 49–51
lifetime
    client cookies 41
    client object 39–40
    request object 35
    session management objects 32
LiveConnect
    calling Java from JavaScript
        application 87
    development history i, 85
    employee sign-out board
        application 89–96
    instances of Java classes 85–86
    Java/application
        incorporation 85–96
    JavaScript/Java data value
        conversion 88
    passing Java data types to
        JavaScript 98
LiveWire
    defined 2
    ODBC drivers 50–51
    ODBC support 49–51
    online resources 195
    supported database
        servers 49–50
    three-tier framework 6
LiveWire objects
    Connection 264
    Cursor 265
    DbPool 265–266
    ResultSet 268
    StoredProc 270
local files 78–83
    accessing 78–79
    binary/text data
        conversions 81
    file position 79–80
    information retrieval 81
    locating/changing
        position 79–80
    locking 81
    opening 78
    reading from/writing to 80–81
Lock class, lock object creation 34
lock method 34, 228–229
Lock object 32, 228–229, 267
    creating as instance of the Lock
        class 34
    critical section protection 33
    local file locking 81
    unlocking 34
    uses 34–35
locking, local files 81
log hours form page
    do_log.html file 162–163
    log.html 161–162
log hours page
    described 113
    interface design 125

log.html file 161–162
login form, login.html file 154–156
login.html file 155–156

M

main menu page
    described 112
    interface design 124
    mainmenu.html file 157–158
mainmenu.html file 157–158
majorErrorCode method 71, 229–231
majorErrorMessage method
    71, 231–232
menu pages
    interface design 124
    Web-based applications
        156–161
menus, Web-based applications
    156–161
method property 36, 232
methods
    array 73
    beginTransaction 68, 201–202
    byteToString 81, 204–205
    call 256
    clearError 81, 206
    close 78, 207–208
    columnName 208–209
    columns 62, 209–210
    commitTransaction 68, 210
    connect 210–211
    connected 211–212
    connections 213
    cursor 214
    deleteRow 217–218
    destroy 218
    disconnect 218–219
    displayForm 161
    employee object 119
    eof 80, 219
    error 81, 219
    errorCode 74
    errorMessage 74
    eval 256
    execute 220
    exists 81, 220–221
    expiration 40, 220–221
    finalize 257
    flush 80, 222
    getLength 81, 223
    getMember 257
    getPosition 79, 224–225
    getPostData 84
    getSlot 257–258
    getWindow 258
    hours object 120–121
    httpdHeader 83–84
    insertRow 227
    JSException 258
    lock 228–229
    lock 34

majorErrorCode 71, 229–231
majorErrorMessage 71, 231–232
minorErrorCode 71, 233
minorErrorMessage 71, 233–234
next 234–235
open 235
open 78–79
outParamCount 236
outParameters 236
project lock 46
read 80, 239
readByte 80–81, 239
readln 80, 240
release 241
removeMember 260
report objects 121–122
ReportHours object 123
resultSet 243–244
returnValue 244
rollbackTransaction 68, 244–245
send 74, 245
setMember 260–261
setPosition 79, 246–247
setSlot 261
SQLTable 56–57, 248
storedProc 64, 249
storedProcArgs 64, 250
stringToByte 81, 250
timeClient object 120
toString 251–252, 261
unlock 34, 252–253
updateRow 253
write 80, 254
writeByte 81, 255
writeHttpOutput 262
writeln 80, 255
minorErrorCode method 71, 233
minorErrorMessage method 71, 233–234

N

Name field, Application Manager 22
Netscape Enterprise Servers
 adding applications to 185–189
 cross-platform support 2
 database-driven applications 1
 jsa.conf file 187
 multiple database connection support 49
 netscape.javascript package 87
 netscape.net file 87
 netscape.server package 87
 obj.conf file 129
 ODBC connectivity 2
 ODBC drivers 50–51
 platform independence 3
 security features 4
 server3_0.zip file 87

server-side JavaScript activation 15–16
Netscape, online resources 195
netscape.javascript package 87
netscape.net file 87
netscape.server package 87
NetscapeServerEnv class 97
NetscapeServerEnv object 260
new function
 file object creation 78
 Java class instance creation 88
newsgroups, DevEdge 196
next method 234–235
NT system, CLASSPATH environment variable 86
N-Tier Web applications
 described 7–8
 versus client-server applications 6–8

O

obj.conf file, application directory creation 129
object framework. See session management objects/objects
object properties, access methods 73
objects
 application 119–123
 client 32, 38–44, 206–207, 263
 Connections 212, 264
 Cursor 58–62, 213–214, 265
 DbPool 51–52, 215, 265–266
 employee 119, 130–135
 File 78–83, 82–83, 221–222, 266–267
 header 84
 hours 120–121, 142–145
 implementing 129–152
 Java 88
 JavaScript 11, 97–98
 JavaScript creation 130
 js (JavaScript) filename extensions 11
 JSObjects 259
 lock 32, 81, 228–229, 267
 NetscapeServerEnv 260
 Packages 88
 project 32, 45–46, 81, 237–238, 267
 properties 73
 report 121–122, 145–150
 ReportHours 123, 150–152
 request 32, 83–84, 242, 268
 ResultSet 243, 268
 SendMail 74–77, 245–246, 269
 server 32, 46–48, 246, 269–270
 session management 31–48
 StoredProc 64, 248–249, 270
 timeClient 120, 136–142
 user tracking 38

ODBC drivers
 feature capabilities 51
 supported types 50–51
ODBC, LiveWire supported database servers 49–51
online example, viewing 275–276
online resources 195–196
open method 78–79, 235
operators
 assignment 39
 var 194
Oracle databases, stored procedures 63
outParamCount method 236
outParameters method 236
output parameters, stored procedures 67

P

Packages object, Java class instance of creation 88
parameters, Add Application form 186
pointers, JavaScript non-support bugs 193–194
port property 47, 237
procedures, stored 62–67
project lock method, project object 46
project object 32, 45–46, 237–238, 267
 client data sharing 45
 client tracking 45
 local file locking 81
 locking 46
 properties 45
properties
 agent 36, 200
 Bcc 201
 Body 204
 Cc 205–206
 client object 39–40
 From 223
 host 47, 225
 hostname 47, 225
 ImageX 38, 226
 ImageY 38, 226
 ip 36, 227
 Java objects 88
 method 36, 232
 object 73
 port 47, 237
 project object 45
 protocol 36, 47, 238
 report objects 121–122
 ReportHours object 123
 SendMail object 74
 server object 46–47
 Smtpserver 247
 Subject 251
 To 251
protocol property 238
 request object 36
 server object 47

Index

prototypes, stored procedures 64
publications
    Comprehensive Guide to VBScript, The 6
    Official Netscape Communicator 4 Book, The 3
    Official Netscape Enterprise Server 3 Book 2
    Official Netscape JavaScript 1.2 Book, The 6
    Official Netscape JavaScript 1.2 Programmer's Reference ii

Q

queries
    cursor objects results display 59–60
    database display 56–57
    table data relationship reduction 10
query string, described 41

R

read method 80, 239
readByte method 239
    binary data 81
    next file byte return 80
readers, book assumptions i–ii
readln method 80, 240
redirect function 240
redirect root function 240
registerCFunction function 240–241
registerCFunction root function 240–241
release method 241
removeMember method 260
report object 121–122, 145–150
report.html file 167–169
ReportHours object 123, 150–152
ReportHours.java file 150–152
reportObj.js file 145–150
request body, accessing 84
request header, accessing 83–84
request object 32, 35–38, 242, 268
    assigned properties 37
    creation circumstances 35
    default properties 36
    image maps 38
    lifetime 35
    properties 36–38
    request body access 84
    request header access 83–84
    request-specific properties 37
    response header access 84
    URL encoding 37–38
request-specific properties, request object 37
resources, online 195–196
response header, accessing 84
result sets, stored procedures 66
resultSet method 243–244

ResultSet object 243, 268
return values, stored procedures 66
returnValue method 244
rollbackTransaction method 68, 244–245

S

scope, session management objects 32
scripting, client-side 5–6
security
    client browser restrictions 12
    client certificates 1–2, 4
    client-side processing 12
    extranets 12–13
    firewalls 13
    intranets 12–13
    SSL (Secure Sockets Layer) 13
    user authentication 1–2, 4
    Web development concerns 4
    Web-based application levels 2
semicolon (;) characters, statement ending 57
send method 74, 245
SendMail object 74–77, 245–246, 269
    error codes 74–76
    properties 74
    uses 76–77
serial approach method, database connection pools 53
server <SERVER> HTML tag 17
server cookies
    See also cookies
    client object maintenance 43
    maintenance advantages/disadvantages 44
server object 32, 246, 269–270
    assigned properties 47
    client data sharing 46
    default properties 47
    locking 48
server URL encoding 43–44
server3_0.zip file, built-in Java classes 87
server-side JavaScript
    administrative server activation 15–16
    advantages over CGI program i
    CLASSPATH environment variable 86
    development history i
    LiveConnect functionality 85
    object properties 73
    object reference 263–270
    online resources 195
    reference 199–262
    server <SERVER> HTML tag 17
    versus client-side JavaScript 184

server-side methods, client object maintenance 42–43
session management objects 31–48
    client 32, 38–44, 263
    described 31
    lifetime 32
    Lock 32, 267
    object framework description 31
    project 32, 45–46, 267
    request 32, 35–38, 268
    scope 32
    server 32, 46–48, 269–270
    threaded architecture 31
    uses 32
setMember method 260–261
setPosition method 246–247
    arguments 80
    changing a file position 79
setSlot method 261
shell scripts, build 18–19, 129
signin.html file, employee sign-out board 93–94, 104–105
signout.html file, employee sign-out board 94–95, 105
Smtpserver property 247
SQL statements 56–57
    database table creation 127–128
    executing 57
    query display 56–57
SQLTable method 248
    Customize and Mimic 209
    database query display 56–67
SSL (Secure Sockets Layer) 1, 13
standard method, database connection pools 53
start page
    start.html file 153
    start.js file 153
start.html file 93, 103, 153
start.js file 153
stateless connections 4
statements
    control 57
    data definition language 57
    ending semicolon (;) character 57
    SQL 56–57, 127–128
static methods, Java objects 88
stored procedures 62–67
    benefits 62
    DB2 database registration 63–64
    Informix database 63
    Oracle database 63
    output parameters 67
    prototype definitions 64
    result sets 66
    return values 66
    returned data handling 65–67
    running 64–65

Sybase database 63
    using 62–65
StoredPoc object 270
storedProc method 64, 249
StoredProc object 64, 248–249
storedProcArgs method 64, 250
stringToByte method 81, 250
Subject property 251
sun.net file, netscape.net file
    replacement 87
Sybase databases, stored
    procedures 63

T

tables
    data relationships 10
    database design 9–10
    types/uses 9–10
templates
    application 25
    dynamic content design 11
terms 273–274
text data
    binary data conversion 81
    described 81
threaded architecture, session
    management objects 31
threading, Java code 98
three-tier framework, LiveWire
    applications 6
time tracking, application map
    113–114
timeClient object 120, 136–142
timeClientObj.js file 136–142
To property 251
top page, login page 154
top.html file 154–155
toString method 251–252, 261
transactions
    database 67–68
    database error tracking 195
    described 67
    explicit management 68
    uses 67

U

UNIX system, CLASSPATH
    environment variable 86
unlock method 34, 252–253
updatable cursors 60–61
updateRow method 253
URL encoding, request object 37–38
Usenet newsgroups, DevEdge 196
user authentication
    access security 4
    described 2
    Web-based application access
        restrictions 1
user IDs, Web-based application access
    types 1

users
    client object tracking 38–44
    database connection pools
        sharing 53–54
utils.js file 18, 180

V

var operator, variable scope problem
    tracking 194
VBScript for Internet Explorer,
    client-side scripting support 6
versions, application development 191
view hours form page
    do_view.html file 165–166
    view.html file 164–165
view hours page
    described 113
    interface design 125
view reports form page
    do_report.html file 169–171
    report.html file 167–169
view reports page
    described 113
    interface design 125
view.html file 164–165
    employee sign-out board 106
    employee sign-out board 95
visits.html file 17
Visual JavaScript 16

W

Web
    development platform
        advantages 2–4
    security concerns 4
    stateless connections 4
    ubiquitous client software 3
Web browsers
    advanced HTML tag support 5
    application feature set
        support 3
    client-side scripting handling
        concerns 5–6
    cookies support 5
    documentation support 3
    rich feature non-support access
        restrictions 4–5
    version number support
        information 6
Web File Path field, Application
    Manager 23
Web pages, application map 112–113
Web sites
    DevEdge 85
    LiveWire resources 195
    Netscape DevEdge 195
    online example 275
    server-side JavaScript
        resources 195
    server-side JavaScript
        support 195

Web-based applications 1–14
    adding to servers 185–189
    administrative access
        forms 125–126
    application map creation
        111–114
    application objects 119–123
    browser rich feature
        non-support access 4–5
    browser version number
        support information 6
    client certificates 1
    client-side versus server-side
        JavaScript 184
    database table creation 127–128
    database tables 115–118
    database-driven 9–13
    debug messages 191
    debugging 189–191
    development advantages/
        disadvantages 2–4
    development version
        creation 191
    directory creation 128–129
    display.js file 181–184
    forms 161–180
    general access forms 124–125
    interface design 123–126
    Internet access 1
    JavaScript functions 180–184
    menu pages interface 124
    menus 156–161
    object implementation 129–152
    pages 112–113
    running 188–189
    security levels 2
    SSL (Secure Sockets Layer) 1
    testing 188–189
    testing options 196
    user authentication access
        restriction 1
    utils.js file 180
    writing HTML pages 152–180
write function 78, 254
write method 80, 254
write root function 254
writeByte method 255
    binary data 81
    character write based on number
        passed 80
writeHttpOutput method 262
writeln method 80, 255

VENTANA

http://www.vmedia.com

VENTANA

Official Netscape Enterprise Server 3 Book

Richard Cravens
$49.99, 480 pages, part #: 1-56604-664-5

- Detailed examination of web-site security issues and benefits.
- Complete coverage of installation, configuration and maintenance, along with troubleshooting tips.
- Shows how to enrich web sites with multimedia and interactivity.

CD-ROM contains sample HTML editors, HTML references, current Netscape plug-ins.

For Windows NT & UNIX • Intermediate to Advanced

Official Netscape Technologies Developer's Guide

Luke Duncan, Sean Michaels
$39.99, 352 pages, part #: 1-56604-749-8

- Guide to the most critical ONE SDKs and APIs—CORBA/IIOP, IFC, plug-ins and server-side JavaScript.
- Overview of Internet/intranet application development with IFC.
- Example plug-in project to integrate multiple aspects of Netscape ONE.

All Platforms • Intermediate to Advanced

VENTANA

Official Netscape LiveWire Book

$49.95, 744 pages, illustrated, part #: 1-56604-382-4

Master web-site management visually! Now even new webmasters can create and manage intranet and Internet sites. And experienced developers can harness LiveWire's advanced tools for maintaining highly complex web sites and applications. Step-by-step tutorials cover all LiveWire components. Learn to design powerful distributed applications—without extensive programming experience.

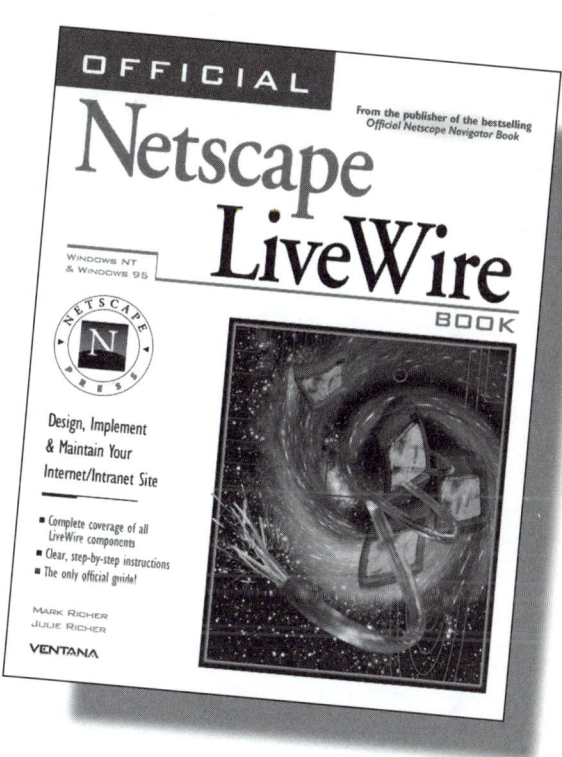

Official Netscape LiveWire Pro Book

$49.99, 800 pages, illustrated, part #: 1-56604-624-6

High-end database management and connectivity techniques highlight this examination of LiveWire Pro, featuring sophisticated site development and mangement skills that ease the task for webmasters. Learn to maintain databases, update links, process online orders, generate catalogs and more. The CD-ROM features all the code from the sample applications in the book.

VENTANA

Official Netscape JavaScript 1.2 Programmer's Reference

$39.99, 496 pages, illustrated, part #: 1-56604-757-9

Peter Kent/Kent Multer
Windows, Macintosh & UNIX
Intermediate to Advanced

- Complete reference to all JavaScript expressions, objects, properties, methods, statements, reserved words and color values.
- In-depth explanations and examples, including syntax and usage.
- Encyclopedic listing, extensively cross-referenced for quick access to information.

CD-ROM: Searchable hyperlinked version of the book.

Official Netscape Server-Side JavaScript for Database Applications

$39.99, 544 pages, illustrated, part #: 1-56604-745-5

Luke Duncan
Windows NT & UNIX
Intermediate to Advanced

- Designing and implementing Internet/intranet applications for Netscape Enterprise Server 3 using server-side JavaScript.
- Using Java with LiveConnect to create browser-independent applications.
- Troubleshooting tips, advanced topics and productivity-enhancing examples.

VENTANA

Official Netscape SuiteSpot 3.0 Book

*$49.99, 400 pages, illustrated
part #: 1-56604-794-3*

*Larry Budnick/Richard Cravens
Windows NT/95, UNIX
Intermediate*

- Integrate SuiteSpot 3.0 with existing network components.
- Create custom applications and features.
- Covers all nine SuiteSpot 3.0 servers plus LiveWire Pro and Visual JavaScript.

CD-ROM: Sample code from the book and helper applications for servers.

Official Netscape ONE Book

*$49.99, 400 pages, illustrated
part #: 1-56604-632-7*

*Luke Duncan, Sean Micheals
All Platforms
Intermediate to Advanced*

- Helps you harness ONE to create integrated Web solutions that balance ease of use with economy of resources.
- Highlights all of the ONE SDKs and APIs.
- Demonstrates how to integrate multiple aspects of Netscape ONE into a single example plug-in.

CD-ROM: All the code examples from the book; complete step-by-step plug-in example.

VENTANA

Java 1.1 Programmer's Reference

Daniel I. Joshi, Pavel Vorobiev
$49.99, 1000 pages, illustrated, part #: 1-56604-687-4

The ultimate resource for Java professionals! And the perfect supplement to the JDK documentation. Whether you need a day-to-day reference for Java classes, an explanation of new APIs, a guide to common programming techniques, or all three, you've got it—all in an encyclopedic format that's convenient to refer to again and again. Covers new Java 1.1 features, including the AWT, JARs, Java Security API, the JDBC, JavaBeans, and more, with complete descriptions that include syntax, usage and code samples. **CD-ROM:** Complete, hyperlinked version of the book.
For all platforms • Intermediate to Advanced

Migrating From Java 1.0 to Java 1.1

Daniel I. Joshi, Pavel Vorobiev
$39.99, 600 pages, illustrated, part #: 1-56604-686-6

Your expertise with Java 1.0 provides the perfect springboard to rapid mastery of Java 1.1 and the new tools in the JDK 1.1. Viewing what's new from the perspective of what you already know gets you up to speed quickly. And you'll learn not only what's changed, but why—gaining deeper understanding of the evolution of Java and how to exploit its power for your projects. **CD-ROM:** All the sample Java 1.1 programs, plus extended examples.
For Windows NT/95, Macintosh, UNIX, Solaris
Intermediate to Advanced

The Comprehensive Guide to the JDBC SQL API

Daniel I. Joshi, Rodney Runolfson
$49.99, 456 pages, illustrated, part#: 1-56604-637-8

Develop high-powered database solutions for your Internet/intranet site! Covers the basics of Java and SQL, interface design with AWT and instructions for building an Internet-based search engine. **CD-ROM:** OpenLink Server-side JDBC driver, SQL databases and tables from the book, sample code, JDBC API specification and example sites.
For Windows 95/NT • Intermediate to Advanced

VENTANA

Java Programming for the Internet
$49.95, 816 pages, illustrated, part #: 1-56604-355-7

Master the programming language of choice for Internet applications. Expand the scope of your online development with this comprehensive, step-by-step guide to creating Java applets. The CD-ROM features the Java Developer's Kit, source code for all the applets, samples and programs from the book, and much more.

The Visual Basic Programmer's Guide to Java
$39.99, 450 pages, part #: 1-56604-527-4

At last—a Java book that speaks your language! Use your understanding of Visual Basic as a foundation for learning Java and object-oriented programming. This unique guide not only relates Java features to what you already know—it also highlights the areas in which Java excels over Visual Basic, to build an understanding of its appropriate use. The CD-ROM features comparative examples written in Java & Visual Basic, code for projects created in the book and more.

VENTANA

The Mac OS 8 Book

$34.99, 658 pages, part #: 1-56604-688-2

Craig Danuloff and Mark R. Bell
Macintosh
Intermediate

- Covers installing, updating third-party add-ons and troubleshooting tips for Mac OS 8.
- Shows how to connect to the Net and publish on the Web with Mac OS 8.
- Includes a complete overview of all commands and features.

Plus—online updates for up-to-the-minute patches and fixes for Mac OS 8, as well as updates to the book.

The Metrowerks CodeWarrior Professional Book, Macintosh Edition

$39.99, 500 pages, illustrated, part #: 1-56604-733-1

Dan Parks Sydow
Intermediate to Advanced

- Illuminates each phase of development through aspects of a single example program.
- Examines alternative programming methods, with a special look at Java classes and the Java API.
- Covers porting Macintosh programs to Windows 95/NT, along with tips on programming.

CD-ROM: All source code for the book's main example, lite version of CodeWarrior, EarthLink Network TotalAccess Internet connection package with the Netscape browser.

VENTANA

The Mac Web Server Book

$49.95, 662 pages, illustrated, part #: 1-56604-341-7

Get the most from your Internet server with this hands-on resource guide and toolset. Learn to choose the right server software; set up your server; add graphics, sound and forms; and much more. The CD-ROM includes demo software, scripts, icons and shareware.

The Windows NT Web Server Book

$49.95, 680 pages, illustrated, part #: 1-56604-342-5

A complete toolkit for providing services on the Internet using the Windows NT operating system. This how-to guide includes adding the necessary web server software, comparison of the major Windows NT server packages for the Web, becoming a global product provider and more! The CD-ROM features Alibaba™ Lite (a fully licensed web server), support programs, scripts, forms, utilities and demos.

The UNIX Web Server Book, Second Edition

$49.99, 684 pages, illustrated, part #: 1-56604-480-4

Tools and techniques for building an Internet/intranet site. Everything you need to know to set up your UNIX web site—from basic installation to adding content, multimedia, interactivity and advanced searches. The CD-ROM features Linux, HTTP, CERN Web Server, FTP daemon, conversion software, graphics translators and utilities.

VENTANA

HTML Publishing on the Internet, Second Edition

$39.99, 700 pages, illustrated, part #: 1-56604-625-4
Brent Heslop
Windows 95/NT & Macintosh
Intermediate

- Create a home page and hyperlinks; build graphics, video and sound into documents.
- Save time and money by downloading components of the new technologies from the Web or from the companion CD-ROM.
- Highlighted throughout with examples and templates, and tips on layout and nonlinear organization.

CD-ROM: HTML authoring tools, graphics and multimedia utilities, textures, templates and demos.

The HTML 4 Programmer's Reference

$39.99, 376 pages, illustrated, part #: 1-56604-730
Robert Mullen
All Platforms
Intermediate to Advanced

- Detailed descriptions of every HTML tag, attribute and value, with syntax and examples.
- Advanced techniques including tables, frames, cascading style sheets and browser-specific extensions.
- Encyclopedic listing, extensively cross-referenced for easy access to information.

CD-ROM: Hyperlinked version of the book.

VENTANA

Official HTML Publishing for Netscape, Second Edition
$39.99, 800 pages, part #: 1-56604-650-5

Windows 95/NT, Macintosh • Intermediate

Make the Most of the Latest Netscape Features!
Learn how the latest developments in Netscape Navigator and HTML enhance your ability to deliver eye-catching, interactive Web pages to a broad audience, and how to harness new technologies to create a compelling site. Includes:
- Playing to Navigator's hottest features, including tables, frames, plug-ins and support for Java applets.
- Guidelines for designing great Web pages.
- New material on style sheets, sound, multimedia and databases.

The CD-ROM contains an example Web site on the Net, sample JavaScript, clip objects, backgrounds and more.

Official Netscape JavaScript 1.2 Book, Second Edition
$29.99, 592 pages, part #: 1-56604-675-0

All platforms • Beginning to Intermediate

Brew up instant scripts—even if you're not a programmer!
Learn all the skills you need to perk up your Web pages with multimedia and interactivity. Fully updated for Netscape Communicator, this bestseller now includes:
- Basic programming techniques.
- Tips for using existing scripts and building your own from scratch.
- Nearly 200 script samples and interactive tutorials online.

Official Netscape FastTrack Server Book
$39.99, 432 pages, part #: 1-56601-183-9

Windows NT • Intermediate to Advanced

Turn your PC into an Internet/intranet powerhouse!
This step-by-step guide to the hottest server software on the Net provides all the instructions you need to launch your Internet or intranet site, from technical requirements to content creation and administration. Learn how to exploit FastTrack Server's high-performance server architecture to easily create and manage customized web sites. Plus, enhance your site with FTP and Telnet; ensure security for online transactions; and import and convert documents.

VENTANA

Principles of Object-Oriented Programming in Java

$39.99, 400 pages, illustrated, part #: 1-56604-530-4

Move from writing programs to designing solutions—with dramatic results! Take a step beyond syntax to discover the true art of software design, with Java as your paintbrush and objects on your palette. This in-depth discussion of how, when and why to use objects enables you to create programs—using Java or any other object-oriented language—that not only work smoothly, but are easy to maintain and upgrade. The CD-ROM features the Java SDK, code samples and more.

The Comprehensive Guide to Visual J++

$49.99, 792 pages, illustrated, part #: 1-56604-533-9

Learn to integrate the Java language and ActiveX in one development solution! Master the Visual J++ environment using real-world coding techniques and project examples. Includes executable J++ sample projects plus undocumented tips and tricks. The CD-ROM features all code examples, sample ActiveX COM objects, Java documentation and an ActiveX component library.

VENTANA

TO ORDER ANY VENTANA TITLE, COMPLETE THIS ORDER FORM AND MAIL OR FAX IT TO US, WITH PAYMENT, FOR QUICK SHIPMENT.

TITLE	PART #	QTY	PRICE	TOTAL

SHIPPING

For orders shipping within the United States, please add $4.95 for the first book, $1.50 for each additional book.
For "two-day air," add $7.95 for the first book, $3.00 for each additional book.
Email: vorders@kdc.com for exact shipping charges.
Note: Please include your local sales tax.

SUBTOTAL = $ _____
SHIPPING = $ _____
TAX = $ _____
TOTAL = $ _____

Mail to: International Thomson Publishing • 7625 Empire Drive • Florence, KY 41042
☎ US orders 800/332-7450 • fax 606/283-0718
☎ International orders 606/282-5786 • Canadian orders 800/268-2222

Name _____
E-mail _____ Daytime phone _____
Company _____
Address (No PO Box) _____
City _____ State _____ Zip _____
Payment enclosed ___VISA ___MC ___ Acc't # _____ Exp. date _____
Signature _____ Exact name on card _____

Check your local bookstore or software retailer for these and other bestselling titles, or call toll free

800/332-7450
8:00 am - 6:00 pm EST

Technical support for installation related issues only provided by Ventana. The Ventana technical support office is open from 8:00 A.M. to 6:00 P.M. (EST) Monday through Friday and can be reached via the following methods:

World Wide Web: http://www.netscapepress.com/support

E–mail: help@vmedia.com

Phone: (919) 544-9404 extension 81

FAX: (919) 544-9472

America Online: keyword **Ventana**